Law and teachers today

Law and teachers today

Second edition

Neil Adams

Neil Adams has taught in secondary modern, grammar and comprehensive schools. He took Law in his degree and has lectured for many years on the legal aspects of school management. He has been a Head for twenty-two years and, since 1974, the Head of the John Taylor High School at Barton-under-Needwood in Staffordshire.

Hutchinson
London Melbourne Sydney Auckland Johannesburg

Hutchinson & Co. (Publishers) Ltd

An imprint of the Hutchinson Publishing Group

17–21 Conway Street, London W1P 6JD

Hutchinson Publishing Group (Australia) Pty Ltd
PO Box 496, 16–22 Church Street, Hawthorn,
Melbourne, Victoria 3122

Hutchinson Group (NZ) Ltd
32–34 View Road, PO Box 40–086, Glenfield, Auckland 10

Hutchinson Group (SA) (Pty) Ltd
PO Box 337, Bergvlei 2012, South Africa

First published 1983

Second edition 1984

Reprinted 1984 with revisions

Set in Linotron Times

Printed and bound in Great Britain by
Anchor Brendon Ltd,
Tiptree, Essex

British Library Cataloguing in Publication Data
Adams, Neil
Law and teachers today. ——2nd ed.
1. Law—England
I. Title
344.204′78 KD661

ISBN 0 09 156720 3

For Jean

Contents

5 Parents

6 Parent substitutes

7 Negligence and supervision

11 Defamation, records and references

12 Copyright, licensing and lotteries

Appendices

Acknowledgements

I would like to record my thanks to Harold Barry, Fred Tye and John Buckley of the North West Educational Management Centre without whose encouragement over the years this book would not have been written; David Parkes, barrister, for his constructive criticism; and Barbara Elson for her immense patience in typing the manuscript.

Thanks are due to the following for permission to use copyright material.

Staffordshire LEA; Times Newspapers Ltd.; the Controller of HMSO; the National Union of Teachers; the Council of Local Education Authorities; the Yorkshire Post; the Joint Matriculation Board; the National Federation of Parent Teacher Associations; the Universities Central Council on Admissions.

Preface

I first became a head teacher in 1962 and at that time the legal problems confronting heads, senior staff and indeed all teachers were comparatively few. All this has changed. The growth of large comprehensive schools, the raising of the school-leaving age, the ramifications of present employment law, the increasing interest in parental rights and concern over the accountability of schools have forced all involved in the running of the education service to become more aware of the legal implications of what they do (or don't do!)

When I talk to groups of teachers on school management courses their increasing anxiety becomes obvious. This book is written largely because of that concern and because it has been suggested to me by many teachers that they would welcome a book that presents information, is interesting and readable, poses realistic problems related to the everyday life of schools and gives practical advice. This is what I have tried to do.

I owe my thanks not only to those persons acknowledged already but also to all those teachers on courses in the North West and Midlands who have supplied me over the years with a fund of experience and problems. The law here is as up-to-date as I can discover it but, since law is in a constant state of change, inevitably there will be inaccuracies. I am entirely to blame for any mistakes or deficiencies and the opinions expressed are my own. I must apologize for the use of 'he' throughout the book but it seemed clumsy to write 'he or she' so frequently. Most of what I have said applies equally to both sexes, of course.

N.A.

1 Introduction

1.1 Law and order

The farmer, the lawyer and the politician were arguing. Whose profession was the oldest?

The farmer spoke with a rich burr (farmers always do in stories): 'When God expelled him from the Garden of Eden Adam took to tilling the soil. Farming is the oldest profession.'

The lawyer spoke carefully (lawyers always do): 'In the beginning Order was created out of Chaos. To create Order you need laws and lawyers. Mine is the oldest profession.'

The politician was not dismayed (politicians never are): 'And just who do you think created the Chaos in the first place?'

The politician, as might be expected, had the last word. The lawyer was, however, explaining and justifying his profession. Any society, however simple, however small, needs order and certainty and thus a structure of rules of conduct. In a primitive society the rules may be unwritten – the foundation of our own common law lies in such customs. A modern urbanized and industrialized society such as ours, however, will inevitably need a mass of written laws. As our society becomes more complex so does the law relating to it.

Law, then, might be defined as a system of rules which governs the conduct of members of a given society. It is the servant of that society and must develop according to the changing needs and beliefs of that society. Once the death penalty was in force for stealing a sheep and an old bridge in Dorset still bears a metal plaque announcing that any person found damaging the structure is liable to transportation for life. We have abolished the death penalty for murder (though theoretically it may still be imposed for treason) and corporal punishment for criminals. In Pakistan recently a schoolgirl taken in adultery with the driver of a school bus was sentenced to 100 lashes and her lover sentenced to death. Britain is now the only western European country to retain corporal punishment in schools. The Scottish 'tawse' case at the European Court of Human Rights and other cases due to come before the same court could well mean that by the time this book is published corporal punishment may be banned in British schools.

The growth of a modern welfare state such as ours has meant a volume of law dealing with taxation, national insurance, employment, health and safety, discrimination on grounds of sex or race, and the rights of consumers. But the changes have not been confined to the introduction of new areas of law. As times goes on we see shifts of emphasis in existing law – our concept of liability towards others in negligence for example. The Unfair Contract (Terms) Act of 1977 has made it illegal for one party to a contract to exclude liability in negligence for death, personal injuries or any other factor which the court considers unreasonable. *British Railways Board* v. *Hetherington* (1972) and *Pannett* v. *McGuiness & Co.* (1972) are two cases which have increased substantially the liability in negligence towards child trespassers – particularly where the defendant is a public body or large corporation; over the last twenty years the law relating to divorce has changed almost beyond recognition; there has been a slow acknowledgement through cases involving children that the welfare of the child must be the paramount concern; and recently there have been significant changes in the rights of an accused before and during a criminal trial.

Mr Bumble thought the law an ass – and he had his reasons for saying so. Mostly, the law is founded on common sense and reasonableness. But it is slow to change and what is appropriate for one generation may not be so for the next. When laws are outworn and irrelevant they may indeed appear ridiculous.

1.2 Changing law

Some believe the law to be rigid and certain. This is far from true. It is often flexible and often unpredictable. In a criminal case a jury must believe an accused guilty beyond a reasonable doubt before they convict him. In civil cases the judge must weigh the case for the plaintiff against that for the defendant. It is no exaggeration to say that in some cases a different judge or a different presentation of the case by a different counsel might well produce a different result. The uncertainty of the law is well illustrated by the introduction of laws relating to breathalyser tests on motorists and the many technicalities on which drivers have escaped conviction.

As we have said, the law is in a constant state of development and change. This happens in two ways.

1.3 By statute

The obvious way in which change is brought about is by the introduction of an Act of Parliament. This may come about through the direct policy of the government taking office, through the influence of official inquiries and reports (often because of the lobbying by pressure groups), or through the persistence of an individual Member of Parliament.

The Act that has affected schools and teachers so much in modern times is, of course, the Education Act 1944. If, however, we examine it closely we find that some facts – the setting up of county colleges for example – have never been implemented and that other creations – such as the tripartite system of grammar, modern and technical schools – have disappeared because of suc-

Education Act 1980

CHAPTER 20

ARRANGEMENT OF SECTIONS

School government

ELIZABETH II

Education Act 1980

1980 CHAPTER 20

An Act to amend the law relating to education.

[3rd April 1980]

BE IT ENACTED by the Queen's most Excellent Majesty, by and with the advice and consent of the Lords Spiritual and Temporal, and Commons, in this present Parliament assembled, and by the authority of the same, as follows:—

School government

Change of nomenclature. 1944 c. 31.

1.—(1) The members of the body constituted for a primary school under subsection (1) of section 17 of the Education Act 1944 (governing bodies of county and voluntary schools) shall be known as governors instead of managers and the instrument providing for the constitution of that body as an instrument of government instead of an instrument of management.

(2) The rules in accordance with which a primary school is required to be conducted under subsection (3)(*a*) of that section shall be known as articles of government instead of rules of management.

(3) The enactments mentioned in Schedule 1 to this Act shall have effect with the amendments there specified, being amendments consequential on the provisions of subsections (1) and (2) above.

(4) For any reference in any other enactment or document to the managers, foundation managers, instrument of management or rules of management of any primary school to which the provisions of subsections (1) and (2) above apply there shall be substituted, as respects any time after the coming into force of those provisions, a reference to the governors, foundation governors, instrument of government or articles of government of the school.

ceeding changes in the law. Such changes are not only brought about by amending Acts of Parliament but also by the use of delegated legislation – that is where ministers, statutory corporations, local authorities and other bodies have power under an Act to make legislation through the use of statutory instruments. Thus the Secretary of State for Education and Science in recent years has issued statutory instruments relating to sex discrimination in schools, remuneration of teachers, scholarships and grants, provision of clothing, handicapped pupils, holidays and so on. Under the 1980 Act by means of a statutory instrument, The Education (School Information) Regulations 1981, he has laid down detailed conditions and guidelines for the publication of information regarding each school, as required by the Act.

The 1980 Act is the latest example of an attempt at major changes in the working of the system of education. It came about through public interest and pressure, particularly through the Taylor Report. For some time there had been a feeling that the public, parents and teachers should have a greater say in the running of schools. The Taylor Report recommended the reform of governing bodies and some of its suggestions were included in the 1980 Act. Tory policy before the last election was to involve parents and teachers and encourage more decision-making at local level. Parents were to be given a wider choice of schools for their children. Whether the Act has really brought about major changes and could be described as a 'parents' charter' is very doubtful. Only time will tell.

Governors

The Act abolishes 'managers'. All schools maintained by a local authority must have governors and an instrument and articles of government. It is still possible for schools to be grouped under one governing body. The governors must include members of the teaching staff and parents. There is no provision for pupil governors.

Choice of school

The Act makes it compulsory for local authorities to make arrangements for parents to express a preference for the school they wish their child to attend, though they must give reasons for their choice. For the first time parents will have a right to opt for schools outside their own county boundary.

Appeals

Under the 1944 Act s.76 parents had the right to have their children educated according to their wishes. The Secretary of State could only interfere if an appeal was made to him under s.68. The 1980 Act now requires authorities to set up special appeal committees and rules are laid down as to their composition.

Information

So that parents may make their choice of school, local authorities must publish

Main provisions of the 1980 Act

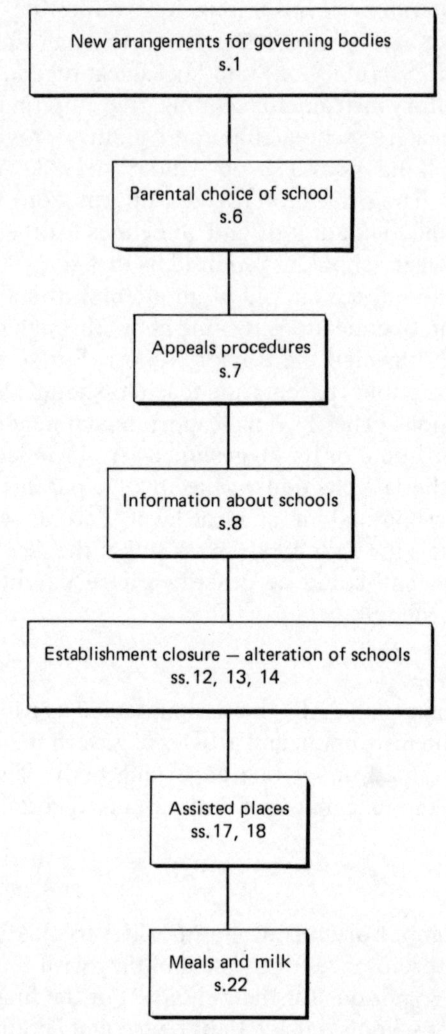

in good time the numbers to be admitted to each county or controlled school, their policy over admissions and various details relating to particular schools. Governors of aided and special agreement schools must make similar arrangements.

Establishment closure – alteration

The Act lays down new arrangements for the publication of proposals, the hearing of objections and the determination of proposals.

Assisted places

A limited number of 'assisted places' are to be available for selected pupils to

STATUTORY INSTRUMENTS

1981 No. 630

EDUCATION, ENGLAND AND WALES

The Education (School Information) Regulations 1981

Made - - - -	15*th April* 1981
Laid before Parliament	1*st May* 1981
Coming into Operation	25*th May* 1981

In exercise of the powers conferred on the Secretary of State by sections 8(5) and (7) and 35(4) and (5) of the Education Act 1980 (**a**) the Secretary of State for Education and Science, as respects England, and the Secretary of State for Wales, as respects Wales, hereby make the following Regulations:—

Citation, commencement and effect

1.—(1) These Regulations may be cited as the Education (School Information) Regulations 1981.

(2) These Regulations shall come into operation on 25th May 1981 but shall not have effect so as to require the publication of any information or particulars in relation to a school year beginning before the first day of the autumn term at a school in 1982.

Interpretation

2.—(1) In these Regulations, unless the context otherwise requires, the following expressions have the meanings hereby respectively assigned to them, that is to say—

"the Act of 1980" means the Education Act 1980;

"education authority" means a local education authority and, in relation to such an authority, "the offices" means the education offices;

"primary education" does not include such education provided in a middle school;

"relevant education authority", in relation to a school, means the education authority by whom the school is maintained;

"school" means a school maintained by an education authority other than a nursery school.

(2) In these Regulations any reference to a Regulation or a Schedule is a reference to a Regulation contained therein or a Schedule thereto and any reference in a Regulation or a Schedule to a paragraph is a reference to a paragraph of that Regulation or Schedule.

(**a**) 1980 c.20; relevant transitional provisions are contained in paragraph 1 of Schedule 3 to the Education Act 1980 (Commencement No. 2) Order 1980 (S.I. 1980/959).

SCHEDULE 1

GENERAL INFORMATION TO BE PUBLISHED BY AN EDUCATION AUTHORITY

PART I

MISCELLANEOUS MATTERS

1. The addresses and telephone numbers of the offices of the authority to which inquiries, in respect of primary and secondary education in their area, should be addressed.

2. The arrangements for parents to obtain the information particularised in Schedule 2 in the case of individual schools other than special schools.

3. As respects each school maintained by the authority, other than a special school—

(a) the name, address and telephone number of the school, and

(b) the expected number of pupils thereat and their age range.

4. The classification of each such school as—

(a) a county, controlled, aided or special agreement school;

(b) a primary, middle or secondary school or a sixth form college;

(c) a comprehensive, secondary modern, grammar or bilateral school;

(d) a co-educational or single-sex school;

(e) a day or boarding school or a school taking both day and boarding pupils;

so, however, that for the purposes of sub-paragraph (b) or (c) other terminology may be used.

5. The affiliations, if any, of each such school with a particular religious denomination.

6.—(1) This paragraph shall only apply in the case of a Welsh education authority.

(2) The authority's general arrangements and policies as respects the use of the Welsh language in schools other than aided or special agreement secondary schools—

(a) in the whole or in different parts of the authority's area;

(b) in all such schools or in different schools;

(c) by pupils of all age groups or of different age groups.

(3) The information required by this paragraph shall, in particular, include information as respects—

(a) the use of Welsh as the language in which instruction is given in all or any subjects forming part of the curriculum;

(b) any normal requirement that pupils should learn Welsh, and

(c) the circumstances in which pupils are excepted from any such requirement and the alternative instruction, if any, provided for pupils so excepted.

7. The authority's arrangements for transfer between schools maintained by them other than special schools, otherwise than at a normal admission age, including, in particular—

(a) the respective functions of the authority and governors of schools as respects admission on transfer, and

(b) the policy followed in deciding transfers.

8. The authority's general arrangements and policies in respect of transport to and from schools other than special schools (including non-maintained schools attended by pupils in pursuance of arrangements made under section 6 of the Education (Miscellaneous Provisions) Act 1953(**a**) including, in particular—

(**a**) 1953 c.33.

attend those independent schools participating in the scheme. Assistance is limited to tuition and other fees, but boarding fees are excluded.

Meals and milk

The Act gives authorities the power to make arrangements for the provision of school meals but does not lay a duty on them to do so – the 1944 Act had imposed such a duty. They must, however, provide facilities for the eating of meals brought to school by children and they must provide a free midday meal for pupils whose parents are in receipt of supplementary benefit or family income supplement. Charges for meals are at the discretion of the authority.

Similar rules apply to the provision of milk.

1.4 By case law

Once an Act has been passed that is not an end of the matter. It has to be interpreted. No matter how hard the legal draftsmen have tried there will be ambiguities and anomalies. If you use the word 'driving' do you mean the person steering, or the one propelling it by touching the accelerator with a foot? On odd occasions they had not been the same! Can you 'drive' a car by pushing it from outside with your hand through the open window and holding the steering wheel? What is meant by terms like 'recklessly', 'carelessly', or 'negligently' in certain contexts? Such problems have to be settled by case law.

Under Section 68 of the 1944 Act the Secretary of State may intervene if a local authority acts 'unreasonably'. Before 1977 the DES seems to have thought that this meant a broad discretion, which it was always reluctant to use. In the Tameside case concerning school reorganization the House of Lords decided that it did not mean that at all. It meant that the administrative act of an authority must not be unreasonable. If the action itself was reasonable then the Secretary of State could not intervene merely because he believed the policy behind the act was unreasonable.

Case law has to deal with such problems of clarification and interpretation. It works like this.

When a set of circumstances is not covered by existing law, or the law relating to it is not clear, and a legal action is brought then it is the task of the court to decide what the law is in that particular case. The court will listen to both sides in the argument and to the results of previous cases (precedents) which counsel for both sides may say are relevant. It will give judgment and that judgment itself may constitute a precedent, to be quoted in subsequent cases. A precedent is the decision of a court on a point of law. Our system of courts is a hierarchical one and a system operates where, broadly speaking, lower courts are bound to follow decisions of higher courts and may follow decisions of courts of equal or lower standing if they feel it appropriate to do so. Thus a precedent may be binding or persuasive. Decisions of the European Court on matters covered by the Treaty of Accession are binding on British courts but otherwise decisions of foreign courts and bodies like the Judicial Committee of the Privy Council, which are outside our system, are only persuasive.

The system of appeals means that a court may refuse to accept the finding of a lower court or a precedent set by such a court. Even the House of Lords itself has not, since 1966, been bound to follow its own decisions as the final court of appeal in Britain, although usually it will do so. A case that comes close for teachers is *Ward* v. *Hertfordshire County Council.*

Timothy Ward arrived at school at about 8.50 a.m. Together with some friends he had a race across the playground. The playground wall was made of flints – some of which jutted out. Apparently this method of building walls is common in that part of Hertfordshire. Timothy fell against one of the flints and injured his head. At the first hearing in the Queen's Bench Division of the High Court, the judge ruled that the council had been negligent both as regards the flint wall and the lack of supervision in the playground before the commencement of school. In effect the decision meant that education authorities would be responsible for the direct supervision of pupils from the moment the first child arrived on school premises and that such supervision must be able to prevent such an accident happening.

The Court of Appeal reversed the decision. The judges in the appeal court held that it was common practice to build walls in such a way, that the fact that there was no direct supervision in the playground before school did not amount to negligence and that even if there had been such supervision it could not be expected to prevent some accidents occurring. Since the judgment here was concerned mainly with the dangers of a playground wall, it should not be assumed that it would necessarily constitute a precedent regarding supervision.

LAW REPORT DECEMBER 18

COURT OF APPEAL

PLAYGROUND WALL NOT DANGEROUS

WARD v. HERTFORDSHIRE COUNTY COUNCIL

Before Lord Denning, the Master of the Rolls, Lord Justice Salmon and Lord Justice Cross

The boundary wall of a village school playground, about 3ft. 6in. high, and built in common form of brick and flint in 1862, was not "inherently dangerous" such as to make the education authority liable in negligence when an eight-year-old boy taking part in a race up and down the playground shortly before school began stumbled, and fell, striking his head against a jagged flint, and suffered serious head injuries. Nor was the authority negligent in not supervising the children at the time, for even if a master had been in the playground he would not have been under any duty to stop the children from racing up and down.

Their Lordships so decided in allowing an appeal by Hertfordshire County Council, as the education authority for Sarratt Primary School from Mr. Justice Hinchcliffe (The Times, March 15; [1969] 1 W.L.R. 790), who had awarded to Timothy Roy Ward, suing by his father, of Sarratt, damages of £950 for personal injuries sustained on April 29, 1966, when he was aged eight.

Mr. Hugh Griffiths, Q.C., and Mr. John Griffiths for the council; Mr. Colin Ross-Munro for the infant.

The MASTER OF THE ROLLS said that Timothy's mother left him and his younger sister at the school at about 8.50 and school started at 8.55. Timothy and the other boys decided to have a race up and down the playground. As he was running he stumbled and fell headlong against the wall. The wall was of a very common type, built about 100 years ago, with brick pillars and flint and mortar in between. It was only 3ft. 6in. high and the flints came up to about 2ft. 3in.

Timothy's head hit one of the rather jagged flints. Though he had made a remarkable recovery, he had had to have a plate in his head and there were a number of things he would not be able to do.

The judge found that the wall was inherently dangerous and that the education authority should have rendered the wall or put up railings or netting or something to prevent a child falling against it; and he also held that the masters should have been supervising the children in the playground from the time they began to arrive.

His Lordship found it impossible to say that the wall was inherently dangerous. It was the commonest type of wall of the period when flints were taken out of the ground and put into walls everywhere. A third of the houses in Sarratt and 16 of the schools in Hertfordshire had flint walls and goodness knew how many in the country at large, for all the church schools at that time were made in the same way; and all such walls had their angle points.

It was said that the danger of the wall was shown by previous accidents; but when the three of which evidence had been given were examined—all the witnesses now being grown men—they were just the ordinary sort of thing that happened in any playground. Timothy's accident was far more serious, but even his mother had said it never occurred to her before it that the wall was dangerous.

As to supervision, the headmaster, who took charge of the children from the moment school began until they were let out, had said that the teachers were indoors before school but that if he himself had been outside he would not have stopped the race. It could not be said that there was any want of supervision in the present case. Great as was his Lordship's respect for the trial judge and his judgment on such matters, he could not go with him in the present case.

It was one of those unfortunate cases where a small boy playing at school hurt himself more badly than usually happened. But the school authorities should not be held liable. Much as his Lordship sympathized with Timothy and his parents the appeal should be allowed.

LORD JUSTICE SALMON, concurring, confessed that he had tried hard to find in favour of a charming little boy who was to be denied many pleasures such as football and boxing which other little boys of his age enjoyed. But generations of children in Sarratt had played in that playground and suffered no serious injury; and it would be straining sympathy too far to find any real negligence against the school authorities. The fact that there was no master in the playground was also irrelevant for there was no duty to prevent the children from playing in the way Timothy was playing.

LORD JUSTICE CROSS, though considering that the wall in question was marginally less suitable as a boundary wall to a school playground than an ordinary brick wall, could not bring himself to think that a wall which had stood in the village school since 1862 was such a source of danger that those in charge were guilty of negligence in not having it rendered or fenced in any way.

The council did not ask for costs.

Solicitors: Berrymans; Matthew Arnold & Baldwin. Watford.

The Times
18 December, 1970

1.5 The teacher in law

Mr Handy

Mr Handy, who teaches biology at the Coletown Comprehensive School, is fond of slapping the senior girls for the slightest breach of discipline. There is nothing obviously sexual about this but Mr Freud, the headmaster, is convinced that Mr Handy enjoys his excess of zeal in administering punishment.

On a particular day Mr Freud observes Mr Handy slapping the plump bare arm of Betsy Bunter, the daughter of Councillor Bunter.

He calls Mr Handy to his office and, in a voice quivering with anger, tells him that in his view such conduct is unprofessional. He gives Mr Handy a clear instruction that under no circumstances is he ever to inflict corporal punishment on a child again.

Mr Handy is a member of a powerful union and knows his rights. He tells Mr Freud that in common law he is in *loco parentis* and thus he has the right to administer reasonable punishment. Betsy has not handed in her homework and, therefore, his punishment was justified. He will continue to administer such reasonable punishment, according to his professional judgment and in spite of Mr Freud's instruction.

How do you assess the situation? Put your views in the box below, if you wish.

Comment

As far as the common law is concerned Mr Handy is correct. When a child is in school the teacher assumes the mantle of a parent – that is what in *loco parentis* means. He must take responsibility for the child in the way that a good and sensible parent would. He may also discipline a child in the way in which a reasonable parent might do. It is unlikely that any court in Britain would hold that it was unreasonable for a parent to smack his child. The power of a teacher generally in relation to corporal punishment will have to be removed by a legal ruling from the European Court, an Act of Parliament or by powers vested in a local authority.

However, Mr Handy is an employee of the local authority and therefore subject to all the law concerning employers and those who work for them. An employee works under a contract of service, which will be discussed in detail in

Chapter 3. One of the conditions implicit in such a contract is that an employee must obey reasonable instructions. It would seem reasonable that the local authority through its agent, the headmaster, should be entitled to decide which of its staff should administer corporal punishment. Providing that the court agrees that Mr Freud's instruction is reasonable the LEA may take disciplinary action against Mr Handy, perhaps eventually dismissal.

It should be pointed out that should a teacher be in court on a charge of assault, on grounds that the punishment he gave was unreasonable, then the local authority's regulations might be evidence as to what was 'reasonable' in a school situation.

Conclusion

Mr Handy's case illustrates the rather strange dual personality that teachers have under the law. On the one hand they are employees and affected by the law of contract and the mass of employment legislation passed in recent years: on the other hand they are parent substitutes, exercising the rights and responsibilities of parents while pupils are in their charge. As in the case of corporal punishment, the two roles can present something of a legal tangle. Much of this book will be devoted to examining the implications of the two roles.

1.6 Civil courts

Already in this book we have mentioned 'court' several times and the use of 'precedent' in a hierarchical system. To understand these references the reader will need an explanation of the main systems of courts in use in England and Wales – civil and criminal.

The highest civil court in Britain is the House of Lords. The entire House does not sit as a court, only the Lord Chancellor, the nine Lords of Appeal in Ordinary (The Law Lords) and any other member with experience of high judicial office. There is a quorum of three in both civil and criminal cases. The Law Lords, who must have had fifteen years at the Bar or two years as a Supreme Court judge, are drawn from Scotland and Northern Ireland as well as from England and Wales. The House hears appeals from the Court of Appeal (Civil Division) or in certain circumstances direct from the High Court. In order to appeal permission must be given either by the House or the court hearing the case. Since 1966 the House of Lords has had the power to reverse its own previous decisions, though it is usually reluctant to do so.

The Supreme Court of Justice is divided into the Court of Appeal and the High Court of Justice.

The Court of Appeal (Civil Division) consists of the Master of the Rolls and sixteen Lords Justices of Appeal. Again there is a quorum of three. Appeals lie to this court from the Divisions of the High Court, the County Courts and such courts as the Employment Appeal Tribunal (which itself hears appeals

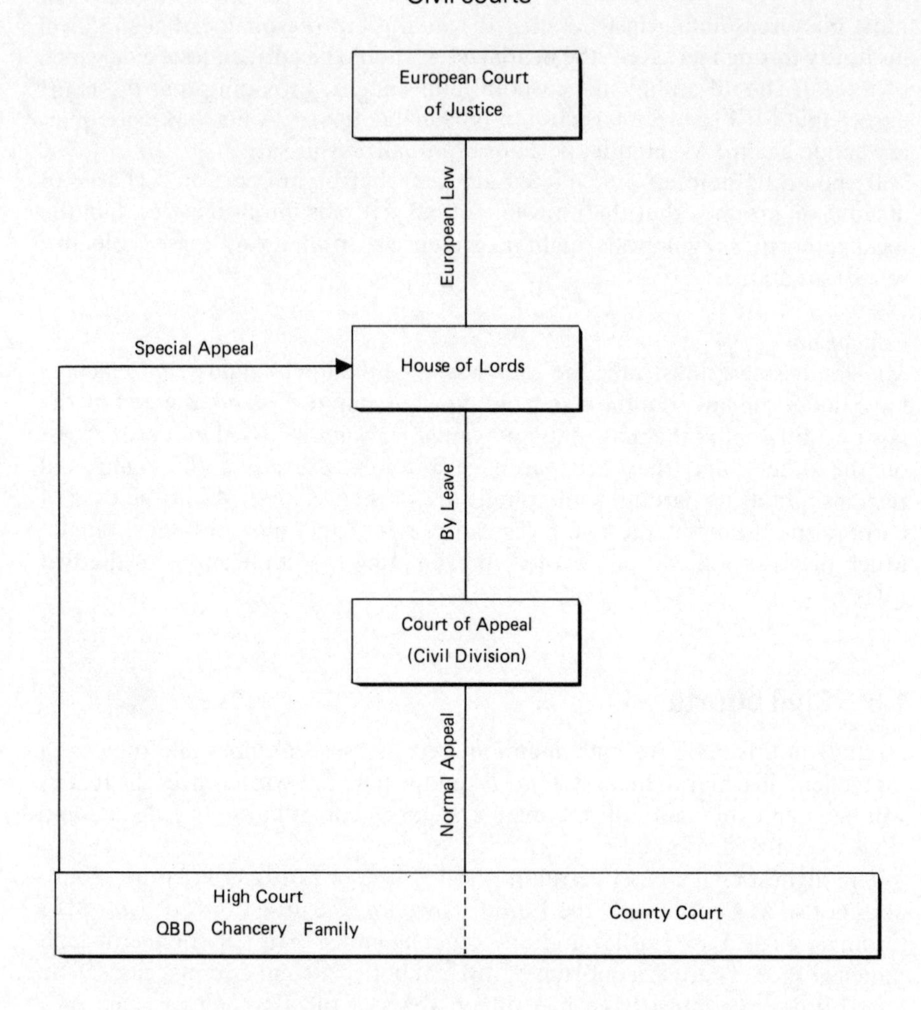

from industrial tribunals), the Restrictive Practices Court and the Court of Protection.

The High Court has three main Divisions – the Queen's Bench, Chancery and Family. All may hear cases for the first time (first instance) or hear cases on appeal from lower courts. A case of first instance will be heard by a judge sitting alone but when hearing appeals it is usual for three to sit.

The Queen's Bench Division is the busiest of these courts and, indeed, any case not falling to the other two may be allocated to it. It deals with cases in tort (see 3.3) and contract. Also, for historical reasons it retains some criminal jurisdiction and it also has powers to issue what are known as prerogative orders. These are methods of preventing an abuse of power by inferior courts, government departments, corporations, organizations or individuals. There are three orders. A *Mandamus* may be used to order something to be done, e.g. forcing an LEA to carry out its statutory duty for the provision of free school transport. A Prohibition prevents something being done, e.g. preventing an LEA from exceeding its powers, such as charging for music lessons. A *Certiorari* is used to transfer cases to the QBD from inferior courts where such courts are in error, have exceeded their jurisdiction or are disregarding the principles of natural justice, e.g. a magistrate hearing a case in which he has a financial interest or knows one of the parties. The Court also deals with applications for the use of Habeas Corpus, which orders the release of a person unlawfully detained, e.g. when a local authority refuses to allow a child to return to parents who have been granted rights of custody. Apart from its criminal powers, the Court also hears appeals from the Solicitors Disciplinary Committee and other tribunals.

The Chancery Division deals with matters relating to trusts, mortgages, partnership and bankruptcy. It also deals with contentious probate business – where there is an argument over the validity or meaning of a will, or problems relating to intestacy. It hears appeals from county courts on bankruptcy matters and from the Commissioner of Taxes.

The Family Division deals with defended divorce cases, those involving the validity and dissolution of marriages, the wardship of infants and judicial separation. It deals also with non-contentious probate matters. Appeals to it lie from magistrates' courts on matrimonial matters.

The lowest (and busiest) civil court is the County Court of which there are more than four hundred in England and Wales. In spite of the name, they are not tied to county areas, though each serves its own immediate locality. They are staffed by circuit judges, assisted by registrars who must be qualified solicitors or barristers. County courts have a wide jurisdiction over many civil matters. Usually they deal with such matters where the sums involved are below a certain level, cases involving sums above the level being heard in the High Court. Cases on contract and tort, trusts, mortgages, recovery or possession of land, dispute over wills may all be dealt with. County courts also deal with undefended divorce cases and other matrimonial causes such as nullity and the adoption of children. An action by a pupil claiming damages for injury through negligence against a teacher or local authority would therefore be brought in the County Court if the sum claimed was below the present level of £5000. If the sum claimed was greater, then the case would go to the QBD unless both parties agreed that the matter should be dealt with in the County Court.

1.7 Criminal courts

The highest criminal court in Britain is the House of Lords. It deals with criminal appeals on points of law only from the Court of Appeal (Criminal

Criminal courts

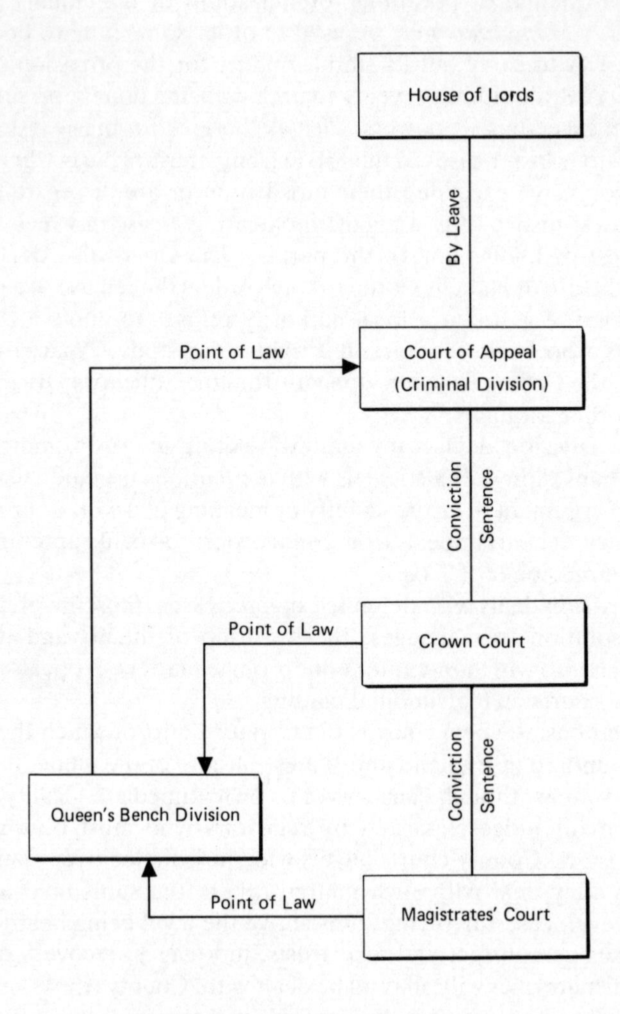

Division) or the QBD. Either of these courts may give leave for appeal and they must certify that a point of law of public importance is involved.

The Court of Appeal (Criminal Division) hears appeals from the Crown Court against conviction or sentence. It is staffed by the Lord Chief Justice and judges of the QBD with a quorum of three. It has the power to quash a conviction and to increase or decrease a sentence. In some circumstances it may order a re-trial.

The Divisional Court of the Queen's Bench Division still retains some criminal jurisdiction. It hears appeals from magistrates' courts or crown courts on 'case stated', that is on a point of law only. Thus in *R. (The Crown)* v. *The Newport Justices* (1929) a headmaster had caned a pupil for breaking a school rule which banned smoking. The boy had been off school premises at the time and the parents maintained that because of this the head had no right to inflict corporal punishment. At the parents' insistence an appeal was made to the QBD on a point of law, i.e. whether a school's authority extended to matters away from the school premises. The court decided that it did.

Crown Courts were set up by the Courts Act of 1971 and replaced the old assize and quarter sessions. Though first tier crown courts may also try civil cases, their main function is to try indictable criminal offences. These may be very serious crimes such as murder, rape or arson, which have to be tried in the crown court, or lesser crimes such as petty theft or handling stolen goods, where the accused has chosen crown court trial by jury instead of summary trial by the magistrates. Trial is by a judge – a High Court judge, a Circuit judge or a Recorder (a part-time judge), according to the seriousness of the offence – and a jury of twelve persons sworn in for the purpose. The judge decides on the law and the jury gives a verdict on the facts. The criminal jurisdiction of the Crown Court is unlimited and it may impose any sanction that is allowed under the criminal law. That could be life imprisonment, though technically the death penalty is still in force for treason or piracy. The crown court hears appeals from magistrates' courts against verdict or sentence.

Magistrates' courts exist in almost every town of any size and they deal with a wide variety of matters in their own areas. They have some civil jurisdiction such as in the adoption of children and in domestic matters. They exercise wide administrative or quasi-legal powers over licensing. Formerly a school wishing to use its hall for music and dancing had to be licensed by the magistrates to do so. However, under the Local Government (Miscellaneous Provisions) Act 1982 this may now be done by application to the appropriate local authority.

However, the main function of magistrates is to deal in the first instance with criminal offences. This happens in two ways. If the crime is a serious indictable offence, such as murder, the magistrates conduct what is known as a preliminary hearing, or committal proceedings. In effect, their task is to examine the evidence and decide whether there is a case to answer. If they believe that there is not then they may dismiss the case. If they believe that there is enough evidence to warrant a trial then the matter is remitted to the crown court.

Many lesser offences are triable either upon indictment in the crown court or summarily by the magistrates and the accused may be given the option of a hearing by the magistrates or a trial by judge and jury. It may be a difficult decision. The accused may feel he has a better chance if tried by twelve ordinary members of the public. However, the crown court's powers of punishment are unlimited whereas the magistrates may only impose fines of up to £1000 or imprisonment up to six months. Actually, where indictable offences are concerned, magistrates always leave the option open to remit convicted persons to the crown court for sentencing.

Other offences are only triable summarily by the magistrates. This category includes many traffic offences such as speeding or failing to tax a vehicle. Failure to cause a child to be educated is also a summary offence.

Appeal against conviction or sentence lies to the Crown Court and appeal on a point of law to the Queen's Bench Division.

There are a few stipendiary magistrates (paid, full-time, legally qualified persons) but most magistrates are members of the public appointed by the Lord Chancellor on the recommendation of advisory committees for local authority areas. They are appointed under what is known as the Commission of the Peace. Magistrates may only serve in the area to which they are appointed. They receive expenses only and are not legally qualified, though it is usual for them to have some part-time training.

At least two magistrates must sit when a case is being tried (usually there are three). They act as both judge and jury. They have a clerk to assist them, who must be a qualified barrister or solicitor. He may advise them on the law but may not assist them in reaching a verdict. The clerk is responsible for the general administration and procedure of the court.

Juvenile courts are separate sittings of the magistrates' courts and occupy a considerable amount of their time. They will be discussed in some detail in Chapter 10.

1.8 Tribunals

Strictly speaking these are not courts but in practice they act in a very similar way. They are hearings set up to deal with problems in specific areas largely created by modern legislation such as rents, land, income tax and employment. These are called administrative tribunals and their composition, procedure and powers vary considerably. However, all exist under the Tribunal and Enquiries Act 1971 and control may be exercised over them by the Queen's Bench Division by means of prerogative orders. Most have provision for appeals.

There are also what are known as domestic tribunals. These are disciplinary hearings for certain professional groups such as barristers, solicitors, doctors and dentists. If, eventually, a central teachers' council should be established, then it would certainly wish to have its own disciplinary tribunal. Occasionally, local authorities have been known to set up a domestic tribunal in order to deal with a particularly difficult situation in relation to schools. Unless such tribunals are flouting the basic rules of our law, the courts will not interfere with them. Their procedure, therefore, may vary widely and this has led to criticism. In one such tribunal set up by an education authority the 'accused' and his representative were not allowed to cross-examine parents and children giving damaging evidence against him.

The tribunal that may be of real concern to teachers and other employees is the industrial tribunal dealing with employment law – particularly problems related to dismissal, redundancy, sex and race discrimination. Such a tribunal has a legally qualified chairman and two lay members and appeal lies from it to the Employment Appeal Tribunal, which has the status of a Division of the High Court, and thence to the Court of Appeal itself.

1.9 European Law

The European Economic Community was established by the first Treaty of Rome in 1957. Great Britain joined in 1972. British courts may ask for rulings on points of Community Law and courts of final instance, such as the House of Lords, must do so. In matters of European Law the European Court of Justice supersedes the House of Lords so it is no longer true to say that the latter is the final court of appeal on all matters. Clearly, as time goes on, European Law will have an increasing effect on our affairs.

In 1950 Britain was a signatory to the European Convention of Human Rights. It is possible, therefore, for matters covered by this Convention to be referred to the European Court of Human Rights. Refusal to comply with a direction from this Court could possibly lead to a state being expelled from the Council of Europe.

2 The English system of education

2.1 Parliament and the DES

Our Parliament is supreme. It can make new laws, change existing laws, or completely reverse the decisions of previous Parliaments. Mostly change takes place as the result of public pressure or when a new government takes over and attempts to implement promises it has made during the election. The Education Act of 1980 is a good example of this. The Conservatives had promised parents a greater involvement in the running of schools and local authorities more discretion as to the services they need or need not provide.

Certain Acts stand out as watersheds of change – the Reform Act of 1832 which extended the suffrage, the Education Act of 1870 which introduced free education for all or the National Insurance Act of 1949. The 1944 Education Act is in this category.

Today the public system of education in England and Wales is based upon this great Act, largely the work of Lord Butler. It set up the Ministry of Education, now the Department of Education and Science; it gave wide powers to local authorities over a wide range of educational provision; and it made arrangements for the inclusion of denominational schools within a national system.

There have been a number of amending Acts ranging from the 1946 Act to the recent Acts of 1980 and 1981. Other Acts have brought about minor changes such as the Act of 1973 which legalized Work Experience and the Act of 1976 which changed the pattern of leaving dates.

The Act of 1964 set up the Department of Education and Science and authorized the appointment of the Secretary of State with delegated powers to create rules and regulations by means of statutory instruments. It is the duty of the Secretary to, 'promote the education of the people in England and Wales . . . and to secure the effective execution by local authorities, under his control and direction, of the national policy' 1944 Act Section 1 (i).

The work of the Department is dealt with in a number of branches. The school's branch deals with primary and secondary education. Through its teams of HMIs and other officers it takes an overall view of school provision and is responsible for seeing that the statutory requirements in relation to schools are adhered to. It also deals with such matters as secondary reorganization, assisted places and independent schools, nursery schools and the provision for immigrant children. The special services branch deals with the education and further education of handicapped pupils and the school health and dental services. The teachers' branch deals with teachers' qualifications, conditions of service and salaries. It is responsible for policy regarding the demand and supply of teachers. It also has responsibility for teacher training and the probation of teachers. It deals with all matters relating to pensions. Other branches are universities, further education, science, architects and building, finance, planning, legal, arts, intelligence and external relations.

The Secretary of State has the duty of inspecting schools at appropriate intervals and such inspections are carried out by members of the Inspectorate, who are servants of the Crown. For obstructing an HMI the penalty is a fine not exceeding £20 on a first offence, or, for subsequent offences, a fine of £50 or three months' imprisonment.

The Inspectorate is organized in geographical areas each headed by a divisional inspector in charge of a team. There are also staff inspectors who are responsible for particular subjects or sectors of the educational system.

Inspections may be of three types – general, specialist or district. General inspection concerns the overall inspection by a team of HMIs of a particular institution or a group of schools or colleges, though in recent years this type of inspection seems largely to have disappeared. Specialist inspection concerns particular subjects or specific areas such as the provision for deaf children. District inspection concerns the range of educational provision in an LEA's area. An individual HMI may be concerned with more than one type of inspection. According to his particular experience, interest and qualifications he may act as a specialist inspector over a wide area, as well as a general inspector over his own district.

HMIs have no powers of compulsion – they visit mainly in an advisory capacity but, of course, they may submit reports to the LEA or other appropriate authority. Perhaps the most valuable functions carried out by HMIs at the present time lie in the national surveys undertaken and the dissemination of new ideas from one school to another.

The main control exercised by the Department over local education authorities is a financial one. In order to ensure the most economic use of the country's money, the Department only permits new building projects in carefully drawn up 'Building Programmes' – even though the LEAs are spending from their own limited resources.

Advisory councils have been set up for England and Wales. The Secretary of State refers questions of educational theory and practice to them as he sees fit and asks for their advice.

In 1964 the Schools Council was established. Its function is to initiate and to encourage research into curriculum development and other educational problems and to co-ordinate secondary school examinations. It is now to be replaced by two separate bodies – one dealing with examinations, the other with curriculum matters.

2.2 Local authorities

Section 6 (1) and (2) of the 1944 Act put the actual provision and administration of education into the hands of local education authorities. They were allowed to divide their areas into smaller units called divisions, to be administered by local committees, called divisional executives. The powers given to divisional executives varied from one area to another. Since 1st April 1974, however, divisional executives have ceased to exist and county authorities have taken responsibility for education in full – most of them devising their own systems of delegation to various districts within their own areas. Metropolitan authorities like Manchester and Liverpool give full responsibility for education to each of their districts.

The LEA is responsible for the day to day working of the education system. It has powers to adopt its own policy towards education. Thus many authorities are now fully comprehensive – some have taken very few steps towards a change. There is the financial control mentioned above. Also, by Section 99 (1) of the 1944 Act there is the right of the Secretary of State to order an authority to comply with his directions, although this is very rarely used. The Secretary may do this at his own instigation or on the complaint of an interested person. Under Section 68 of the same Act, he may exercise the same powers over governors of schools.

LEAs may make regulations on a wide range of matters and these are discussed in later sections.

Perhaps it is typical of us that our system is not really a national system at all. It is a collection of local systems, loosely similar, with some control and direction from the centre.

There are disadvantages. If his family were on the move, a child could possibly attend a first school, a primary school, a middle school (eight to twelve or nine to thirteen), a secondary school (eleven to sixteen, twelve to sixteen, eleven to eighteen or thirteen to eighteen) or a sixth form college. The curriculum range, staffing provision and teaching methods could vary enormously and so could the provision of other facilities. For example, Authority A is well known for its excellent provision of sports halls and the assistance it gives to representative teams but its libraries are dreadful whereas in Authority B the reverse happens.

What an LEA must do

1 Appoint a chief education officer.
2 Enforce the education of children between five and sixteen years.
3 Provide all books and equipment.
4 Provide efficient and suitable schools.
5 Provide facilities for further education.
6 Arrange for special educational treatment.
7 Comply with DES standards over school premises.
8 Provide for the health and safety of staff and pupils.

9 Appoint governors.
10 Make instruments and articles of government.
11 Organize free transport for those qualified.
12 Allow medical and dental inspections.
13 Arrange for collective worship and religious instruction.
14 Implement mandatory awards.
15 Supervise the part-time employment of children of thirteen to sixteen years.

What an LEA may do

1 Create, amalgamate or close schools.
2 Group schools under one board of governors.
3 Control secular instruction.
4 Control the appointment and dismissal of teachers.
5 Provide education otherwise than at school.
6 Organize school or college inspections.
7 Provide meals or milk.
8 Arrange work experience.
9 Pay for board and lodging of pupils.
10 Provide free clothing.
11 Make awards for 'assisted places'.
12 Provide nursery schools.
13 Make discretionary awards.
14 Purchase land compulsorily.

2.3 Schools

Section 8 of the 1944 Act requires LEAs to provide sufficient schools for their areas, and these shall

> 'not be deemed to be sufficient unless they are sufficient in number, character and equipment to afford for all pupils such variety of instruction and training as may be desirable in view of their differing ages, abilities and aptitudes'.

The 1944 Act lays down that the system shall be organized in three successive stages: primary, secondary and further. The primary stage includes nursery, infant and junior schools; the secondary stage includes grammar, modern and technical schools, and various hybrid forms, although most of these have now changed to the various forms of comprehensive school; and further includes all vocational and non-vocational education for those who have left school – but it does not include the universities. According to their age range, middle schools may now be classified as either primary or secondary schools. In addition, LEAs must provide facilities for all children needing special educational treatment. These may be within the normal school system, such as centres for

ESN children attached to ordinary schools, but they may consist of day or boarding special schools.

Schools in which the LEAs have a financial interest are described as maintained. These may be county schools, where the LEA has complete control and responsibility, or they may be voluntary.

2.4 County schools

Here the LEA is entirely responsible for the provision and maintenance of the school. The school is governed by an instrument and articles of government. Under the 1980 Act the governing body must include governors appointed by the education authority and at least two parent governors elected by parents. There must be teacher governors – at least two where the school has 300 pupils or more and one in schools where the figure is below 300. The staff governors must be elected by the staff from the school. The head teacher must be a governor of the school unless he elects otherwise. When a county primary school is in the area of a wider authority such as parish or district council that authority must provide at least one governor, who does not necessarily have to be a member of that local authority.

Religious education in county schools must be undenominational and according to the agreed syllabus.

2.5 Voluntary schools

These may be either 'aided', or 'controlled', or 'special agreement'.

Aided

The school was not established by the LEA and the governors have provided a proportion of the cost of bringing it up to standard. They are also responsible for the maintenance and repair of the exterior of the building with an 85 per cent grant from the LEA which has complete responsibility for the interior and the grounds and playing fields.

The governing body must include foundation governors who must outnumber the other governors by two if the total number of governors is eighteen or less and by three if the total is more than eighteen. At least one foundation governor, at the time of appointment, must be the parent of a child at the school. The head must be a governor unless he elects otherwise.

Religious education is controlled by the governors according to the trust or the custom in a school before it became aided. However, if a pupil attends such a school because no county school is readily available then his parents may request that he be taught according to the agreed syllabus. Usually the act of worship is denominational.

Staff salaries are paid by the LEA which also has the right to prohibit the appointment of any teacher engaged to give secular instruction and the right to require the dismissal of such a teacher. Caretakers, cleaners and other ancillaries are usually appointed by the governors but the LEA appoints school meals staff.

The LEA has a limited right to free use of the building for educational purposes outside normal school hours.

Controlled

Here the LEA bears the entire cost of maintenance, improvements and additions but if the school is on its original site the ownership must be vested in the trustees.

At least one fifth of the governing body must be made up of foundation governors and the rules as to parents, teachers and the head are the same as for county schools.

The agreed syllabus for religious education must be used but the school has to provide denominational instruction for not more than two periods per week if parents request it. Where the staff of a controlled school exceeds two, 'reserved' staff for the teaching of religious education must be appointed, up to one fifth of the total staff. The head is not a 'reserved' teacher but the LEA, which appoints all other staff, must hear representation from the foundation governors before his appointment. The act of worship may be denominational.

The governors have special rights over the use of the school on Saturdays and Sundays.

Special agreement

The rules as to governors and the maintenance of premises are the same as for aided schools, as are the provisions for religious education. The act of worship may be denominational.

Provisions for staff appointments are as for controlled schools and the LEA appoints all non-teaching staff.

The LEA has limited rights over the use of the premises outside school hours.

2.6 Special education

Largely as a result of the recommendations of the Warnock committee, the Education Act of 1981 was passed, establishing new provisions for special educational treatment. No doubt many of these will take some time to come into effect, but an explanation of them may be found in DES circular 8/81 of 7 December 1981.

The Act introduces a concept of special educational provision based on the special needs of individual children (previously there were various categories of handicaps). Perhaps up to 20 per cent of pupils might now be affected (as against 2 per cent previously) since the concept of 'special educational need' is intended to be a fairly wide one and includes children with a learning difficulty significantly greater than the majority of children of the same age. The only difficulty excluded is that imposed by belonging to a linguistic minority.

Subject to the views of parents, the resources of the school and the LEA and the effect on other pupils, provision is to be made in ordinary schools. LEAs may still provide special education by special schooling or home tuition.

The LEA has a responsibility to identify children who have special educational needs from the age of two upwards, to make an assessment, issue a statement and then arrange suitable special educational provision. It may insist on medical examination. Parents may claim an assessment for children under the age of two, have a right to make representations to the LEA and the right of appeal to the Appeals Committees set up under the 1980 Act, and ultimately to the Secretary of State.

Health authorities are under a duty, where they believe a child under five has special educational needs, to inform the parents and the LEA.

The Secretary of State has power to make new regulations for special schools.

2.7 Independent schools

The 1944 Act s.70 deals with independent schools, which are those not receiving financial help from an LEA (except under the 'assisted places' scheme). They may exist under a trust deed or simply as a commercial undertaking but they must be registered. Failure to register may result in a prosecution – a successful action being brought against one school in 1970.

Since 1977 it has not been possible for independent schools to be inspected and 'recognized as efficient'. However, they are still liable to inspection by HMIs and the Secretary of State may take action if they are found to be housed in defective or unsuitable accommodation, if the instruction is inadequate, or the proprietor or teachers are not 'proper persons'.

The other control of independent schools is exercised by the Independent Schools' Tribunal, set up under the 1944 Act. A tribunal, which may consist of either a legal or educational panel, acts under the control of the Council on Tribunals in accordance with the Tribunal and Enquiries Act 1971. Its powers include the removal of an independent school from the register.

2.8 Governors

Under the 1944 Act all schools must have governors though the composition of the governing body varies according to the type of school. Also the composition of the governing body may vary from one LEA to another.

The LEA delegates the management of schools to governors by means of an instrument and articles of government and proceedings must comply with The Education (School Governing Bodies) Regulations 1981.

The Taylor Report (1977) made a number of recommendations regarding the composition of governing bodies and attempted to increase the opportunities for real involvement in the running of schools. The 1980 Act certainly allows for increased representation on governing bodies by parents and teachers but such representation is limited and many authorities have, for some time, been allowing parents, teachers and even pupils to sit as governors anyway. No attempt has been made to give governors real power or to deal with the difficult problem of the separate powers of governors and head teachers. Nor has any attempt been made to deal with that blight on governing bodies – the political appointee who has no interest in the school or its locality.

While governors may have functions in encouraging and supporting the work of a school and bringing a sensible layman's views to the running of what may be something of a closed community, their powers are very limited, as an examination of the instrument and articles of government will show.

Both of these documents are drawn up by the LEA in the case of county schools and where secondary schools are concerned the approval of the Department of Education and Science must be obtained. The Department does not insist on absolute uniformity so, while regulations tend to be similar from one authority to another, they may not necessarily be so. Teachers have a right to see the instrument and articles for their school. From 1 September 1985 instruments and articles must comply with the 1980 Act.

2.9 Instrument of Government

This is the constitution of the governing body. It lays down the number of governors to be appointed, special governors, e.g. parents or the representatives of universities, the method of removing governors and the arrangements for filling casual vacancies.

Before the passing of the 1980 Act many instruments allowed for a teacher representative elected by the teaching staff. The teacher was usually appointed for one year and had no vote. He was asked to leave the meeting if discussion was to take place of the appointment of teaching staff, disciplinary action against staff equal or senior in status to himself, or for any 'good cause' decided by the governors. Under the new Act, teachers have full powers as governors unless of course they have an interest in proceedings e.g. over a personal promotion.

The instrument lays down rules for the appointment of chairman and vice-chairman. The appointment of chairman is particularly important to the head of a school. Since the governors normally meet as a body only once a term, the head must be in regular contact with the chairman over the running of the school and the possibility of calling special meetings. The most frequent of these will be for the appointment of staff but they may also be necessary when some crisis has occurred. If the head wishes to suspend a pupil then he will need the backing of his chairman, even where county regulations give him the right himself to impose a short suspension.

The instrument lays down rules for the calling of meetings, for procedure at meetings, and defines the duties of the clerk to the governors.

2.10 Articles of Government

The Articles deal with the powers of the governors in relation to the running of the school.

There is a section dealing with finance but since governors in county schools rarely exercise any financial control except over sums of money given to the school or raised by it, the high sounding phrases have a hollow ring to them.

The governors must report to the LEA on the condition and repair of the premises and usually they have responsibility for the letting of the fields and buildings outside school hours.

The Articles will lay down the provisions for the appointment and dismissal of the headmaster, the teaching staff and ancillaries of the particular school. Other matters dealt with include occasional holidays and the transfer, admission and suspension of pupils.

Articles for secondary schools are drawn up by the local authority but must have the approval of the Department of Education and Science. However, the Department does not insist on Articles being identical for different secondary schools. Articles drawn up for primary schools are not subject to DES approval though, of course, the Secretary of State has ultimate control over them. It is in dealing with such matters as the curriculum and the suspension of pupils that there may be slight but significant differences between various Articles of Government.

2.11 Problems

The Karl Marx Comprehensive School and the Samuel Pickwick High School are secondary schools of a similar type and organization but situated in different authorities.

The Karl Marx Comprehensive School

Extracts from the Articles of Government:

'The local education authority shall determine the general educational character of the school and its place in the local education system, subject thereto the governors shall have the general direction of the conduct of the school and the welfare of the pupils.'

'The headmaster shall control the internal organization, management and discipline of the school, and shall exercise supervision of the teaching and non-teaching staff, and shall, after consultation with the Chief Education Officer, have the power of suspending pupils from attendance for any cause which he considers adequate, but on suspending any pupil he shall forthwith report the case to the governors who shall consult the local education authority.'

The Karl Marx School has a most vociferous body of left wing governors who are determined that the school shall turn over to a system of complete mixed ability teaching. Politics is to be introduced as a subject from Year 1 onwards. The head and staff are opposed to both changes.

How do you assess the situation? Write your comments below.

The Samuel Pickwick High School

Extracts from the Articles of Government:

'The local education authority shall determine the general educational character of the school, its place in the local educational system and the main lines of policy which shall determine its curriculum.'

'The headmaster shall control the internal organization, management and discipline of the school, shall exercise supervision over the teaching and non-teaching staff, and shall have the power of suspending pupils from attendance for any cause which he considers adequate following consultation with the chairman, or the vice-chairman of the governors but on suspending any pupil he shall forthwith report the case to the governors who shall consult the local education authority. No pupil shall be expelled or otherwise withdrawn from the school at the request of the governors without the prior approval of the local education authority.'

The head of the Samuel Pickwick High School wishes to suspend Samuel Weller who has declared in a loud voice for all to hear that the music master, Mr Tracy Tupman, is of doubtful parentage. Samuel is a thorn in the flesh of many staff at the Samuel Pickwick School and after this latest insult there is strong pressure on the head 'to do something about it'. He decides to suspend Samuel Weller and consults his chairman of governors. But, unfortunately, the chairman will not agree. Privately he agrees with the comment regarding Mr Tupman and suggests that a strong warning be given to Samuel Weller and the matter be left at that.

What is your reaction to this? Write your comments in the box.

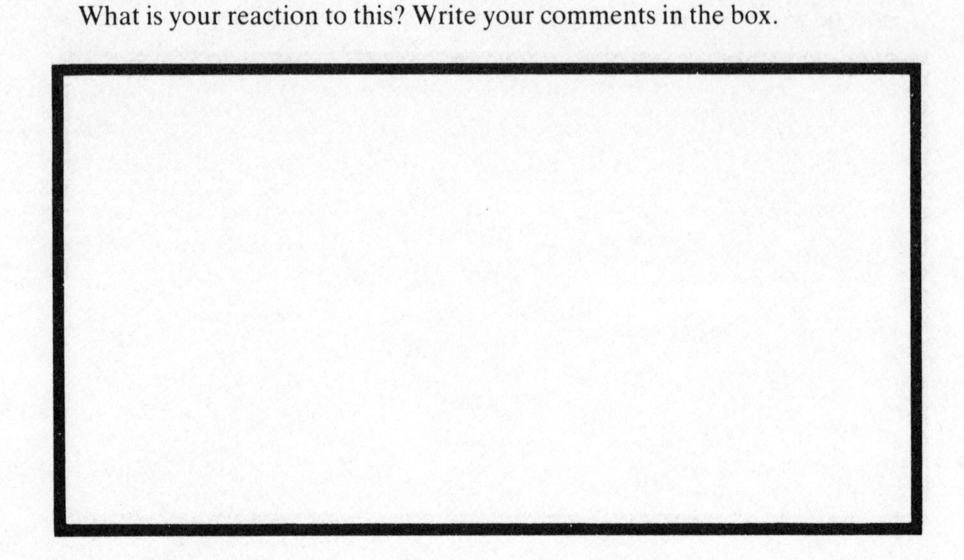

2.12 Comments

The Karl Marx School

The word 'curriculum' is not used in the Articles of Government. The governors have the general direction of the 'conduct of the school and welfare of the pupils'. They seem to have a case for saying that they may decide on the curriculum and perhaps to add that a study of politics is important for the welfare of pupils. The head is responsible for the 'internal organization and management'. He has a case for saying that decisions of curriculum matters are, therefore, his. The terms used are so vague that various interpretations are possible and a court case would be needed to decide what they meant.

The Articles of Government of the Samuel Pickwick School at least leave the 'main lines of policy' over the curriculum to the LEA but it is doubtful if even that would solve the problem at the Karl Marx School. Is a teaching strategy like mixed ability grouping covered by 'curriculum'? Is the introduction of politics covered by 'main lines'? Very doubtful.

The Samuel Pickwick School

The head of this school has the power of suspending pupils after consultation with the chairman or vice-chairman of governors. Does this mean that he simply has to discuss the matter and then go ahead with the suspension or may the chairman block the action? The clause suggests that he may defy his chairman but the wording is very unsatisfactory.

In the Karl Marx School the LEA must be consulted but the same problem arises. Can the head suspend in spite of the LEA's view? It might seem so.

3 Teachers and contracts

3.1 Questions

Here are some statements. They are common ones, frequently mentioned by teachers, which stem from the contractual situation in which we find ourselves. Briefly, there are three possible comments – yes, no or perhaps. What are your reactions? Please see the end of the chapter for comments.

Is that true?

1. If a child is injured while in the care of a teacher, the teacher is liable to be sued and may have to pay damages.
2. An authority may move a teacher from one school to another.
3. You only have to do what your contract says you have to do.
4. A teacher is required to work a five hour day.
5. Staff must carry out supervision duties.
6. This includes supervision before and after school sessions.
7. Because of the Employment Protection Act teachers cannot be sacked.
8. A head can ban a female member of staff from wearing trouser suits and insist that male teachers wear a tie.
9. Teachers are entitled to the same holidays as pupils.
10. Taking part in out-of-school activities is absolutely voluntary.

3.2 Servants and independent contractors

In law there are two kinds of people who work for others and are paid for it. One kind, known as a 'servant', is not only paid by his employer but is controlled by him as to the manner in which his duties shall be performed and, explicitly or implicitly, accepts such control when he makes his contract. He is employed under a contract of service. The other kind, the independent contractor, is also paid but is left to organize the work himself and is not subject to close control by his employer. He is employed under a contract for services. A paid employee is then either a servant or an independent contractor – it sometimes needs a court to decide into which category a particular person falls. It might be thought that the amount of real control exercised over a teacher – that is over what and how he teaches in the classroom – is rather slight but an education authority does control the time, the place, routine and conditions under which a teacher works and so it is accepted that a teacher is a servant. Architects and solicitors would be independent contractors, as would a teacher giving private tuition in his own house.

The distinction between the two categories is important as in almost every case an employer is not liable for the torts of his independent contractors but he is vicariously liable for the torts of his servants committed within the course of employment.

3.3 Torts

A tort is a civil wrong, dealt with in the civil courts, as distinct from a criminal wrong which is an offence against the state, punished by the state in the criminal courts. Some wrongs, such as assault and battery (crime or trespass to the person), may be both crimes and torts – the distinction depending on whether the action is brought in a civil or criminal court. In criminal actions there may be a number of purposes – punishment, protection of society, deterring of others or reform of the criminal. In tort there is normally one object – compensation in cash for an infringement of a right. Torts that may concern teachers in particular are negligence – damage suffered by others through one's careless behaviour; trespass in its various forms; or defamation – damage to a person's reputation by libel or slander.

3.4 Course of employment

An employer is not usually liable for the crimes of his employees (though the special situation under the Health and Safety at Work Act will be discussed in Chapter 4). If a teacher assaults and batters a pupil and a criminal prosecution is brought the authority cannot be joined in the action. However, if the action is brought in a civil court as an action for assault and battery (forms of trespass to the person) then the employer may well be joined. It depends on whether the teacher was acting 'within the course of his employment'. If he was, then under the principle of vicarious liability the authority may be sued alone, or the two may be sued together. If the teacher was not acting within the course of his employment then he is on his own. If an authority loses an action where it is held to be vicariously liable, then it may recover some of the damages from the teacher.

When is an employee acting within the course of his employment? The basic answer is when he is carrying out any activity which a court might reasonably conclude is a part of the job for which he was employed and, either directly or by implication, was authorized by the employer. It has been held that an employee driver who, for his own purposes, deviated from the express route given to him by his employer was putting himself outside the course of his employment. It has been held that an employer is liable for the torts of his employee even when the employee was carrying out his duties in a manner expressly forbidden by the employer. In each case the court decides whether the act was within the course of employment or not.

If Mr Chips, the woodwork master, sends a boy out of school to fetch coffee for the staff of the department, then he is acting outside the course of his employment. But if Mrs Pastry, the home economics teacher, sends a girl to fetch materials to use in the demonstration lesson, then she may well be acting within the course of her employment.

Many education authorities divide school activities into those that are compulsory or 'curricular' and those that are voluntary or 'extra curricular'. In the voluntary category are usually included activities such as supervising inter-school matches, visits to the theatre, visits abroad, visits to museums, factories, art galleries and so on. Compulsory activities are those that are an essential part of a school course. Schools that did not provide the so-called voluntary activities today would be considered very poor schools indeed and it is suggested that in a test case today a court would certainly consider them to be authorized by the employer as an incidental part of a teacher's duties and therefore the employer would be vicariously liable.

3.5 The contract

There is no clear definition of a contract of service. Until recent times the situation was largely one governed by the law of contract. The terms agreed between the parties when the contract was concluded were all that mattered. However, a spate of modern legislation has changed this position considerably. Most of the statutory provisions relating to contracts are discussed in Chapter 4.

Contrary to popular belief, very few contracts have to be in writing (even contracts for the sale of land have only to be evidenced in writing). Therefore a contract of employment may be made orally. However, under the Employment Protection (Consolidation) Act of 1978, within thirteen weeks from the commencement of employment all employers must give their employees written details of the appointment. This rule does not apply to employees working less than sixteen hours a week.

Most teaching posts are advertised either locally or nationally, particularly in the *Times Educational Supplement*. The practice of 'internal' advertising is growing, however, and this entails advertising only within an authority's existing schools. The usual procedure is for teachers to obtain details of the post and an application form which requests details of education, qualifications, training, DES number, teaching experience and employment outside teaching. A space is left for any further details the applicant may wish to include to further his cause. Some authorities which have not updated their forms for some time continue to ask applicants for senior academic posts if they can play a musical instrument. Over-anxious candidates have been known to put forward their proficiency on the bugle or harmonica as of value in their applications for head of mathematics or head of science posts!

The names of referees are required but the request for written testimonials has now been dropped by most authorities.

Appointment is by interview. Sometimes all governors have a right to be present, sometimes an appointments sub-committee has been formed. In practice, interviews for junior posts will be conducted by the chairman of governors and two or three others while very senior posts will be conducted by the entire governing body. In county and voluntary schools a representative of the authority, an inspector or an adviser, is usually present and also the head but only the governors present have a vote. Some authorities include senior staff, such as heads of department, on the panel but they have no vote.

An offer made to a teacher at interview is invariably subject to ratification by the local authority and a written offer to the candidate. In county schools this comes from the authority, in voluntary schools from the governors. The teacher is then in a position to accept or refuse the offer. While it is unusual for authorities to refuse to confirm an appointment recommended by the governors, it is safer for a teacher not to tender his resignation from an existing post until a formal offer of the new post is received. The contract is complete once the acceptance has been posted – not when it is received by the authority.

Teachers may be offered full-time posts, part-time or temporary posts (formal interviews are not always conducted for these) or even fixed term contracts.

In most schools the offer of a post comes from the governors who are not the employers so they are not parties to the contract. In aided schools, however, it is said that the governors are the employers. If the governors are the employers then of course they may be vicariously liable for the torts of their teachers if committed within the course of employment.

3.6 Express terms

Certain terms are stated clearly in a contract but even these may vary from one contract to another. Some authorities appoint teachers to the service of the authority, others to a specific school. It might be a breach of contract (and possibly a constructive dismissal) for a teacher appointed to a specific school to be moved to another without his or her consent.

Some authorities use written formal contracts for the appointment of teachers and others appoint by an offer and acceptance in writing but, whichever method is used, under the Employment Protection (Consolidation) Act 1978, certain particulars must be given to each employee within thirteen weeks of commencing employment.

These are:

1 The title of the post.
2 Details of salary, including the rate of pay and intervals at which payment is to be made. A teacher must be told the scale at which the post is to be paid.
3 Regulations for sick pay, payment because of injury and pension rights.
4 Hours of work and holiday entitlement.
5 The length of notice to be given by either the employer or the employee.
6 Particulars of disciplinary rules, including the relevant grievance procedure.

Eyebrows may well be raised at no. 4. There are no clear rules for teachers as to hours of work and holidays. No. 1 also creates a problem.

Ben Jonson

Mr Jonson applied for the post of second in the English department, scale 3. The post was advertised in the *Times Educational Supplement* and the head of the school sent Mr Jonson details of the English department and explained the duties to be carried out by the person appointed. Mr Jonson was offered the post and accepted. When he received the formal contract it merely stated his appointment as assistant teacher, scale 3.

Can Mr Jonson be switched from English to some other subject? If he signs the contract as it is then it might seem so. The courts have never considered whether an advertisement for a teaching post is a term of the contract or not.

Other matters would amount to express terms. The conditions of tenure (an agreement drawn up between the local authorities and teacher associations) are given to all newly appointed teachers. These give conditions relating to dismissal, salaries, notice to be given, retirement and provisions relating to maternity leave.

The last two of these will be dealt with in Chapter 4.

3.7 Dismissal

Teachers, like most other employees, enjoy the advantages of the Employment Protection Act but their conditions of tenure gave them considerable protection long before the Act was introduced. As far as dismissal is concerned the conditions state:

Dismissal of Teachers

1 Apart from those set out in individual articles of government or rules of management there are various obligatory duties, rights and procedures imposed on and enjoyed by employers and employees under existing legislation in industrial relations; the more important of these are referred to in Appendix I. In addition to the procedures stipulated in the articles of government and rules of management an authority shall have a formal procedure for the hearing of such dismissal cases as follows:

2 Before any decision is taken to dismiss a teacher, or in the case of a voluntary aided school, before any decision is taken to give consent to the dismissal of a teacher (where such consent is required of the local education authority), the local education authority shall at his/her request grant the teacher a hearing, and at his/her option allow him/her to be represented by a friend.

3 At least seven days' notice of the time, date and place of such hearing shall be given to the teacher; and if his/her dismissal is to be considered on the grounds of some charge, complaint or adverse report affecting his/her conduct or capacity he/she shall at the same time be supplied in writing with a statement of such charge, complaint or adverse report.

4 The hearing shall take place before a sub-committee of the Education Committee appointed for the purpose or such other body as may be agreed locally by the

authority and the recognised teachers' organisations.

5 All proceedings shall be confidential until the decision of the local education authority has been made and only the operative decision shall be published or made public in any way. The decision and the reasons for it should be communicated in writing to the individual.

6 In the event of emergency on allegation of misconduct or for any other urgent cause a teacher may be suspended pending the decision of the authority. In the event of such suspension steps shall be taken for a meeting of the appropriate committee to be held as soon as possible so that the suspension may be terminated by dismissal or reinstatement or otherwise as may be decided. Payment of full salary during periods of suspension shall be regarded as the normal procedure from which departure shall be made only when the employing authority expressly decides that there is a compelling reason for so doing.

7 The provisions relating to hearing before decisions to dismiss teachers are taken are intended to apply not only to cases of summary dismissal but also cases of dismissal on due notice under contract.

8 The above provisions will apply to the vast majority of cases, since the dismissal of any teacher will, in general, require the consent of the authority. Where the consent of the authority is not required the authority should ensure that provision is made for a similar procedure to be followed whereby the teacher concerned shall at his/her request be accorded a hearing and representation by that body which has the power of dismissal with the consent of the authority vested in it, either under statute or by delegation from the authority.

(*Conditions of Service for School Teachers in England and Wales*, CLEA/ST)

The 'friend' mentioned in 2 could be either a solicitor or a Union representative. The procedure does not remove the right to bring an action at an Industrial Tribunal for unfair dismissal.

3.8 Salary

Teachers are paid by monthly instalments and for each full term's service the teacher must receive not less than one third of the annual salary. For this purpose the terms are constituted as follows:

Summer – 1 May to 31 August
Autumn – 1 September to 31 December
Spring – 1 January to 30 April

Adjustments between authorities may be made, for example a teacher taking up a new appointment as from 21 April would be paid up to 20 April by his old authority and from 21 April by his/her new one.

Teachers taking up their first appointments are paid from 1 January, the first day of the summer term if this is before 1 May, or from 1 September (or from the first day of the Autumn Term if this is before 1 September).

Salaries are based on the Burnham Scale (set by a joint negotiating body of representatives from the local authorities and the teacher associations).

Teachers are paid on scales ranging from 1 to 4. In addition there is a senior teacher scale, deputy head teacher scales and head teacher scales.

According to a rather complicated formula based on points given for different age groups, schools are given a unit total and are placed in a group. The groups are reviewed on a triennial basis and necessary adjustments made. The groups range from one to fourteen. The salaries of heads and deputies are related to the group the school is in. Each group is given a 'points score'. This is a range of points and indicates the minimum and maximum number that an authority may allocate. For example: a school with a unit total of 2800 is in group ten with a points score range of forty-seven to sixty. To make matters even more complicated a scale 2 post counts one point, a scale 3 post two points and scale 4 and senior teacher posts count three points each.

Generous authorities award the maximum number of scale points per group, parsimonious ones the minimum. Most strike the half way mark. This explains why it seems possible to get a scale 4 for geography, say, in one authority rather than in others and why some primary schools seem so blessed with points in comparison with others.

Appointments to all scale posts are in the hands of the governing body, subject to the authority's approval, and posts may be advertised at a certain scale or internal promotions may be made in some circumstances. Usually those above scale 1 have specific responsibilities attached to them but the reasoning behind the allocation of such posts in some schools may often seem rather strange.

When a teacher is promoted to the next higher scale he moves to the same salary level on the new scale and up by two increments. If at the time of promotion an increment was due anyway, then this takes effect before the salary is calculated on the new scale.

When as a result of a review a points score is reduced, heads, deputies and other teachers may be protected but where the number of points is exceeded and a teacher holding a post above scale 1 leaves, then the points are lost. In a situation of falling rolls this could become a serious problem in the management of schools in the future.

The system of points and groups for special schools is a different one and details of this and all matters relating to salaries, unit totals, groups and scale posts may be found in the current Burnham report.

3.9 Notice

All assistant teachers are under at least two months' notice, terminating at the end of a school term. All head teachers are under three months' notice, terminating at the end of a term. Where the date of termination is 31 August then an additional month's notice is required. The terms are as defined in 3.8.

A teacher who breaks his contract by failing to give the correct period of notice may be sued for damages for the loss of his services. He cannot be forced to serve out his time as the courts will not decree specific performance when they are unable to supervise the carrying out of the contract.

3.10 Implied terms

Mr Vogler

In 1975 Mr Clement Vogler was dismissed by the Hertfordshire Education Committee because he had been having intercourse with a sixteen year old girl pupil at the school where he was employed. In effect, a major element of Mr Vogler's defence was that there was nothing in his contract that forbade such a state of affairs. His defence failed.

(Apparently Vogler is German for birdcatcher and anyone wishing to read an amusing commentary on this case is invited to consult Bernard Levin's article in *The Times* of 11 November 1975, entitled 'A just price for a teacher's passion'.)

Mr Vogler's dismissal was upheld because his behaviour was not fitting for a person in the responsible position of a teacher of the young and vulnerable. This was not spelt out at the time of his agreement with the authority. It was what is known as an 'implied' term, that is, a term which any reasonable person would naturally have assumed to be part of the contract when it was entered into.

Contracts cannot cover all eventualities, neither do they have to state the obvious. It is always an implied term that a person employed to do a job will perform his task in a reasonable, fitting and professional manner, whether he is a doctor or a dustman. It is always an implied term that an employee will be 'loyal' to his employer – whatever loyalty means. Betraying an employer's trade secrets would clearly come into this category. In one case a teacher wrote to his local newspaper complaining of the poor discipline within his school. The authority dismissed him on the grounds of disloyalty and the dismissal was upheld. Punctuality would be an implied term. Keeping reasonable class control and marking books in one's own time are probably implied terms. Perhaps the advertisement for a teaching post is an implied term in the final contractual agreement. Only the courts can decide.

3.11 Local authority regulations

In law, by implication, local authority regulations would form part of a teacher's contract and he would be expected to be conversant with them. Sometimes they are contained in the handbook of administration which is to be found in each of the authority's schools. Sometimes they consist of circulars issued at various intervals. Topics dealt with would probably include such matters as discipline, regulations governing educational visits and insurance, supervision of pupils, methods of accounting for both official and unofficial funds, school records, ordering furniture and equipment, attendance of pupils, courses for teachers, travelling expenses for teachers, times of opening and closing, school holidays, regulations affecting non-teaching staff and procedures in case of accidents.

To illustrate the importance of understanding and following such regulations it would be useful to examine the case that occurred in Cheshire some time ago. A PE teacher was taking a number of boys for athletics practice. He had divided them into groups, each working on a different activity in various parts of the school field. One group was practising javelin throwing. As one boy threw the javelin, a boy from another group sprinted suddenly into the line of fire. The javelin went right through him. Some months later he died.

The javelin throwers had been given clear instructions and were obeying them. However, the teacher at the time was with another group thirty or forty yards away from the javelin group. Had he been present he could have done nothing to prevent the accident but the authority's regulations stated, 'there must be no throwing at all unless the teacher is actually at, and in direct charge of the group during the javelin throwing'. The teacher was in breach of contract. A settlement was made out of court but there is no doubt that, if an action had been brought for negligence, the fact that the teacher had not been carrying out the authority's instructions would have been of significance in deciding what was reasonable supervision.

Whether expressed or not the courts assume certain duties owed both by employers and employees.

3.12 Duties of an employer

1 To pay the wages or salaries agreed. To pay sick and holiday pay according to the agreement as well as that for maternity leave. To observe the provisions of the Equal Pay Act 1970.
2 To allow time off with pay for officials of recognized trades unions to carry out their duties and undergo training. To allow time off for employees declared redundant to seek other jobs. (There would be an implied duty to allow a teacher time off to attend an interview for another post.)
3 To provide work. There is also the right to return to work after pregnancy.
4 In common law an employer is bound to take reasonable care and provide safe premises, equipment, a safe system of work and competent fellow employees. In addition the Health and Safety at Work Act lays down many stringent rules for employers.
5 To insure his employees against injuries sustained during the course of employment and to indemnify them for losses incurred whilst carrying out instructions in the course of employment.

3.13 Duties of an employee

1 To act honestly and in good faith. (To teach pupils on school premises

during normal school sessions for personal reward would be a breach.)

2 To carry out the work for which he is paid, as implied by the contract. (To refuse to take a normal lesson as scheduled on the timetable would be a breach.)

3 To take reasonable care in performing his duties. (To fail to mark exercise books might be a breach here.)

4 To obey the lawful and reasonable orders of his employer. (It has been held that a teacher refusing to supervise at a morning break was in breach.)

3.14 Conditions of service

No doubt the reader will have concluded already that the conditions of service under which teachers in schools work are vague. He would be right. Those who work in the field of further education have their hours of work and other conditions set out much more clearly. Whether it is advisable for teachers' conditions of employment to be laid down more strictly is debatable. Some feel that the traditions of voluntary service in running school teams, producing plays and organizing clubs and societies might well be lost if a teacher's service was on a more precise and perhaps mercenary basis. Others feel that the present system takes advantage of teachers' goodwill and that parents, authorities and pupils take all the extra time for granted. The parent who believes that teachers are paid overtime is still not uncommon!

Attempts have been made between representatives of the authorities and the teacher asssociations to agree on some conditions of service but stumbling blocks such as the supervision of school meals seem to be impossible to solve as yet.

In November 1978, the first edition of the booklet *Conditions of Service for School Teachers in England and Wales* was produced, although limited agreements of a similar kind had existed before. The booklet, in the form of a purple file, has now been sent to all schools. It was produced by the CLEA/school teachers' committee – the agreed negotiating committee for conditions of service of teachers employed by LEAs.

The bodies involved in the negotiations were:

Associations of County Councils (ACC)
Association of Metropolitan Authorities (AMA)
Acting through the Council of Local Education Authorities (CLEA)
Assistant Masters and Mistresses Associations (AMMA)
National Association of Head Teachers (NAHT)
National Association of Schoolmasters/Union of Women Teachers (NAS/UWT)
National Union of Teachers (NUT)
Secondary Heads' Association (SHA)

The conditions do not exclude other conditions that may be laid down by individual authorities, and the legal force of some of the conditions is doubtful.

Certainly, they may be evidence as to what is an implied term or is reasonable in particular circumstances. The sections that are legally enforceable are taken directly from employment legislation, such as conditions of employment, employment protection, equal pay, health and safety at work, redundancy, race relations, sex discrimination, trade union and labour relations and superannuation.

As far as hours of work, duties and holidays are concerned there are no positive statements whatsoever.

The statutory provisions will be discussed in the next chapter but we shall now take a look at four of the 'grey' areas.

3.15 Duties

As an employee, a teacher must carry out the reasonable instructions of his employer. As a substitute parent, he must take such care of his charges as a reasonable parent would.

What will amount to reasonable instructions in a school situation? Obviously, anything contained as an express term in the agreement but also anything implied as a term. The duty to teach according to the timetable, to behave in a professional manner, to maintain adequate class discipline, to mark books and to arrive on time would all seem to be included. Are some supervision duties also implied terms?

The courts have declared that continuous supervision of children during breaks and lunch-hours cannot be expected, neither can teachers be expected to supervise from the moment the first child arrives on the premises. (Whether pupils should be left unsupervised in a classroom during normal lesson time has not been tested.) However, 'adequate' supervision must be provided throughout the school-day.

The teacher associations seem to accept that there must be a reasonable amount of supervision before and after school sessions, according to local circumstances. For instance, in rural schools where pupils arrive early on buses and have to wait for transport at the close of the day.

It is a compulsory duty to supervise during morning and afternoon breaks. The courts have ruled so. Lunch-times remain a 'grey' area though. As a result of *Price and Others* v. *Sunderland County Borough Council* (1956) it is clear that teachers cannot be compelled to collect dinner money. As a result of a working party which reported in 1968, the power of local authorities to require teachers to undertake, 'supervision of pupils taking the school meal' was withdrawn. The report says that teachers, 'having oversight of pupils during the midday break should be entitled to a free school dinner'. This would include any teacher supervising a club, team or extra coaching session or running the school library. The report also suggests additional supervisory assistance by ancillaries. It does not, however, deal with the problem of midday supervision of school premises away from the dining hall. Whether teachers can be forced to undertake lunch-time supervision of corridors, playgrounds, fields and classrooms being used by sandwich eaters has yet to be tested.

The liability of a teacher in negligence for failing to act as a reasonable parent will be discussed later but if he disobeys the lawful instructions of his employer over duties then he is in breach of contract and liable to be dealt with under disciplinary procedures and possibly dismissed.

Teachers may not be called upon to perform any duties except those connected with the work of the school, neither may they be required to abstain outside school hours from any occupations which do not interfere with the due performance of their duties as teachers.

3.16 Holidays

Teachers' contracts do not specify holiday entitlement. A case in the West Country involved a teacher who resigned from his post as from 31 August. His new employers invited him to take up duties as from 1 August. He agreed. The first authority claimed that as they were paying him until the end of August he was in their employ, could be recalled and could not take up other employment. The court ruled against the authority and decided that the teacher was entitled to his summer holiday and could do as he wished during it. Unfortunately, no consideration at the time was given to Christmas, Easter, or half-term breaks.

The recent case (1982) of Mr Evans, the rugby-playing teacher of Monmouth may now have helped to clarify the situation. Mr Evans forfeited pay in order to take part in a rugby trip to the USA. The tour included his half-term break and the local authority tried to deduct pay for this holiday period as well as for the school days that he missed. The court ruled that Mr Evans was entitled to his pay for the holiday period.

It would seem then that there is an implied term that a teacher is entitled to the same holidays as his pupils. If so, attendance at a staff meeting on the day before term commences is voluntary.

3.17 Hours of work

In 1978 as part of a pay dispute the members of the NAS/UWT in some areas decided to work a five hour day. As a part-time teacher is paid on the basis of a twenty-five hour week, the conclusion was that teachers were only required to work a five hour day. Normally, many teachers work for longer than this. A number of authorities responded by docking a proportion of the salary of those involved in the action.

Doncaster was one of those authorities and it cut the pay of Mr Brewster who taught in a comprehensive school. Mr Brewster sued the council in breach of contract for the sum of £22.16p, the case being heard in Doncaster County Court. The court ruled against Mr Brewster. It was true that no specific hours of work had been laid down but there was an implied term that he would work the normal hours for which his particular school was open. By working less he was in breach of his contract.

It would seem that different teachers have different hours of work. An infant teacher works fewer hours than a secondary school teacher and, indeed, the hours may vary even between schools of a similar type.

3.18 Parents' evenings and staff meetings

In recent times government and local authorities have encouraged greater involvement of parents in school matters and greater consultation between teachers and parents. This can only be achieved by holding arranged meetings between staff and parents to discuss pupils' work and progress. Can attendance at such meetings be made compulsory for teachers?

Increasing emphasis has been laid on the management of schools and curriculum planning and development. Can teachers be required to attend staff or departmental meetings outside school hours for these purposes?

Such problems have not been argued in the courts as yet. Most of the teacher associations would consider it acceptable for members to attend a reasonable number of such meetings, given adequate notice, but would be reluctant to admit that such attendance was compulsory. Some authorities take the view that they are contractual, but others, usually reluctant to pay travelling expenses, still claim they are voluntary.

Again, in the light of custom and the nature of the organization of present-day schools, one might feel that attendance at a number of such meetings was implied in the contract.

The recent case of *Donnelly (Inspector of Taxes)* v. *Williamson* (1981) would seem to dispel this idea. An attempt had been made to tax Miss Williamson on the travelling expenses she received for attending parents' evenings. The court ruled in the teacher's favour. It did not ask whether attendance at such meetings was voluntary – it assumed so without question:

'In connection with her teaching duties she attended voluntarily certain out-of-school activities, namely parents' evenings. Those activities did not form part of the duties of her employment and she was not paid for them.'

3.19 Religion

The vicar who asks about one's church-going habits and the trade unionist who puts a probing question about political affiliations are well known characters quoted by interviewees. Both religion and politics are taboo where the appointment of teachers is concerned unless, of course, the appointment is to an aided school or that of a 'reserved' teacher to give denominational instruction at a controlled or special agreement school.

Section 30 of the 1944 Act states:

'No person shall be disqualified by reason of his religious opinions, or of his attending or omitting to attend religious worship, from being a teacher',

and

'No teacher shall be required to give religious instruction or receive any less emolument or be deprived of, or disqualified for, any promotion or other advantage by reason of the fact that he does or does not give religious instruction or by reason of his religious opinions or of his attending or omitting to attend religious worship.'

Mr Ahmad

Mr Iftikhar Ahmad was a teacher employed by the ILEA, his school being open from Monday to Friday with a break for lunch from 12.30 to 1.30 p.m. Mr Ahmad was a devout muslim and his religion required him to attend the nearest mosque for prayers every Friday, the time for prayers being from 1 to 2 p.m. He was unable to return to school until the middle of the afternoon and thus in practice required every Friday afternoon off. The authority would not accept this state of affairs and decided to pay him as a part-time teacher, working four and a half days a week, though they arranged to have his pension rights safeguarded. Mr Ahmad refused to accept this arrangement and resigned in protest.

Quoting Section 30 of the 1944 Act, he took action against the authority claiming unfair dismissal since their conduct had forced him to resign. He lost at the Industrial Tribunal, Employment Appeal Tribunal and in the Court of Appeal. He was last heard of heading in the direction of the Court of Human Rights in Strasbourg.

Section 30 was intended to protect teachers from dismissal because of their religions beliefs or their connection (or lack of it) with particular religious establishments. It was also intended to prevent conditions of a religious nature being made over appointments. It did not anticipate cases such as Mr Ahmad's. It does mean that, unless appointed for the purpose, no teacher can be forced to give religious instruction and no teacher can be forced to take a religious assembly or indeed attend such an assembly. Teachers who do not attend assemblies could, of course, be given other duties to perform, such as those involving supervision of some kind.

Where the taking of assemblies is an express or implied term of the contract, such as in the case of a head teacher or deputy, then the use of Section 30 as an escape clause may be somewhat doubtful.

3.20 Qualifications

The Education (Teachers) Regulations 1982 give the Secretary of State power to require that all maintained schools shall be suitably and adequately staffed by qualified teachers including a headteacher.

Qualified teachers are those persons who have undergone an approved course of initial training for teachers or a course considered comparable.

Persons with approved special qualifications may be granted qualified status (this could include untrained graduates of shortage subjects). If they are to teach in primary schools or special schools the qualifications must have been gained before 1 January 1970 – if they are to teach in secondary schools the qualifications must have been obtained before 1 January 1974.

The DES grants qualified status and employing authorities must check the qualifications of those they appoint. False claims to qualified status are not unknown. Special cases for consideration may be put to the DES by the authority, not the teacher, and qualified status may unusually be granted on grounds of particular qualifications and experience.

Teachers in special schools are subject to special regulations laid down in the same document.

As from 1979, the three-year course for the Certificate in Education has been phased out and all trainees will take a degree of some kind thus leading to an all-graduate profession. There is now a requirement that all entering a teacher training course shall have 'O' level passes at Grade C or better, or a Grade 1 pass at CSE, in both English language and mathematics as well as the other qualifications that individual institutions may lay down. The same rule applies to those with special qualifications where that qualification was obtained after 31 August 1984.

3.21 Instructors

During the times of desperate teacher shortage, it was made possible to appoint certain people as 'instructors' where it had proved impossible to find a suitably qualified teacher. Their appointment was on a temporary basis and had to be reviewed from time to time. The method was most often used to find teachers of handicrafts, commercial subjects and music but was sometimes used for modern language teaching, the teaching of religious instruction and other subjects. The appointment of instructors is still possible but such a person may not be appointed to teach general subjects. Their rate of pay is, of course, considerably less than that of qualified teachers and they may only be employed on a temporary basis.

3.22 Health

Unless a teacher is a person registered as disabled then at the beginning of his first appointment he must satisfy the Secretary of State as to his physical fitness for teaching.

3.23 Probation

All qualified teachers must complete a period of probation and the onus is on the individual teacher to demonstrate his ability to reach the standards required. For full-time teachers trained in the United Kingdom the normal period of probation is one year. For other teachers the period is two years. For part-time teachers the period is usually up to three years.

The responsibility for supervising probation lies on the employing authority. Before the end of the period, they must recommend whether the teacher should pass, that the period of probation should be extended, or that the person should no longer be employed to teach. If the teacher passes the authority will inform him. If an extension or failure is suggested then this must go in the form of a report to the Secretary of State who will make the decision. The teacher must be told of the contents of the report. If a further extension or termination is suggested, then the teacher must be given the chance to put his case, before a final decision is reached by the Secretary of State.

Untrained qualified teachers, who would normally have to undergo two years' probation, may pass their probation in one year if they satisfy HMI as to their obvious competence. Similar reductions are possible for part-time teachers.

Recently a teacher who failed his probation claimed unfair dismissal at a hearing of an Industrial Tribunal. It was ruled that a tribunal has no power to hear such a claim.

A teacher who fails probation and leaves his post may not teach elsewhere without the express permission of the Secretary of State. If such permission is given then the probationary period commences afresh.

3.24 Withdrawal of recognition

The Secretary of State may bar a person from teaching on medical grounds, on educational grounds or on grounds of that person's misconduct (whether or not this is evidenced by conviction of a criminal offence). He has the power to direct an authority or other body concerned to suspend or terminate a teacher's employment or make his continued employment subject to specified conditions. He may bar the teacher from working in any other school. If this action is taken on grounds of misconduct the teacher concerned must be given an opportunity to make representations to the Secretary of State.

Thus, if an authority dismisses a teacher because of misconduct or conviction of a criminal offence (or the teacher resigns on these grounds), then the facts must be reported to the DES. If such a matter is reported to the DES then withdrawal of the right to teach may take place, even if the authority itself does not wish to terminate the teacher's employment.

The misconduct or conviction does not necessarily have to be in relation to a school matter. It is sufficient if the conduct involved could affect the suitability of the teacher in carrying out duties in a professionally acceptable way, or where his or her conduct might place children at risk. A teacher involved in theft, in soliciting in a public lavatory, in abandoning an illegitimate child or being engaged in a street riot are all examples of such dismissals.

The DES maintains a list of those banned from teaching and this is circulated to authorities.

3.25 The head

Head teachers in British schools are in a very powerful position, perhaps too powerful. Under his contract, the head is usually responsible for the internal organization, management and discipline of the school and the control of the teaching and non-teaching staff. A very wide brief. He is responsible to a body of governors, many of whom will know little of the working of the school or even of the education system itself. Some will take an interest – others will see the position of governor as some kind of reward for political service and will make only token appearances.

It is comparatively easy, therefore, for a head to have his own way, particularly so if he has the confidence of his governors. His influence over appointments, internal promotions, organization and curriculum matters is obvious. He must follow his authority's regulations since these are part of his contract, though these will be far from comprehensive and often vague. The only other legal restraint is that he must act reasonably. For example, *Spiers* v. *Warrington Corporation* (1954) (which will be referred to again later) makes it very clear that the head has powers to make any reasonable school rules. The test of reasonableness could be applied to all the head's rulings that are not covered by the express or implied terms of his appointment. Obviously what is reasonable is frequently debatable.

Staff appearance often seems to cause friction. It would be unreasonable to expect the engineering or pottery teacher to wear his best suit while carrying out his duties. It would also seem unreasonable to attempt to ban female teachers from wearing trouser-suits. The head of a boy's school might be tempted to insist that attractive young lady members of staff wore trousers rather than short skirts! It would seem reasonable to expect teaching staff to be clean and tidily dressed.

Other reasonable instructions by the head might include the keeping of records, writing reports, preparing schemes of work, going to lessons on time, teaching to a certain syllabus and not administering punishment.

The female bank clerk who insisted on serving at the counter whilst wearing a device on her sweater that advertised her lesbian inclinations was held to be fairly dismissed. Since her conduct was an affront to the public that she served perhaps a really scruffy or dirty appearance would be an affront to pupils or parents with whom a teacher came into contact.

A head who banned a teacher from parking his car on school premises because the back window carried an advertisement for Durex was probably acting in a reasonable fashion. So was the head who banned a teacher from making potent home-made wine with his class in a science laboratory. So was the head who banned a domestic science teacher from getting her classes to do her own family wash and baking.

The head who tried to insist that one of his handicraft teachers should mend the roof of the head's house was acting unreasonably, so was the education authority that tried to rescind the appointment of a headmaster after it discovered that he spent his spare time in running a public house.

Other unreasonable instructions by the head might include a requirement that all staff remained on school premises beyond school hours on a regular basis or that all staff were required to take morning prayers.

3.26 Professional associations

Teachers do not have to belong to an association though some authorities when making appointments encourage them to do so. However, in a time like the present with annual pay bargaining, falling rolls and difficult parents, most teachers join an association, if only as a means of self-protection. It is unfortunate that this attitude is taken since most of the associations offer services beyond legal advice and protection which teachers might avail themselves of. The National Union of Teachers, for example, has its own library, newspaper, insurance company and building society as well as a benevolent fund and homes for retired teachers in difficult circumstances and for those suffering from physical handicaps. It also produces reports on educational matters and gives professional advice of all kinds.

It is difficult to obtain accurate membership figures for the teacher associations, since the numbers fluctuate and the associations tend to present their figures in the most favourable light. Certainly by far the largest is the NUT. This is followed by the NAS/UWT and the AMMA. A smaller union is the Professional Association of Teachers, the union which is committed never to strike. The largest association of head teachers is the NAHT followed by the Secondary Heads Association. The Headmasters' Conference is a body largely representing the heads of public schools.

Most education committees have representatives of teachers and these are usually appointed through consultation with the teacher associations. Often there is a joint consultative committee which consists of representatives of the associations and of the authority, where matters of policy and administration are debated. A further development is the appointment by election of teacher representatives at local level to deal on the spot with matters affecting teachers and their employers.

In recent times there has been an increase in militancy amongst teachers over such issues as the supervision of school meals, out-of-school activities, teacher participation and staff consultation and these have often posed serious problems of management. It must be said, however, that improvements in conditions of service that have taken place have been largely due to the efforts of the teacher associations. Unfortunately, infighting between them too frequently slows progress for the profession as a whole.

From time to time the suggestion is raised of a teacher's council. Such a body, representing all teachers, would monitor entry into the profession and deal with matters of professional discipline and conduct – as happens with doctors and others. There seems little likelihood of such a development in the near future. Most of the associations do however, have a code of professional conduct and members who are in breach of this code may be disciplined or expelled from the association.

The NUT's code is a typical example.

NUT code of professional conduct

The following is a list of actions already declared to be unprofessional but this list is not exclusive. All actions which are alleged to be injurious to the interests of the profession or the professional honour of any member can be referred to the Committee for adjudication.

(a) For any teacher to take an appointment from which, in the judgement of the NUT Executive, a member of the Union has been unjustly dismissed.

(b) For any teacher* to make a report on the work or conduct of another teacher without at the time** acquainting the teacher concerned with the nature of it, if it be a verbal report, or without showing it, if it be written and allowing the teacher concerned to take a copy of it.***

(c) In any case of dispute between members of the NUT settled by arbitrator under Rule 53 for any member not to abide by the decision.

(d) For any teacher to censure other teachers or to criticize their work in the hearing of the pupils and other persons not directly involved in the running of the school.

(e) For any teacher to seek to compel another teacher to perform outside the ordinary school hours any task which is not essentially connected with the ordinary work and organization of the school.

(f) For any teacher to impose upon another teacher, out of the ordinary school hours, an excessive and unreasonable amount of work of any kind.

* Whilst primarily the word 'teacher' in Article ii of the Professional Conduct Code has been regarded as being applicable to serving teachers and those actively and professionally engaged in education, the Committee reserves the right to examine references to it under the Professional Conduct Code concerning any member of the Union other than those professionally engaged in the service of education.

** When a report is made by a teacher on the work or conduct of another teacher, it should be shown to the teacher concerned before it is submitted, and the teacher allowed to take a copy of it.

*** Where a teacher gives the name of another teacher or member as a referee, he takes, in accordance with normal practice, a risk as to the nature and contents of the reference which the referee may give. Accordingly, any reference so given is not regarded by the Executive as a report within the meaning of the above Article.

3.27 Comments

Here are some observations on the statements made in 3.1 at the commencement of this Chapter.

1 Yes, he may be, but under the principle of vicarious liability if the teacher is acting within the course of employment then the employer will also be liable jointly. Invariably, damages, if awarded, will be against the employer though he has possible rights of action against the employee.
2 Yes, it may. If the appointment is to the service of the authority then clearly it has a right to do so but if the appointment is to a particular school then the authority might not do so without the teacher's consent unless there is a properly negotiated redeployment procedure.
3 Of course you must carry out the express terms of your contract. You must also carry out the implied terms. What is implied is always open to question.
4 The Doncaster case suggests that it is an implied condition that a teacher works the hours for which his particular school is normally open. This was heard in a county court and might not be followed by a higher court.
5 Yes. Though they must be reasonable. This does not include pupils taking the school meal. Other supervision in the lunch-break is a 'grey area'.
6 Yes – for a reasonable time.
7 Untrue. Teachers had a measure of protection before the new legislation. They are, of course, covered by all the new employment laws. This does not preclude dismissal on grounds that are fair.
8 He can make reasonable rules. The banning of trouser suits seems definitely unreasonable. Insistence on ties is arguable.
9 No holiday entitlement has been laid down for teachers. The only case which decided that a teacher was entitled to the summer holiday would suggest teachers may be entitled to the same holidays as pupils.
10 Probably so for most teachers. Could a PE specialist in a secondary school claim that he would not take any matches after school or on Saturdays? It may well have been implied in his contract that he would do so to a reasonable degree. A similar argument could be applied to teachers of some other subjects, such as music or drama.

4 Employment, law and teachers

4.1 Employment protection

Employment, as we have said, is basically a contractual situation which either party may bring to an end according to the terms of the contract. The last ten years or so have seen increasing protection given by the law, mainly to employees, so that it is no longer a simple matter of giving the required notice to effect dismissal.

Much of this law comes under the umbrella of employment protection and is embodied in the Employment Protection (Consolidation) Act of 1978 which brings together employees' rights established under the Redundancy Payments Act 1965, the Contracts of Employment Act 1972, the Trade Union and Labour Relations Act 1974 and the Employment Protection Act 1975. We shall now examine a number of these provisions as they affect teachers in particular.

4.2 Wrongful dismissal

This is where a clear term of the contract is broken, for example where a teacher who is entitled to two months' notice is only given notice of one month.

4.3 Unfair dismissal

This occurs when the terms of the contract are observed but the employee maintains that the grounds for the dismissal are unfair, i.e. the letter of the law may have been observed but an injustice has been done. Most employees have the right not to be unfairly dismissed. Exceptions include – those employees with less than fifty-two weeks' continuous employment; those over sixty-five; those who work for less than sixteen hours per week (those who work eight hours or more per week for five years also qualify); those on fixed contracts who have waived their rights in writing at the time of the making of the contract; and those involved in industrial action at the date of dismissal. The first two and the last one have some protection in special circumstances. Most teachers, therefore, are protected against unfair dismissal.

The following usually amount to an unfair dismissal and if the teacher can prove one of them then he or she has an absolute right to redress.

1 The dismissal was because the teacher joined, or has stated his intention of

joining, an independent trade union. (An independent trade union is one not receiving financial or material support from employers and not under the employer's control.)

2 The teacher had taken part, or proposed to take part, at any appropriate time in the activities of an independent trade union. (Appropriate time means outside working hours or within working hours according to an agreement.)
3 Pregnancy or any reason connected with pregnancy. (If a woman teacher's post has disappeared because of a staffing reduction, then when she is due to return the authority would have to find her alternative employment or make a redundancy payment.)
4 On grounds of sex or race discrimination.

Other categories, which are not relevant to teachers, are because an employee refuses to join a particular union which is not an independent one or where, on grounds of religious belief, an employee refuses to join a trade union where there is a union membership agreement.

Both sides are heard by an industrial tribunal considering a claim for unfair dismissal but, apart from the circumstances just mentioned above, the onus in practice is on the employer to show that the dismissal was fair. He must, in the first place, give a reason for dismissal.

Possible reasons

1 The teacher does not have the skill, health, or mental qualities necessary. He cannot maintain class control. His command of English is not good enough for pupils to understand him.
2 He does not possess the relevant professional qualifications.
3 His work is unsatisfactory – again he cannot control classes or cannot communicate.
4 His misconduct (for example a teacher in breach of authority rules in a workshop, who puts pupils at risk). In a teacher's case this might include conduct outside school, such as having an affair with a boy or girl pupil.
5 Redundancy.
6 The teacher's right to teach has been withdrawn by the Secretary of State.
7 The teacher is replacing another absent on maternity leave or because of ill health, the teacher having been informed of this in writing.

Having proved the reason, the employer must then show that in all the circumstances he acted fairly in using the reason for dismissal. The tribunal does not decide whether the dismissal was fair or not, it is only concerned that the employer in good faith and on reasonable grounds believed it to be fair when he took the action. If the employer was genuinely mistaken this will not necessarily render the dismissal unfair, even if the reason for the dismissal by the employer turns out to be unfair. The dismissal may be unfair if the method of dismissal is considered to be unreasonable. ACAS (the Advisory, Conciliation and Arbitration Service) recommends that employers should draw up a code of practice for disciplinary procedures. This should lay down the various steps that should be gone through before a firm dismissal is given. The pattern adopted by most Education Authorities, which relates to both teaching staff and full time ancillary staff, runs as follows:

Informal oral warning.
Warning confirmed in writing.
Final warning.
Dismissal.

Records should be kept of warnings and final warnings and the employee may arrange for his trade union representative to be present when they are given. The final warning should be expressed to be so. It should be given verbally and then confirmed in writing by the employer and should make it clear that further misconduct will result in disciplinary measures. For serious misconduct the procedure may commence with the final warning and for gross misconduct an employer may dismiss summarily.

Failure to follow the code does not necessarily render a dismissal unfair but it may well do so since the code is, presumably, drawn up on lines of reasonableness.

The method of dismissal may also be unfair if there is some other injustice in the procedure.

The William Tyndale School

Many readers will remember the protracted and much publicized affair of the William Tyndale School, Islington.

There was a strong conflict between members of staff over teaching methods and groups of parents became involved. Some members of staff refused to submit to an inspection or attend a public inquiry. They went on strike and the school was closed for two days. Eventually, the inquiry was held and was critical of the authority and particularly so of the conduct of some of the teaching staff. ILEA, the employer, held a disciplinary tribunal and its recommendation that six of the staff should be dismissed was implemented.

The teachers claimed unfair dismissal on several grounds. One was that, contrary to the principles of natural justice, the education officer laid the complaints before the disciplinary tribunal and therefore acted as prosecutor. He was also available for consultation during the proceedings and it was also his task to write the report. If he had served as a member of the tribunal then clearly this would have been wrong but, claimed the teachers, his dual role was also unjust. The employment appeal tribunal thought otherwise and dismissed the appeal. Mr Justice Kilner Brown said: 'Never in the field of teachers' conduct has so much time been spent by so many on so few.'

There must be arrangements for an employee to appeal against warnings.

It would be appropriate for warnings to be given by the head or in his presence but the authority's representatives should always be involved. While the chairman of governors should obviously be kept informed, it would be unwise to involve him in warning procedures since he would perhaps eventually have to preside over the disciplinary hearing.

Naturally, a contract of employment may come to an end by mutual agreement or by frustration. Frustration is where an event occurs that makes the contract impossible of performance, for example a teacher suffering an accident that causes him to be bedridden for the foreseeable future.

4.4 Constructive dismissal

This occurs when there is no express dismissal but the conduct of either the employer or employee implies that a dismissal has taken place. Recently, a West Indian working in Britain went to his homeland and remained there for some weeks without informing his employers or obtaining their permission. Although he had not resigned, it was decided that by his conduct he had dismissed himself and his contract was at an end.

Mostly, however, the implied dismissal comes from situations where the conduct of the employer suggests that he has no intention of being bound by the terms of the contract or where his conduct towards the employee is so unreasonable that the latter cannot be expected to continue in his work.

A hairdresser became very angry with one of his assistants, threw him to the floor and proceeded to punch him. The assistant claimed unfair dismissal. The hairdresser said that he had never even mentioned dismissal.

The tribunal had to consider this problem: If an employer throws his employee to the floor and attacks him, does this imply that he is dismissing him? The tribunal said that it did.

It has also been held that to say, 'I don't like the way you do your work f . . . off' is a dismissal, whereas, 'If you don't like it here you can f . . . off' is not.

Mrs Fishman

Mrs Fishman was employed to run a resources centre in a secondary school in Redbridge. When a change of head teacher occurred the new head asked her to take twelve English lessons a week. Mrs Fishman agreed. Later she was asked to increase this to eighteen periods of English per week. She refused and claimed unfair dismissal.

The authority maintained that any teacher could be asked to teach any subject and Mrs Fishman could be moved from her work in a resources centre to any other kind of teaching. The tribunal disagreed. The head teacher was justified in requiring teachers to do some work outside the work for which they had been engaged but such requests must be reasonable. In this instance the request was unreasonable since it changed the whole nature of Mrs Fishman's job.

Mrs Fishman was awarded damages.

4.5 Remedies for unfair dismissal

There are three possible remedies awarded by an industrial tribunal.

Re-instatement

The teacher will be treated as if he had not been dismissed. There will be no loss of salary or pension rights.

Re-engagement

The teacher will be given employment comparable to his former post without loss of salary or pension rights.

When considering re-instatement or re-engagement, the tribunal has to take into account the wishes of the complainant, if such action is practicable and, where the complainant has contributed to his dismissal, whether it would be fair to re-instate or re-engage him.

There is no way in which an authority can be forced to re-instate or re-engage a teacher but the failure to do so would lead to additional compensation.

Compensation

Where compensation alone is ordered, the maximum at present is £7500, but the average award in unfair dismissal cases is below £1000. The tribunal may take into account loss of earnings, loss of pension rights and the expenses incurred in finding a new post. Where the tribunal considers that the complainant has caused or contributed to the dismissal then it may adjust the sum as it sees fit, even making a nil award.

This is known as the compensatory award. In all cases of unfair dismissal there must also be a basic award. This is based on the number of years service in continuous employment (maximum twenty years) and the weekly pay (present maximum £145).

4.6 Disciplinary proceedings

Apart from warnings and dismissals, which have already been dealt with, the Code of Practice may deal with other matters. The comments that follow are based on regulations for Staffordshire schools but it is likely that the regulations are similar for other authorities.

The code will set out the procedures for appeals against warnings. These may be made to a person nominated by the chief education officer (someone not previously involved in the case) and if, say, a final warning is given by the CEO personally, then appeal will lie to the chairman of the education committee. Provision is made for warnings to be removed from an employee's record after a certain time at the discretion of the CEO. Rules for suspension of employees are included. Suspension is usually allowed where there is a possibility of criminal proceedings being taken against the employee, and there are doubts as to his fitness to continue his work; where his suspension will facilitate investigation into the incidents; or where there are other reasonable grounds for doing so.

Usually, suspension on full-pay is given pending the result of the suspension or inquiry.

The code lays down arrangements for meetings concerning the disciplinary proceedings, including the notice to be given (fourteen days) and the provision of written statements of the report, charge or complaint to all parties concerned (fourteen days). The respondent must give two days' notice if he intends to appear.

Teacher representatives may not attend but the respondent is entitled to be present, together with any person representing him.

Witnesses may be called by both sides and may be cross-examined and when all parties have been heard all but the governors must withdraw.

The governors may vary these arrangements where it seems just to do so. They will then consider whether they are satisfied that the facts have been established, whether these constitute grounds for disciplinary action and, if so, what action should be taken. They will then submit a report to the council with their recommendation. If a recommendation is made by the governors, then they must inform the respondent either immediately or in writing as soon as possible. He must be informed of his rights of appeal.

If he appeals, this will be heard by a committee appointed by the council for the purpose and the respondent must be given at least fourteen days' notice of the meeting. The procedure will be as for the first hearing. The committee may make such decision as they think fit and this decision is final.

If no appeal is made then the committee may take such action as they think fit. If this is disciplinary action other than that recommended by the governors, then the respondent must be given the opportunity of a re-hearing.

A simpler procedure applies to part-time non-teaching staff.

Where an employee is dismissed summarily for gross misconduct, the dismissal may be reviewed on notice in writing. This review will be carried out by the special committee appointed by the council, not by the governors. The request must be made within fourteen days or later if criminal proceedings are pending.

The regulations do not apply in cases of redundancy, where a probationary period is concerned, for casual employment, termination by expiry of time, frustration or any rule of law.

4.7 Grievance procedures

As a result of discussion between the teacher associations and the local authorities, a model grievance procedure has been drawn up and most authorities have adopted this. A copy is given to each newly appointed teacher.

If a teacher has a grievance against another teacher, the head of department, the head teacher or against the authority itself, the method of presenting such a grievance is laid down.

The model grievance procedure as it applies to Staffordshire schools is contained in Appendix 1 at the end of this book.

4.8 Sickness pay

Although regulations may vary slightly, they are usually very similar from one authority to another since they are based on the principles agreed between the teacher associations and the authorities. Where a teacher moves from one authority to another all service qualifies.

A teacher qualifies from the start of employment. This is 25 days on full pay and after four calendar months of service, 50 working days on half pay. The entitlement rises annually until the maximum is reached after three years. It is then 100 working days on full pay and 100 days on half pay.

Qualifying service commences on 1 April and a teacher who commences duties after that date is presumed to have commenced service on the preceding 1 April.

A teacher who is absent on account of sickness for four, five or six consecutive working days is eligible for statutory sick pay from the local authority. On return to school the teacher should complete a 'self certification' form which should be available from the school office. This should then be submitted to the employer. A teacher who is absent for more than six consecutive days (excluding Sunday) should also obtain a medical certificate and submit this to the employer. A 'self certification' form is also necessary to cover absence from the fourth to the seventh day. In cases of continuing sickness, medical certificates should be obtained as often as required. The employer is responsible for payment of sickness benefit during the first eight weeks of absence.

Teachers who are certified as being fit to return to work during a holiday period should notify the authority in writing.

Where a teacher is absent because he is suffering from a serious infectious illness that he is likely to have contracted at school, or because he is in contact with a serious infectious illness at home, such as polio, then sick leave should not be counted against his entitlement.

Teachers who are absent for a long period or at frequent intervals, may be required to undergo a medical examination though they have a right to have their own doctor present at the time. If the medical evidence is that they are unfit to work, either indefinitely or for a lengthy period, then the contract may come to an end through frustration. In such circumstances, of course, the teacher may apply for a breakdown pension and lump sum under the superannuation scheme.

4.9 Medical examinations

Conflicts may arise where it is alleged that a teacher is unfit for service.

Mrs Kingston

In 1977 Mrs Kingston, who worked at a London school, claimed constructive dismissal on the grounds that her local authority had put pressure on her to resign, part of such pressure being an order to have a medical examination. She underwent the medical but previously had one by another doctor who pronounced her perfectly fit. She did, in fact, pass the authority's inspection but there seemed to be some suggestion that this was 'political' rather than medical.

Her complaint was not heard since it was made out of time.

Miss Davies

Miss Davies became a deputy-head in a Lancashire secondary school in 1975. Relationships within the school involving successive heads, other staff and Miss Davies seem to have become very involved and unpleasant. In 1978 Miss Davies was asked to undergo a medical examination. She refused. A second request was made and this time it was indicated that the authority's consultant psychiatrist would also be present. Miss Davies said that the regulations relating to teachers who were sick did not authorize psychiatric examination. She consented to a medical examination, however, with her own doctor present, provided that the authority would put into writing the reasons why this should take place. The authority was unwilling to do this to Miss Davies' satisfaction. She did not undergo examination, therefore, and the governors recommended the authority to dismiss her.

The industrial tribunal found in favour of Miss Davies. It would not order re-instatement because of the poor relationships within the school but it ordered re-engagement, i.e. the authority had to find a comparable post for her (a group 10 deputy-headship). This the authority refused to do so the only remedy Miss Davies had was financial compensation.

Inability to perform a service because of ill-health may, of course, frustrate the contract and may be fair ground for dismissal.

4.10 Maternity leave

It is unfair to dismiss a woman on grounds connected with pregnancy. She is entitled to return to her job up to twenty-nine weeks after her confinement and if the job has disappeared during her pregnancy, she is entitled to comparable employment or re-engagement or redundancy pay.

Before maternity leave commences she must inform the employer, in writing, of her absence because of pregnancy and of her intention to return (she may change her mind about this later). She will be entitled to six weeks maternity pay beginning from eleven weeks before the expected confinement.

These rights are available to all women employees under the Employment

Protection Act. Teachers, however, are also entitled to maternity leave under their contractual agreement, if they wish to avail themselves of it. Benefits taken under the contractual scheme do not cancel rights under the Act.

Details of the contractual scheme will be found in the Conditions of Service. Benefits include rights for a teacher who has only been in employment for twelve months and a total period of eighteen weeks leave with pay – full-pay for four weeks (less the maternity allowance) and half-pay for the remainder. There is an absolute entitlement to pay for six weeks but pay for the remaining weeks may be recovered at the discretion of the authority if the teacher does not, in fact, return for a period of at least thirteen weeks.

The scheme applies to unmarried mothers and the post-natal provisions may be applied to adoptive parents.

4.11 Redundancy

Redundancy occurs where a post is lost because the employer ceases to carry on business, or intends to do so, or where work of a particular kind has ceased or diminished.

An employee has a right to compensation, known as a redundancy payment, if he has been in continuous employment for a period of two years. Such compensation is not available for those working less than sixteen hours a week (unless they work at least eight hours or more per week and have done so for over five years). Neither is it available under the fixed term contract where the written agreement excludes such a claim in the event of the contract not being renewed. Persons over state retiring age are not eligible and neither are those who refuse a reasonable offer of suitable alternative employment. However, there are sometimes exceptions.

Mr Taylor

Mr Taylor worked for the Kent authority and in 1968 the boys' school of which he was head amalgamated with a nearby girls' school. Mr Taylor was not appointed to the headship though he was offered a post in the new school. This he refused. The authority informed him that his salary was safeguarded and offered him a post as a peripatetic relief teacher. Mr Taylor claimed a redundancy payment at a hearing of an industrial tribunal but this was not allowed. He appealed (at that time appeal was to the QBD) and won.

The court said that status was important to Mr Taylor, not only salary. To guarantee his salary did not make up for the great loss in status that he would suffer and this amounted to redundancy. A post as a relief teacher was not 'suitable alternative employment'.

The above case occurred before the introduction of the Employment Protection Act. Today it might well come under the heading of Constructive Dismissal.

Very few teachers have been concerned in redundancy situations to date, but the problems caused by falling rolls could mean that a number are so involved in the future.

When redundancy does occur the payment is based on age and length of service, with a maximum of twenty years. One and a half weeks' pay is given for each year's service over forty-one years of age, one week's pay is given for each year served between the ages of twenty-one and forty-one and a half week's pay for each other year of employment.

4.12 Premature retirement

Because of the present staffing crisis in schools over falling rolls, authorities are likely to turn more and more to the scheme for premature retirement in order to reduce overall staff numbers.

Details have yet to be finalized but the scheme, which is described in the Conditions of Service Handbook, will apply to teachers over fifty who have completed at least five years of reckonable service, including those working in further education establishments and special schools.

To qualify, the employing authority must certify that the employee has become redundant or that he has ceased to hold his post in the interests of the efficient exercise of its functions.

The benefits would be a pension and lump sum according to the amount of service completed at the cessation of employment with enhancement at the discretion of the compensating authority. There are limits as to the number of years for which enhancement may be given.

4.13 Continuous employment

The term 'continuous employment' has been used at various times in preceding sections. Unless an employee can show that he has been continuously employed, he cannot claim certain benefits. It is important, therefore, to explain the legal meaning of the term.

The general rule is that unless the week can be credited to an employee, continuity is broken. Sickness, injury, pregnancy and industrial action do not count. Neither does approved leave of absence (paid or unpaid).

4.14 Leave of absence

In addition to maternity leave this must be given for jury service or, within limits, for accredited representatives of recognized teachers' associations and for other forms of public service. It may be given for other purposes such as the taking of examinations, acting as examiners and moderators, attending courses or conferences, acting as officials or competitors at major sporting events, or on compassionate grounds such as attending a family funeral or looking after a sick relative.

4.15 Teacher associations

Teachers have a right to belong to a union or not to do so. Union representatives of a certain standing, for example branch secretary, have a right to a reasonable amount of time off with pay in which to conduct affairs between the authority and members of their union, to take part in joint consultation with the authority or to engage in union activities. Individual school representatives are entitled to co-operation over such matters as accommodation for meetings, use of telephones and notice boards and reasonable use of the schools' reprographic facilities.

Larger teacher associations usually operate on a county or authority basis, subdivided into districts. Smaller associations work on a county basis only. In most authorities there is a joint advisory (or consultative) committee consisting of representatives of the authority and the teacher associations. This body meets regularly to discuss aspects of conditions of service within the authority and to set up working parties to produce reports and make recommendations. Members of this body may be appointed to sit on the education committee though some authorities have representatives elected by all teachers within the authority.

Just as there is a grievance procedure which an individual teacher or group of teachers may pursue, so there is a recommended procedure for 'collective disputes'. These occur where an entire county or branch association, or indeed all the associations represented on a consultative committee, are in dispute with an authority. It may also occur when there are disputes at national level. The procedure is laid down as an appendix to the Conditions of Service Handbook.

4.16 Discrimination

In spite of the new legislation, this may still be lawful. Unfair discrimination may be direct or indirect and it is actionable.

Direct discrimination is the treatment of a person less favourably than another on grounds of sex, colour, race, nationality, ethnic origin or marital status. The House of Lords has held that it was discrimination to ban a Sikh pupil from attending school because he wore a turban. An obvious example would be to advertise a teaching post and make a condition that only white applicants (or only black applicants) would be considered. It must be shown that there was an intention to discriminate.

Indirect discrimination is where a condition is applied to all applicants for a job, say, but it is such that only a small proportion of one sex or racial group may apply, as against the proportion of other groups. For example, it was held

Sex Discrimination Act 1975

No job advertisement which indicates or can reasonably be understood as indicating an intention to discriminate on ground of sex (e.g. by inviting applications only from males or only from females) may be accepted, unless

1 The job is for the purpose of a private householder or
2 It is a business employing fewer than six persons or
3 It is otherwise excepted from the requirements of the Sex Discrimination Act.

A statement must be made at the time the advertisement is placed saying which of the exceptions in the Act is considered to apply.

In addition to employment, the principal areas covered by the section of the Act which deals with advertisements are education, the supply of goods and services and the sale or letting of property.

It is the responsibility of advertisers to ensure that advertisement content does not discriminate under the terms of the Sex Discrimination Act.

---

that the age limit of twenty-eight for entry into the Civil Service was discriminatory since a large proportion of women will be having babies at that age. The employer may be able to justify his action, as in the case of the Sikh who was refused a job in a sweet factory, on grounds of hygiene, since he refused to shave off his beard. It is not necessary to prove that an indirect discrimination was intentional.

Some discrimination may be lawful. In schools this could include, under the need to preserve decency or privacy, the necessity to appoint a mistress to be responsible for the welfare of girls and to appoint separate masters or mistresses for boys' or girls' physical education. There are a number of other exceptions under the Sex Discrimination Act and the Race Relations Act but they can hardly be applied to educational establishments. Discrimination against pupils will be discussed in a later chapter.

The claimant is entitled to ask questions and receive answers from the respondent but not have access to confidential documents.

If a tribunal decides that unlawful discrimination has taken place then it may make an order declaring the rights of the parties concerned. It may award compensation – the maximum at present being £6250 – and it may take account of injured feelings. Finally, it may recommend the action to be taken by the respondent to put matters right.

Both the Equal Opportunities Commission and the Commission for Racial Equality have power to issue notices requiring persons or organizations to desist from discriminatory practices. There is a right of appeal against such notices but if the appeal fails the notice may be enforced by an injunction.

Mrs Stott and the scale four post

Mrs Stott taught at a Manchester Comprehensive School. She was a head of year. A vacancy for a head of remedial, scale 4, came up in the school and the head, Mr Schofield, recommended to the authority that a Mr Booth on the staff of the school should be promoted to fill the vacancy. Such recommendations for internal promotion were common in Manchester and Mr Schofield believed that Mr Booth was the only suitable candidate.

Mrs Stott was aware of the vacancy and saw Mr Schofield about it. He told her of the recommendation he had made to the authority.

Although Mr Schofield believed that he was not bound to do so, he agreed with his inspectorate that the scale 4 post should be advertised internally. This was done and Mr Booth and Mrs Stott were the only applicants. Both were interviewed and the panel decided to appoint Mr Booth.

Mrs Stott went to an industrial tribunal claiming discrimination on grounds of sex. She said that there were far more higher scale posts given to men on the staff than to women. Mr Booth was not the better candidate and her rejection had been because she was a woman.

The tribunal found that the members of the panel had been fair and honest. They believed quite genuinely that Mr Booth was the better candidate on merit and there had been no discrimination. The tribunal was not impressed by the argument that more scale posts were given to men. There were more men applicants for senior posts than women, so the imbalance was inevitable.

Mrs Stott lost.

4.17 Health and safety at work

Schools, like other owners or occupiers of premises, have always owed a common duty of care to those who work in them or visit them. Until the passing of the Health and Safety at Work Act in 1974 there were few statutory provisions of great significance affecting staff and pupils over health and safety. Some ancillaries, such as school secretaries, were covered by Acts such as the Offices, Shops and Railways Premises Act 1963 but those enactments like the Schools Regulations of 1959, which did make references to school matters were vague and non-committal.

The Health and Safety at Work Act has changed all this. The Act applies to all places where work is carried on and not only to those who work there – it applies to anyone who has a reasonable right to be on such premises, so for the first time there are strict rules applied to schools, their staffs, their pupils, parents and any other visitors.

An employer must, 'ensure as far as is reasonably practicable, the health, safety, and welfare at work of all his employees'. This is the principal aim of the Act and while it does lay down many conditions its main function, through the Health and Safety Commission, is to consult with interested parties and either draw up codes of practice or encourage groups to draw up their own codes. It is possible, therefore, for an LEA or even a body of governors, where they are the employers, to produce a code. Such a code would probably be based on recommendations made in the various DES pamphlets such as *Safety in Science Laboratories*, *Safety in Physical Education* or other relevant government publications.

The duty of seeing that the Act is observed rests with Her Majesty's Factory Inspectors of the Health and Safety Executive. They have power of entry to any school and may pay a routine visit or inspect as the result of an accident or a complaint from any source whatsoever. They may make recommendations to the employer and suggestions to the Department itself. They may issue improvement notices – these require matters to be remedied within a specific time. They may issue prohibition notices – these order a practice to cease until certain steps have been taken. Failure to observe an inspector's instruction could lead to a criminal prosecution.

Regulations made under the Act allow for the appointment of safety representatives in places of work. The task of the safety representative, who is obviously a person with local knowledge, is to make checks, investigate accidents and make recommendations to the employer. The employer must give any relevant information needed and the representative must be given time off for training. There is no additional legal liability on a safety representative, other than that on every employee.

Each recognized trade union is entitled to a safety representative at the place of work. This means that in a school there could be a representative for each union – of teachers and ancillaries. This could amount to anything from four or five people upwards. It is possible, and usual, in schools for the various unions to agree on one person acting as safety representative.

The Health and Safety at Work Act is a criminal Act. This fact caused considerable panic amongst teachers when the Act was first promulgated since, as we discovered earlier, an employer is liable for the civil wrongs of his employee but not his crimes. The assumption was that where a breach of the Act occurred the teacher would be liable on his own. This is unlikely to be so. The Act lays the duty of complying squarely upon the employer's shoulders and this means that while the CEO may delegate duties to schools he cannot delegate ultimate responsibilities. Statements from the inspectors and answers to questions in Parliament indicate that the prosecution will always be against the employer unless the employee has wilfully disobeyed clear instructions, for example failed to use protective goggles in the science laboratories after a direct instruction from the head or a science adviser to the contrary.

What action should individual teachers take in relation to the Health and Safety legislation?

Teachers should read and follow instructions they are given, particularly where these relate to the use of dangerous and specialist equipment, such as machinery in a workshop, apparatus in a sports hall or gymnasium, dangerous chemicals or acids in a laboratory or electrical equipment of any kind.

Where a potential hazard appears it should be reported to the appropriate person who might be a head of department, the caretaker or the head. It is always wise to let the school's safety representative know of the report, unless it is a very trivial one.

Clear warnings should always be given to pupils and faulty or dangerous equipment should be withdrawn from use and locked away securely until appropriate action is taken.

It should be noted that the Act requires individual employees to have regard for their own health and safety at work and to have concern for what their acts or omissions might do to others.

This major Act is a far-reaching one and if all its provisions were introduced immediately it would lead to the closure of all our schools and many of our factories. Changes will have to be brought about gradually through the codes of practice and through statutory instruments.

4.18 Superannuation

When a teacher is newly appointed he should be given a copy of the DES booklet *A Guide to Teachers' Superannuation*, copies of which may always be obtained from the local authority. This booklet sets out the scheme in detail.

Participation is compulsory and contributions are paid at the rate of six per cent of salary.

The broad provisions are as follows: Unless a teacher's employment is terminated because of redundancy, early retirement or breakdown he must usually retire at sixty-five and may retire at any time from the age of sixty onwards. When he does so he is entitled to a pension and lump sum.

4.19 Pension

This is based on the number of years and days of pensionable service completed, the maximum being forty-five, not more than forty years of which was before the age of sixty. The allowance is based on the highest consecutive 365 days' salary during the last three years of service. One eightieth of salary is allowed for each year's service. The minimum period to qualify for the grant of a pension is five years.

Part-time teachers may count their service pro rata towards pensions but the onus is on them to ask for this to be done.

4.20 Lump sum

This is also based on the number of years service with a maximum of forty-five years but more than forty years before the age of sixty may count providing that the sum related to that service before sixty does not exceed one and a half times the annual salary. Service before 1 October 1956 is calculated at one thirtieth of the highest salary, service for each year after that date counts three eightieths of the highest salary.

The minimum service to qualify for a pension and lump sum is five years, though service for at least twelve months but less than five years may qualify for a short service gratuity. Service may be 'bought in' and overseas service may count if contributions are paid. Allowances may be made for war service.

4.21 Invalidity benefit

Where a teacher retires prematurely on grounds of ill-health or disablement, then benefits are payable. If the twelve months' service have been completed, but less than five years, then the short service gratuity is paid. Service above five years will be enhanced (see p. 15 of the DES booklet mentioned in 4.18).

4.22 Death while in service

Providing that a teacher dies in service, or within twelve months of leaving service, a gratuity is payable. This may be a sum equivalent to the highest consecutive 365 days' salary within the last three years, the lump sum that would have been paid on retirement on grounds of infirmity or an amount equivalent to the teacher's accumulated contributions with 3% compound interest, less the amount of any benefit previously paid. Enhancement is as for invalidity benefits. Short-term payments are payable to widows.

4.23 Widows, widowers and other dependants

The compulsory scheme relating to these commenced on 1 April 1972, though a voluntary scheme was in force before this. Service before 1972 may be bought in.

When a teacher has at least five years of service counting for family benefits, the widow's pension is half of the invalidity pension that would have been paid.

It is a bone of contention (and possibly actionable as discrimination) that a widower does not receive a pension because of his wife's service. A woman teacher may, however, nominate a dependent husband or close dependent relative to receive benefit – as may an unmarried man.

Where there are dependent children the pension for one child is half the widow's pension and if there are two or more dependent children, then the pension is equal to the widow's pension. Again, the minimum qualifying period is five year's service counting towards family benefits.

If orphans are left, one child qualifies for two thirds of the pension, two or more for four thirds.

4.24 Return of contributions

At one time a person who left the profession could withdraw superannuation contributions. This is no longer possible except for those who do not eventually qualify for an allowance and in one or two other exceptional cases.

4.25 How to find out

Entitlements for the majority of teachers are simple enough to calculate but there may be complicated individual queries regarding the various types of service that may be recognized, buying in, re-employment after retirement, rights where there has been a dismissal on grounds of misconduct and so on. Where should a teacher with such problems look for help?

1 The problem may be solved by consulting the DES booklet mentioned above (4.18).
2 Queries may be addressed to the Department of Education and Science, Pensions Branch, Mowden Hall, Staindrop Road, Darlington, County Durham, DL3 9BG.
3 Advice may also be obtained from professional associations, who have officials who are well versed in the intricacies of superannuation problems.

5 Parents

When a pupil attends school the teacher is in *loco parentis*, he takes on the rights and responsibility of a parent. The implications of this will be examined in detail in the next chapter but if teachers are to become substitute parents then it is important to understand the legal implications of the role. Also, with the increase in divorce and the frequent break-up of families, teachers increasingly find themselves involved in the complications that ensue, both for pupils and their parents.

5.1 Marriage

Under English law, in spite of the current divorce rate, there is still the definition of marriage as 'the voluntary union for life of one man and one woman to the exclusion of all others'.

For a marriage to be valid under English law, the parties must be single or legally divorced, or the previous marriage partner must be dead. Death may be presumed by the court after a disappearance of seven years and an applicant must seek a decree to that effect. The parties must be over eighteen. If one or both are over sixteen and under eighteen parental permission to marry must have been obtained. Magistrates have power to overrule parents who refuse permission and may give approval where it is impossible for some reason for parental permission to be obtained. Marriage must not take place between close relatives within the 'prohibited degrees'. Certain formalities must be complied with.

If the marriage is according to the rites of the Church of England then banns must be called or a common licence, special licence or superintendent registrar's certificate obtained. The ceremony must be conducted by a clerk in holy orders between the hours of 8 a.m. and 6 p.m. – except when under special licence. Two witnesses must be present.

Other marriages under a superintendent registrar's certificate may be solemnized in his office or in other places such as non-conformist churches when the superintendent registrar must be present. The building must be unlocked. The Registrar General may authorize a marriage to take place anywhere, for instance in a hospital ward, if he sees fit.

A marriage that does not comply with these rules may constitute a criminal offence, as in bigamy. It may become void, as where one party was under sixteen. This could also be criminal if the woman was under sixteen and the male had intercourse knowing she was under sixteen. It may be voidable, i.e. terminable at the option of one party if, say, at the time of the marriage the second party was suffering from venereal disease, was insane or pregnant with child by another father and the first party was unaware of the fact. Non-consummation also makes a marriage voidable as does the presence of duress before or during the marriage ceremony.

English law recognizes polygamous marriage as valid where the marriage involved foreign nationals and took place abroad according to the laws of the country concerned. Thus a muslim from an Arabic country who arrives in England with two wives, both lawfully wed in his own State, is entitled to have both recognized. If he attempts to marry a third wife in this country that would be bigamy, even though allowable in his own State.

Both parties to a marriage have a right to live together and to have sexual intercourse. There is a mutual right to choose the home. The wife has the right to use her husband's name and to be maintained by him. In some circumstances, such as disablement, the husband may have a right to be maintained by the wife. Husbands and wives may sue each other in tort and they may be convicted of stealing from each other but they cannot be charged jointly with conspiracy to commit a crime.

5.2 Separation

When a marriage runs into trouble divorce is not the only relief that may be given by the courts. An order for judicial separation is possible on the application of one spouse. The effect of such an order is that although the marriage still exists the parties are relieved of their duty to live together. Under such an order a husband can be made to pay money to his wife for the maintenance of herself and her children. The court may also make an order regarding custody of the children and rights of access to them.

If a school knows that a judicial separation order has been made concerning a particular family it is always useful to know who has custody of the children and what are the rights of access of the other parent.

5.3 Divorce

The modern law on divorce dates from the Reforming Act of 1969. The various enactments relating to divorce have been collected in the Matrimonial Causes Act 1973.

There is now only one ground for divorce – the irretrievable breakdown of the marriage. Evidence for this may include adultery, desertion or unreasonable behaviour. Since divorce for separation after five years does not require the consent of both parties, then virtually anyone can obtain a divorce eventually. It is no longer necessary even for parties to appear in court in undefended cases. Recently an attempt was made to obtain a divorce without one party even knowing that the action was to take place – someone had forged his signature on the application.

While divorce may be easy to obtain today the courts have to pay special attention to the welfare of the children involved. The decree absolute may be refused if satisfactory arrangements have not been made for them. The courts will make directions as to maintenance, custody and access.

5.4 Duties of parents

When children are born of a marriage the parents must undertake certain duties. These duties and the rights of parents, together with other aspects of the law concerning children, are to be found in the Children's Act of 1975.

1. They must register the child's birth or cause it to be registered.
2. They must maintain the child, i.e. feed and clothe him adequately. An illegitimate child is entitled to maintenance from his mother and possibly from his father, if an affiliation order has been obtained. A similar duty may lie upon a step-parent.
3. Parents must protect their children.
4. Under Section 36 of the 1944 Education Act they must ensure that the child receives full-time education suitable to his age, ability and aptitude, either by regular attendance at school or otherwise.

5.5 Rights of parents

Although in the past these may have been absolute most are now only limited. They include:

1. The right to physical control of a child – that is custody. This right may be removed by a court as when a child is removed under a court order. On occasion the order may be used against a child who does not attend school and he may be removed from the custody of his parents.
2. Where there is no right of custody there may be a right of access but this will be at the court's discretion.
3. The right to discipline a child by a punishment, including corporal punishment (assault and battery) and restricting liberty (false imprisonment). Discipline is a good defence to a civil or criminal action but only if the correction was reasonable. If not, the parent may be liable.
4. The right to educate a child according to the parents' own wishes. Unless the child is to be educated privately the choice of school is surrounded by difficulties and, apart from religious education, parents have no control over the curriculum.

Other rights include giving consent or refusal to medical treatment, withholding consent to marriage, vetoing the provision of a passport, consenting to adoption, appointing a guardian or administering a child's property. Most of these rights are subject to some control by the courts in some situations.

5.6 Custody

In recent times there has been an increasing effort to make the welfare of the child the first and most important concern in all cases. This is particularly important where custody – the right to physical control – is at issue. The person who has the best legal right in the strict sense may be the worst person to have custody from the point of view of the well-being and happiness of the child. Readers may remember the heart-rending case of the child in Bridport, Dorset, who had lived with foster-parents for as long as she could remember but, upon the real mother asserting her legal rights, was forcibly removed from the foster home.

When deciding custody matters the courts will consider such factors as the behaviour of both parents, the age and sex of the child, the need to keep children of the same family together, blood ties, material and financial considerations, religious beliefs and wishes of the child himself or herself. In the light of all the circumstances, what is best for the child? The decision can be very difficult because it must look to the future as well as the present.

There are two kinds of custody, legal and actual. Legal custody involves the undertaking of the rights and duties in law towards a child. Actual custody means physical possession of the child. The court may award legal custody to one parent. It may allow the other one specified parental rights and duties but not actual custody of the child. It may allow one parent care and control of a child and refuse either custody, thus making the child a ward of court (the court then having legal custody). Social workers and probation officers may also be involved in issues of custody.

5.7 Access

Both parents have an absolute right of access to their children unless this right has been removed or restricted by process of law. As with custody, the most important consideration should be the well-being and welfare of the child. One would expect that normally a child's contact with both parents should be preserved but, clearly, there may be instances where contact with both will only exacerbate the tension and bewilderment in a child's mind and contact with one or other parent only is the best course of action. Contact with one parent may be particularly harmful as in the case of a mother who is a known prostitute.

Custody of young children tends to go to the mother – but not always. Where this happens fathers are often given rights of access at weekends, school holidays or 'any reasonable time'.

Grandparents may be granted a right of access.

5.8 Legitimacy

Illegitimacy was once a serious stigma and also a serious legal handicap in various situations. The situation has changed considerably in recent times, largely under the Family Law Reform Act of 1969 and if the recommendations of the Law Commission are followed then eventually the concept of illegitimacy will disappear entirely. The rate of illegitimate births is still running at nearly 10 per cent of live births but only half of these births are to single women, the remainder being couples who are not married but have some kind of settled relationship.

A child is legitimate if at the time of his conception or birth his parents are legally married. If the marriage is voidable and is later annulled a child still remains legitimate. An illegitimate child whose parents later marry becomes legitimate. Where a marriage is void, if one party believed it to be valid at the time of conception or marriage then the child is legitimate.

The most acute embarrassment to an illegitimate person was often the fact that his birth certificate recorded a mother but no father. The introduction of the 'short' birth certificate has removed this.

5.9 Adoption

An adoption order may be issued by a county court or by a magistrates court. The effect of such an order is to remove all legal rights from the natural parents and award them to the adoptive parents. The courts may, however, make conditions, even allowing access by the natural parents.

Illegitimate or legitimate children may be adopted but in both cases the parent or parents must agree. If a parent disagrees the court may overrule the disagreement if this is unreasonable, or if the parent has neglected, abandoned or ill-treated the child. If one parent cannot be traced or is incapable of consenting, on grounds of insanity, for example, then the court may still issue the order.

Mrs A has two children, and has been divorced. She has custody of the children. She re-marries, to Mr B. Mr B may be step-father to the children but he has no parental rights regarding them.

The new Mrs B has a third child. A happy family is established but after several years Mrs B dies. Mr B has then no right to retain the children of the first marriage.

One way out here is for Mr B and the ex-Mrs A to seek jointly to adopt the children. Mr A's consent will be needed. If the court grants adoption, then Mr B assumes full parental rights and if Mrs B dies then the three children cannot be separated by Mr A.

5.10 Local authorities

All children must have a parent or guardian. If no person will act then some organization such as Dr Barnado's or the Church of England Children's Society may do so. Failing all else, the local authority must assume parental rights and duties and take a child into care. This also applies where a parent or guardian exists but for some reason such as disablement, temporary illness, or insanity is incapable of acting. Children received into care include those orphaned, abandoned, lost or homeless. The receiving of a child into care by a local authority is not compulsory upon parents. It is different from care proceedings and care orders which are made by the juvenile court and will be dealt with in a later chapter. A parent may remove a child from care but if he has been in care for six months then twenty-eight days' notice must be given.

If it appears that a child is an orphan and has no guardian, or he has been abandoned, or his parents are unfit to be responsible for him then the local authority may make a resolution that it shall assume parental rights and duties. If parents or relatives object, then the local authority must satisfy the magistrates court and possibly the High Court of the need for its action.

Even where a local authority has assumed parental rights and duties it has discretion to allow a child to live with parents, relatives or another person.

While parents or guardians are alive, a local authority does not have the power to consent to adoption.

5.11 Domestic violence

The amount of violence, mostly against women and children, that occurs in the home is a constant worry to social workers and teachers since the effect it can have on a child's physical, intellectual and emotional development can be traumatic.

Such violence has always existed, of course. Perhaps it is no worse today than it ever was but the spotlights of publicity and investigation have shown that a deep-rooted social problem exists, whether it be battered wives or battered babies. The work of social services departments, the greater availability of divorce and such measures as the Domestic Violence and Matrimonial Proceedings Act 1976 which may prevent molestation, have all helped to alleviate the problems.

Physical violence towards any other person is likely to be a criminal offence, though it may also be the civil wrong (tort) of trespass to the person. An assault is an act which puts someone in fear of being hit and a battery is the actual application of unlawful force. Usually the two go together but if, for example, someone crept up behind you without your knowledge and struck you on the head you would have been battered but not assaulted. The Offences against the Person Act 1861 also includes drugging, poisoning, choking, endangering life and abandoning a child as offences. Crimes of violence may increase in seriousness from a common assault to wounding, inflicting grievous bodily harm and manslaughter or murder.

Section 1 of the Children and Young Persons Act 1933 states that it is a criminal offence where anyone 'wilfully assaults, ill-treats, neglects, abandons or exposes' a child 'in a manner likely to cause unnecessary suffering or injury to health'. However, the same Section of that Act gives the right to parents, teachers and others exercising lawful supervision over a child the right to administer reasonable punishment. Such a defence is known as 'discipline' or, more pompously, as 'lawful chastisement of a child'. On many occasions, several strokes of a school cane have been held to be reasonable, though it is doubtful if today an ordinary parent would use such a method. Numerous strokes with a whip by a schoolmaster after pupils have taken a cold plunge have been held to be unreasonable!

It is easy to say that a man who hits his wife or a wife who batters her young children are subject to the criminal law but access and proof are not easy and even if a successful conviction is brought the prevention of a recurrence cannot be guaranteed. The police have an unenviable task in dealing with 'domestics' as they are called. Frequently, if police are involved, husband and wife turn upon them together.

Teachers are much more vulnerable than parents since their acts of violence are usually the result of desperation and take place in front of a group of very interested witnesses. Although court appearances are very damaging professionally and upsetting for teachers, they can take comfort from the knowledge that magistrates still seem to take the view that the correction and physical punishment of children is a necessary part of their upbringing.

When violence towards children is reported to the police, they have a duty to investigate. Another method of approach is through the NSPCC which maintains inspectors throughout the country and will investigate matters brought to its notice, even anonymously.

Where a child is obviously beaten up or otherwise abused, then a constable or other authorized person, such as a social worker, may remove the child to 'a place of safety' pending proceedings, such as a request for a care order. In recent times there have been tragic examples where a reluctance to take action in such cases has resulted in the death or permanent disfigurement of children.

5.12 Problems for teachers

Matters dealt with in the last few sections can raise difficult situations for teachers. The following are based on real incidents. Ask yourself what you would do in such situations and record your comments in the boxes provided.

Mr W

Mrs W left home with her children because she said she was being battered and moved into the school's catchment area. She told the school that Mr W did not know where she was and she wanted her address and that of the school kept from him, as she feared physical attack in the home and also that he would take the child away from school and run off with him. She mentioned that there had been a court appearance and another one was pending.

Mr W arrived on the school doorstep accompanied by a large man with biceps bulging under the sleeves of his jacket. Mr W introduced him as his 'legal adviser'. Mr W said that he wished to talk to his son and when the head demurred he became aggressive, saying that the boy was in moral danger because of the mother's promiscuity. Mr W's arguments were punctuated by the loud grunts of agreement from the 'legal adviser'.

Mrs X

Mrs X had re-married after a divorce. She had one son by the first marriage and to avoid confusion and embarrassment for him she wrote to the class teacher saying that in future he was to be known by her present married name, not that of her previous husband.

Mr Y

A school was notified that a girl of fourteen was pregnant. The girl in a state of agitation, went to the senior mistress and without any prompting told her that her own father, Mr Y, was responsible.

Mr and Mrs Z

Mr and Mrs Z had a boy of ten. He came to school irregularly and often in a dirty and unkempt condition. At times he had bruises which he explained in ways which made his class teacher suspicious.

5.13 Comments

Mr W

Both parents have equal rights of access to their children unless a court has decreed otherwise. Since children do not have to attend school but may receive education by some other means, it is suggested that a parent has a right to the possession of his child as against the school and may, therefore, demand that the school release him on request. Technically, the writ of Habeas Corpus would lie where a school refused.

Unless a school knows that a parent does not have the right of access, it must treat both parents equally. In the case of pupils from broken families it is important, therefore, to establish if possible which parent has custody and what are the rights of access for the other.

In Mr W's case the school suspected from his remarks that there might be a court decision and it knew which court had dealt with the matter. Mr W was kept talking while a call was made to the court's probation officer who confirmed that the child was a ward of court and Mr W did not have rights of access. The probation officer told him, over the telephone, that he was not to approach the child and that to do so would prejudice his chances at a future hearing.

Another way of tackling a difficult parent in this situation is to say quickly that one assumes the parent's visit is to discuss the child's work and progress at school. It takes a very determined customer to deny this. The next move is to send for the child's latest report and his form teacher and engage in a civilized discussion over English and mathematics. Even a parent who has no right of access has a reasonable case for knowing how his own child is progressing.

In a situation like this where a parent, who has no right of access, becomes aggressive or makes a suggestion of abduction, then the police should be called immediately.

Mrs X

A child's surname may not be changed except by agreement of both parents or by an order of the court as recent cases have confirmed. Of course, if Mrs X and her second husband had jointly adopted the child there would be no problem, the second husband would have taken over the parental rights of the first one.

In this case the teacher altered the name in the register. This should not be done. An admission register and a class register are both documents that may be required as legal evidence in court. They must be kept carefully and accurately.

A person may call himself by any name he chooses, though this would hardly apply to a minor. Nevertheless, it may be in order to call a child by his new family's name but it would be wrong to note it as such on an official register, or on an examination entry form or certificate or on a passport.

Mr Y

Sexual intercourse between a child and parent is the crime of incest. This also applies after a child reaches the age of consent.

It is usually unwise to promise a child absolute confidence. The senior mistress had not done so – indeed, if she had, by concealing the crime she might have committed an offence herself. The matter was reported to the social services and the police. The girl and her younger sister were immediately placed in the care of the local authority and the father prosecuted.

Mr and Mrs Z

Parents, as we have seen, have a duty to care for, protect and educate their children. Mr and Mrs Z were clearly in breach of these duties.

In this case the class teacher rightly drew the head's attention to the problems. The Education Welfare Officer and local Health Visitor went to the home on several occasions but as no progress was made a prosecution was brought. The parents were fined and the child placed in the care of the local authority.

5.14 Education – parental rights and duties

'Thou shalt not', says the Book of Proverbs, 'get thy teacher into a corner'. Today, some teachers feel that they are trapped in this way – beset by authority regulations, difficult pupils and demanding parents (and demanding headmasters!). The chief worry is often over parents who seem to have increasingly powerful rights and an increasing tendency to interfere with the teacher's work by asserting those rights.

This is a false picture. The real story is that for many years schools and teachers have bluffed parents over their rights. Schools have been closed communities which many parents were afraid of, remembering their own experiences perhaps. Parents have been held at arm's length or even actively discouraged from taking an interest in school affairs. Today, parents are waking up and realizing that they can play an important part in the school as a community by becoming involved in its activities and establishing a rapport with teachers. Of course, there are some parents who behave unreasonably – that is human nature but the stupidity of the few is out-balanced by the good will and interest of the many.

Most of the rights parents seem to have are hollow ones, vague and inconclusive. Their duties are onerous, as we shall see.

5.15 Rights of parents

First let us examine the definite rights that parents have.

To have sufficient schools provided

This says nothing about quality, though presumably since a parent must educate his child according to his age, ability and aptitude, schools must also be able to offer such education. But just what is meant by such vague terms? The statement simply seems to indicate that there must be enough schools to go round.

That schools will provide efficient instruction

Not even teachers could possibly agree as to what constitutes 'efficient instruction'. What must be the content of the curriculum? Which teaching methods qualify for approval?

The recent case of the Harrison family from Tenbury Wells illustrates the problem. The Harrison parents claimed that because their children were dyslexic they were better off being taught at home by the parents themselves, by what was described as an 'autonomous system'. The judge decided that the girl's education complied with the Education Act since she was able to read, write and take shorthand (no mention of mathematics, science, history or geography). There was no evidence that the two boys could read or write so the judge decided that in their case the Act was not being complied with. Incidentally, there had been no suggestion that the Harrison children should be forced to attend school – only that the education authority should be allowed to monitor the education that was taking place.

To choose a school

Some years ago the twin boys of Mr Watt were offered places at a Church of England Grammar School. He was a Roman Catholic and after referring to the 1944 Education Act Section 76 and discovering that 'pupils are to be educated in accordance with the wishes of their parents' he sent his boys to Roman Catholic boarding schools and asked the Kesteven authority to pay the fees. They declined and the court supported them. Mr Watt had not read the entire section. If he had done so, he would have seen the words 'so far as is compatible with the provision of efficient instruction and training and the avoidance of unreasonable public expenditure, pupils are to be educated in accordance with the wishes of their parents'. Mr Watt lost his case.

The court said that Section 76 does not say that pupils must, in all cases, be educated in accordance with the wishes of their parents. It only laid down a general principle to which the county council must have regard. It left it open to the county council to have regard to other things as well, and also to make exceptions to the general principle if it thought fit to do so.

It was held that the public expenditure involved was unreasonable. Other cases have followed the same line of argument and an authority was clearly in a strong position to refuse the choice of school if it wished to do so.

The 1980 Act would appear to strengthen parental choice. It does so, perhaps, by introducing an appeals procedure and a right to opt across county boundaries but the wording is still hedged about with expressions such as 'prejudice the provision of efficient education or the efficient use of resources' and for the first time authorities may set a maximum admission level for each of their schools.

Mr Watt would still lose his case today though his twins might get assisted places.

To withdraw a pupil from religious education and worship

It may be that the vast majority of people in this country do not attend church except to be baptized, married or buried but, nevertheless, christian morality and ethics still underly our way of life. Both religious education and worship are compulsory in our schools under the 1944 Act Section 25 (religious education is the only compulsory subject on the curriculum). Opinion polls have shown that most parents wish these provisions to remain. Parents do have a right to withdraw their children from the morning assembly and religious education lessons if they so wish. Few exercise the option, the most common being Jehovah Witnesses. I remember the Hindu pupils whose parents had left them to decide whether to attend an assembly or not. They decided to join in. 'We like to know what is going on, sir.' That was, perhaps, a commentary on our assemblies.

In many schools 'religious worship' hardly seems an appropriate description of what happens and there can be little doubt that the requirements of the Act are often not complied with. This should not be true of the religious education since this should be taught according to the agreed syllabus and a teacher of religious education who refused to follow the agreed syllabus would be liable to disciplinary action. The agreed syllabus is usually drawn up as a result of consultations between the authority, teachers and representatives of various denominations. It suggests broad approaches and leaves individual schools to decide on details.

To have free transport provided

Pupils under the age of eight have a right to free transport if they live more than two miles from the school. Pupils over eight have a similar right if they live more than three miles from the school. The right is decided on the nearest public right of way, even over cart tracks or bridle paths. The case of *Shackstead* v. *Ward* (1954) reaffirmed this and indicated that safety factors in walking to and from school have no legal significance in relation to free transport.

Of course, authorities may provide transport for pupils who live 'within walking distance' if they wish to do so. Where there are spare seats on buses many authorities allow pupils within the limits to use them.

From time to time, it is suggested that the obligation to provide free transport should be removed from local authorities. An attempt to do this as part of the 1980 Act was defeated.

It is a defence to a prosecution for not sending a child to school that the local authority has not complied with its statutory duty of providing free transport.

For pupils to receive free meals and milk

The 1980 Act Sections 22 and 23, removes in the main the obligation of local authorities to provide milk or meals at all. Milk does not have to be provided and if it is it may be chargeable unless it is provided as part of the free meal to which some pupils are entitled. School meals do not have to be provided (some authorities have abandoned them completely) though authorities must make some reasonable free provision for children from families in receipt of supplementary benefit or family income supplement. School meals that are provided may consist of standard meals or snack meals at the authority's discretion.

The 1980 Act does require authorities to provide facilities for pupils who bring food to eat from home and no charge may be made for this.

To have information about schools

The 1980 Act, Section 8, requires local authorities and schools to provide information for parents regarding their criteria for admission, ways for parents to express their preference of school and methods of appeal. By a statutory instrument, the Education (School Information) Regulations 1981, authorities have been given guidance as to the details that should be given and these include, staffing, curriculum, method of organization (streaming, banding, mixed ability), disciplinary measures (including whether corporal punishment is used), examining boards used and recent examination results, name of the chairman of governors and so on.

To be represented on school governing bodies

As explained earlier, parents must now be represented on governing bodies when new instruments and articles of government are made and they must be elected by a secret ballot of parents not by nomination of the authority. In voluntary schools one parent will be elected and one parent governor will be nominated by the foundation governors.

5.16 Duties of parents

The law lays certain duties very clearly on the shoulders of parents.

To educate their children

Section 36 of the 1944 Education Act reads:

> 'It shall be the duty of the parent of every child of compulsory school age to cause him to receive efficient full-time education suitable to his age, ability and aptitude, either by regular attendance at school or otherwise.'

This lays a very heavy duty on parents. It is their ultimate responsibility, not the State's, to see that their children are educated and that the education is a suitable one bearing in mind the age, abilities and talents of their offspring. All this may seem very vague, as many rights are, but it does mean that a parent whose child is in need of special help of a remedial nature, which is only available at a certain school, will be in breach of the Act if he fails to take advantage of it – unless he can provide a satisfactory alternative education himself.

No child has to attend school. Parents may avail themselves of the 'sufficient schools provided by local authorities' if they wish – that is the theoretical situation anyway. In fact, a number of children do not attend school and each case has to be dealt with individually by the local authority which is responsible for seeing that the law is observed. Clearly, a qualified trained primary school teacher who becomes a mother and teaches her own child at home will be beyond the reach of an authority – though her child will be missing the social contacts that many teachers would think desirable. The position over children of secondary school age is much more complicated but the judgement in the Harrison case mentioned above would suggest that many parents could succeed in educating their children themselves if they chose to do so.

To send children to school regularly

If parents decide to send their children to school, then the attendance must be regular.

The Gilmores

In 1969 the Gilmores were taken to court. Their daughter had been absent on twenty-three occasions out of a possible 114. On twelve of these occasions she had played truant without the knowledge of the parents, though they knew of her absence on the other occasions. In spite of appealing on a point of law to the Queen's Bench Division of the High Court, the parents were found guilty but given an absolute discharge i.e. a criminal verdict of guilty was recorded but no other punishment given.

This case (*Crump* v. *Gilmore*) was important for two reasons.

1 It established that not sending your child to school is an absolute offence. In most crimes the prosecution has to show that there is *mens rea* present – that is a guilty intent to commit the criminal offence. For absolute offences such as those involving weights and measures, food and drugs, some road traffic offences such as speeding and offences such as a landlord serving drink to a person already drunk the fact that the act was committed is enough. Intent does not have to be proved. A parent who sends his child out to school but the child fails to turn up is still liable to be prosecuted.
2 That an absence even for one session without a reasonable cause is actionable.

In an earlier case, *Jenkins* v. *Howells* (1949), it had been established that 'reasonable cause' must be unavoidable and something closely affecting the child and not others. In the case mentioned, the courts ruled that a mother was not entitled to keep her daughter at home because she, the mother, was ill herself. Examples of good reason for absence could be a child's own sickness, a visit to the doctor, dentist or hospital, or possibly attending an interview for a job.

Sometimes an excuse that seems unreasonable may turn out to be acceptable. During the war, one boy came to school with a letter from his mother explaining that he had been absent because of the yak. The school was suspicious but investigation showed that a bomb had dropped on a nearby zoo. A yak had, indeed, escaped and was running wild on a stretch of common land that the boy had to cross in order to reach the school!

Under the Education (Schools and Further Education) Regulations 1981 pupils may be absent for two weeks in each year to go on holiday with parents, relatives or friends. They may also be absent for certain days set aside for religious observance, such as Ascension Day, even though they do not, in fact, attend a church service.

There are two other possible defences to a prosecution for non-attendance:

1 That leave of absence has been given by a person authorized by the governors of the school to do so.
2 That the pupil lived beyond 'walking distance' and the authority had failed to provide transport.

To send children to school on time

In *Hinchley* v. *Rankin* (1961) it was decided that a child who comes to school late is not receiving 'full-time' education. Therefore, the parent is in breach of the law.

It is clear from this and the preceding sections that the prompt and accurate keeping of registers can be vital in providing evidence where parents are prosecuted for breaking the law with regard to school attendance.

To see that children obey reasonable school rules

This is not a statutory duty but it may certainly be inferred from a number of cases that when the parent sends his child to a particular school (he does not have to, remember, he can educate him otherwise) then by implication he accepts rules that are reasonable for the running of the school. Banning slacks for girls, banning jewellery, caning for smoking, or for fighting on the way to school and having hair cut to a certain length have all been held to be reasonable.

5.17 Questionable rights

There are always those who have an unrealistic and highly individual assessment of their rights, for example the lady who visited the school and said that during the next academic year she wished her daughter to be taught mathematics by Mr A, English by Mrs B, history by Mr C and so on. She had been doing her homework – or her child's! When her request was refused she pointed out that pupils were to be educated in accordance with the wishes of their parents. These were her wishes and she would insist on her rights. She did not get her way.

There are at least three areas where there are popular misconceptions over parental rights.

Visiting school

Apart from persons who have direct permission to be on private premises (and schools are private premises) anyone else is either a visitor or a trespasser.

A visitor is a person who has implied legal permission to be on premises, a trespasser has no right to be there at all. The milkman who comes up your drive and wakes you in the morning with his clinking bottles is a visitor. If you tell him to leave the bottles at the end of the drive and he ignores your instruction then he becomes a trespasser. On school premises the head, as the agent of the authority, has power to declare almost anyone a trespasser – staff, pupils and certainly parents. He would not be able to declare an HMI a trespasser since he has right of entry. Neither could he declare an officer of the local authority to be a trespasser. The position of the caretaker is a delicate one!

In the absence of the head, his deputy may declare a person to be a trespasser and the caretaker may do so in the early mornings, evenings, holidays and at weekends.

It has been known for officers of an authority and elected representatives to declare the head himself to be a trespasser and escort him from the premises.

A parent's right to visit a school is, therefore, limited by the law of trespass. Trespass is a tort (civil wrong) the remedies for which are basically damages or an injunction, though an injured person may also use what the law describes as 'self-help'.

'Trespassers will be prosecuted' has no meaning in law because trespass without any other element such as damage, violence or theft is not subject to criminal proceedings, and therefore the police can do little to help. A more appropriate notice would read something like 'Trespassers will be dealt with in accordance with the law'.

The provisions of the Local Government (Miscellaneous Provisions) Act of 1982 have changed this in relation to educational premises, (not just schools). Section 40, Sub Section 1 of the Act reads as follows:

> 'Any person who without lawful authority is present on premises to which this section applies and causes or permits nuisance or disturbance to the annoyance of persons who lawfully use those premises (whether or not any such persons are present at the time) shall be guilty of an offence and shall be liable on summary conviction to a fine not exceeding £50.'

Premises includes grounds as well as buildings. The Act applies whether the institution is in session or not so the dog owner allowing his pet to foul a school playing field on a Sunday afternoon is open to prosecution.

It seems from the Act that either the education authority or the police may institute proceedings. In the case of a voluntary school, the school governors must consent before the authority may bring proceedings and in the case of an aided school or special agreement school, the governors themselves may authorize someone to bring proceedings.

Remember that parents and pupils, possibly ex-pupils, have an implied right to be on school premises as visitors. If action is contemplated, it is useful to declare firmly that the person in question is a trespasser and order him to leave the premises.

Two incidents will illustrate how the Act works.

A costly celebration

Two fifth year boys who had just completed their examinations went to the home of one of them in the lunch-hour and drank half a bottle of whisky between them. They returned to school and staggered about the playground jostling other pupils and causing a minor disturbance. The head was called. He could smell the whisky on their breaths, told them they were trespassing and ordered them to leave the premises. They did so but returned a second time. The police were called.

The next morning the two lads called at the front of the school to apologize and asked the head if he would kindly explain what they had done that was wrong. They couldn't remember a thing.

A prosecution was brought under the 1982 Act and each was fined £25 with £15 costs.

A costly silence

Joe had left school but his girl-friend had not, so he frequently came back during breaks and lunch-hours to see her. He never caused trouble and left the premises when told to do so. This had occurred on a number of occasions.

One day the deputy head came upon Joe in the lunch-hour. He was reclining on the grass, girl-friend by his side, and reading a newspaper. The deputy head ordered Joe from the premises but he continued to read his newspaper and ignored the command. He was not rude or aggressive. The request was repeated several times and eventually the police were called.

Joe was fined £15 with costs for causing a nuisance on school premises.

An owner or occupier owes no duty of care to trespassers though he must not take extreme measures, such as shooting at them or setting man-traps. If the vexatious parent or marauding ex-pupil are injured by some defective school property or equipment then they have no redress. The law relating to child trespassers is rather different, particularly where very young children are concerned.

If a school is aware that trespassing on its property takes place by young children and that there is a danger to them, e.g. an old car, a cracked man-hole cover or potentially dangerous climbing equipment then the authority may well be liable if an accident occurs. Notices are of little use as a defence if the trespasser is aged three or four. Good fencing, locked gates and a letter to the parents, if they can be identified, would all help to avoid liability.

Parents and parents' associations

A teacher refusing to write reports for parents at reasonable intervals or refusing to discuss the child's work or progress with parents might be in breach of an implied term in his contract. That would certainly be the most that a parent would be legally entitled to in the way of contact with his child's teachers.

When a parent comes to school to complain, if he or she is prepared to discuss the problem in a reasonable fashion, then a talk with the teacher concerned may well be the best way of dealing with the matter. Whether an angry parent should have a meeting with a teacher is, in the first place, a matter for the head to decide and if he feels it to be advisable then the consent of the teacher must first be obtained. As a last resort, the police should be sent for to deal with violent or threatening parents.

Face to face meetings in a small room, accompanied by a cup of tea or a cigarette, can often work wonders. The teacher is not the fearsome ogre that Johnny or Mary has made him out to be and the face of the angry father when he is introduced to the attractive, blonde, female dragon who has been victimizing his offspring is a sight to be remembered.

The parent has a right to a report but a judge in a recent case assumed, without question, that attendance at parents' meetings by teachers was purely voluntary.

Do parents have the right to form a parents' association? The answer is 'no'. An association could be formed but to have meetings on school premises or undertake activities on behalf of the school requires the consent of the head.

Today, the majority of schools have such an association though sometimes it is known by some other title such as Friends of the School. Such a title is sometimes used so that ex-pupils, for example, may become members but, whatever the title, the group should have a constitution and this may be arranged to cover almost any kind of membership. Heads are sometimes worried about the possible pressures that may be put on them by parents and parents' associations and use the unusual title to prevent the association from legally being one of parents and thus causing problems. In law, it makes little difference since PTAs, as they are usually known, have no legal powers, their status being rather similar to that of a sports or social club.

Rarely is it possible for a PTA to own property of any value since most authorities insist that gifts of minibuses and equipment become the property of the authority so that they have ultimate control over the use. Authorities usually lay down the type and make of equipment that may be provided, e.g. of television sets, video recorders and so on. The equipment always has to be purchased through the authority in order to escape the payment of VAT.

Where a PTA does own a minibus, this has to be registered in the name of one of the officers – perhaps the headmaster – as president. In such a situation, the head should remember all the legal responsibilities he has undertaken with regard to the bus – as if it were his own car.

In law, a PTA is what is known as an unincorporated association, which means that it cannot sue or be sued in its own capacity but actions must be taken by or against its officers. Thus where at a PTA function someone is injured through negligence the plaintiff might sue the individual responsible or an officer of the PTA, such as the chairman or secretary. It is advisable for PTAs to have insurance cover and this may be arranged through an insurance company. A better and cheaper way of obtaining insurance is by joining the National Federation of Parent Teacher Associations, which arranges insurance cover as part of membership. The Association also produces a model constitution for PTAs which is very useful for those setting up such an association. It is given as Appendix 2 to this book.

Control over the curriculum

We have said that a parent has the right to withdraw his child from religious education and worship. Does he have any other rights over the curriculum?

In a primary school in Exeter the head decided to introduce sex education lessons. A parent objected – he did not wish his child to be involved. The court found against him. In a comprehensive school recently a parent complained about the system of options at the end of the 3rd Year. His child wished to take a combination of subjects that was not possible under the system. The court found against this parent but the local authority had, in the meanwhile, negotiated a transfer to another school which offered a combination of subjects acceptable to the parent.

If a parent sends his child to a school then he must accept the curriculum the school offers, except as regards religious education. It is always open to a school to allow a pupil to opt out of certain areas of the curriculum if he wishes. The most frequent problem seems to be with sex education about which some parents hold strong views. During the passage of the 1980 Act through Parliament an attempt was made to give parents the right to withdraw children from sex education lessons but this was lost. Under the 1980 Act information regarding the sex education given must be supplied to parents and an evening to explain the school's policy and show the films etc. that are used can often help to put parents' minds at rest.

Another situation that sometimes causes friction between school and parent is that of examination entries. Is the pupil to be entered for 'O' level or CSE? Is a 6th former to be entered for 'A' level at all? Rigid attitudes by some schools, such as restricting entry to 'A' level after a two years' course to those who have obtained 35 per cent or more in 'mocks' do not help.

The head of the school, or someone to whom he delegates the duty, has to sign the entry forms for examinations. There is at least a moral duty to enter only those who have a chance of success but all teachers know how difficult it is to be sure on this point. The final decision is with the head. Where a school refuses to enter a pupil for 'O' level rather than CSE it is open to a parent to find a centre that will accept the youngster as an external candidate on the payment of a fee.

Some schools ask parents to pay the examination fee in such circumstances and some demand fees for pupils who fail to arrive for an examination and who do not produce satisfactory evidence explaining their absence. Both practices are of doubtful legality unless the approval of the authority has been obtained.

6 Parent substitutes

6.1 In *loco parentis*

When Mary Jones or Robert Smith come to school then their teachers take over some of the legal rights and duties of parents – rights such as those of control and discipline, duties such as those of protection and care. Teachers are parent substitutes, standing in place of the natural parents. This seems straightforward enough but the realities of relating to particular pupils and particular situations may be somewhat complicated.

6.2 The teacher's role

The role of the teacher as a parent substitute was first defined in *Williams* v. *Eady* (1893).

Kenneth Williams

Kenneth Williams attended a private school in Surrey. In a room at the school a number of bottles were left amongst other equipment, including some cricket gear. One of the bottles contained phosphorus.

The room was kept locked but pupils had easy access to the key. Another pupil got hold of the bottle of phosphorus, put a match to it and shook it up. The bottle exploded and Kenneth was burned. Not surprisingly, the school was found liable in negligence.

It is not for this that the case has become well known, however, it is because it is the first occasion on which a court has pronounced on the duty that teachers owe to their pupils:

> 'The school master was bound to take such care of his boys as a careful father would take of his boys, and there could be no better definition of the duty of a school master.'

In spite of the obvious male chauvinism present this is also applied to women teachers and girl pupils and has become the standard definition of the duty of care owed by a teacher in common law to his or her pupils.

This definition has been followed in case after case. Recently it was applied to the education authority itself in *Myton* v. *Wood and Others* (1980):

> 'The duty of a local education authority in the provision of transport for children attending schools in accordance with its statutory duty under Section 55 of the Education Act 1944, is to take such care as a reasonably careful father would take for his own children.'

6.3 Particular or general?

A head was addressing a meeting of new parents and during the course of his talk he explained that corporal punishment was used in the school. No comment was made at the time by any of the parents but the next morning a father rang the school.

He said that he believed in good behaviour and firm discipline but on grounds of conscience he could not agree to his son receiving corporal punishment. The head could punish the boy in any other way that he wished.

The head replied that he could not run a school on the basis of certain parents dictating which form of punishment might or might not be used for particular pupils. This would be unfair to the vast majority. The position over corporal punishment had been made clear and if the parent sent his boy to the school there was an implied acceptance that corporal punishment might be administered. If the parent demanded an undertaking that the boy would not receive corporal punishment, then the head would refuse to admit him.

The father gave in and the boy attended. The question of corporal punishment never arose, for which the school must have been grateful. However, if it had arisen it might have made legal history.

The law is not clear when it states that a teacher stands in place of parents. Does this mean the particular parents of Danny Doolittle or some imaginary 'reasonable parent'? If the former is the case the individual parents could hedge about the delegation of parental powers with all kinds of qualifications. If the latter is true then, providing the teacher acts in what society (or a court) considers the way in which a reasonable parent would have done, then he can ignore the whims and fancies of unconventional and overprotective parents. There is no English case on the problem.

The leading authorities on tort do not agree. Winfield and Jalowicz in *Tort* seem to support the ability of the particular parent to withdraw certain rights from the teacher. Street *Law of Torts* takes a different view, saying that a parent has no legally enforceable right to limit the correction of his child by local education authorities. The defence of discipline may be used by teachers where such action is necessary to preserve good order in a particular school. He quotes the rather outlandish Australian case of *Craig* v. *Frost* (1936) where a teacher ordered a boy not to gallop his horse to and from school and the father told him that he could do so. The action was reasonable for the general safety of pupils and the school could override the wishes of the parent. Being an Australian case *Craig* v. *Frost* is only a persuasive precedent and an English court would not be bound to follow it.

Another view sometimes put forward is that in maintained schools the teacher's authority is derived from the State and only the State can withdraw those rights.

It seems reasonable to conclude that a school cannot be expected to observe the individual wishes of all parents in relation to such matters as punishment and that, providing the disciplinary measures are both careful and reasonable, a parent must comply or educate his child 'otherwise'. A case confirming this view would be welcome.

6.4 The careful parent

If a teacher must behave as a reasonable and careful parent would then just how do we identify what this rather mysterious character might or might not do? The simple (or not so simple) answer is that the court will apply the test of the careful parent to each case that comes before it and will come to a decision in the light of all the circumstances.

Perhaps the best commentary on the role of the careful parent comes from Mr Justice Hilbery in *Hudson* v. *the Governors of Rotherham Grammar School and Selby Johnson* (1937).

Mr Selby Johnson and the cricket roller

The playing field at Rotherham Grammar School had been placed out of bounds for the time being. Mr Selby Johnson had done a tour of supervision and gone back into the school. No boys had been breaking bounds while he was outside but after his departure two of them went on to the cricket pitch and began pushing the roller. Ralph Hudson joined them and by some means the roller was pulled over him. He suffered a fractured skull and other injuries. The action against the school and Mr Selby Johnson was lost.

In giving his reasons for dismissing the case the judge said:

'What has a reasonably careful parent to do? Supposing a boy of yours has some other little boys who are friends of his, coming to tea on a Saturday afternoon and you see them all playing in the garden. Suppose your garden roller happened to be there. Would you consider you had been neglectful of your duty to the parents of those other boys because, for five minutes, you had gone into the house and two of them had managed to pull the roller over the third?

Would you think that, in those circumstances, you had failed to exercise reasonable supervision as a parent? These things have got to be treated as matters of common sense, not to put on Mr Johnson any higher standard of care than that of a reasonably careful parent.

If boys were kept in cotton wool, some of them would choke themselves with it. They would manage to have accidents: we always did, members of the jury – we did not always have actions at law afterwards.

You have to consider whether or not you would expect a headmaster to exercise such a degree of care that boys could never get into mischief. Has any reasonable parent yet succeeded in exercising such care as to prevent a boy getting into mischief and – if he did – what sort of boys should we produce?'

6.5 Natural high spirits

The theme that boys will be boys and girls will be girls, that accidents will happen and that it is not natural for normal parents to curb excessively the high spirits of children echoes through numerous cases.

John Murrell and the trolley [*Murrell* v. *Bexley Borough Council* (1979)]

John was a pupil at a school in Bexley. One day he was in the playground at break and some older boys began to play about with a heavy trolley that was used for moving dishes. They pushed it into John and the result was that his leg was broken.

There was a teacher on supervision duty and she had visited the playground to see that all was well but, at the time of the accident, she had left to inspect another area of the school.

In the High Court the judge dismissed the claim for damages in negligence against Bexley Borough Council. All reasonable care had been taken and it was impossible to expect all parts of the playground and buildings to be under continuous supervision during breaks. He also said that although school teachers have a duty to take reasonable care to prevent injuries from horseplay, they do not have to impose a regime that suppresses the ordinary high spirits that children display. This echoes similar remarks in earlier cases such as in *Jeffrey* v. *London County Council* (1954):

> 'School authorities, when they are considering the care of children, must strike some balance between the meticulous supervision of children every moment of the time when they are under their care, and the very desirable object of encouraging the sturdy independence of children as they grow up. . . .'

Perhaps, though, the judge who remarked, 'It is better that a boy break his neck than allow other people to break his spirit' was overstating the case. One hopes that schools can avoid both these eventualities.

6.6 The careful parent and pupils en masse

How is it possible to compare the actions of the parent dealing with one or two children and teachers dealing with large groups of pupils?

William Beaumont and the elastic [*Beaumont* v. *Surrey County Council* (1968)]

William was a pupil at a school in Surrey. He was eating his biscuits in the playground one morning when the unfortunate accident occurred in which he virtually lost the sight of one eye.

A PE master had taken a long strip of worn elastic from a trampette in the gymnasium and had thrown this into a waste bin. Two other boys had found it and began to fool about with it. The elastic was stretched and when released it flicked to one side and hit William in the eye.

The judge found in favour of William. He laid stress on the fact that this was no ordinary piece of elastic but a heavy and potentially dangerous part of a piece of specialist equipment. He also went on to discuss the problem of relating supervision and care to large masses of children and his comments have been quoted in succeeding cases:

'The duty of a headmaster towards his pupils is said to be to take such care of them as a reasonably careful and prudent father would take of his own children. That standard is a helpful one when considering, for example, individual instructions to individual children in a school. It would be very unwise to allow a six year old child to carry a kettle of boiling water – that type of instruction; but that standard when applied to an incident of horseplay in a school of 900 pupils is somewhat unrealistic, if not unhelpful.

In the context of the present action it appears to me to be easier and preferable to use the ordinary language of the law of negligence, that is, it is a headmaster's duty, bearing in mind the known propensities of boys and indeed girls between the ages of eleven and seventeen or eighteen, to take all reasonable and proper steps to prevent any of the pupils under his care from suffering injury from inanimate objects, from the actions of their fellow pupils, or from a combination of the two. That is a high standard.'

Clearly then the behaviour of the teacher as a reasonable parent may be seen in two contexts – one in relation to one or two pupils (almost in a true domestic situation) and one where he is dealing with large groups in special situations and where his professional training and expertise should warrant a greater degree of care than could be expected from an ordinary parent.

6.7 The domestic

The teacher is in the position of the parent of individual children and in school may ask them to assist in the life of the school as a community. Children do not come to school just to undertake academic work, they are also there in a 'family' situation.

Sandra Cooper and the pot of tea [*Cooper* v. *Manchester Corporation* (1959)]
Sandra was a pupil at a school in Moss Side, Manchester. It was the custom in the school for the older girls to take turns in making tea for the staff. One day Sandra was carrying a large pot of tea, about half a gallon, to the staff room just before break when a small boy burst unexpectedly out of a room and ran into her. She was scalded by hot tea. On appeal the action against Manchester Corporation for damages in negligence was lost.

In this case the judge said that this was an ordinary domestic operation which it was reasonable to ask a child to perform. It was not being carried out in a large group or amongst masses of pupils in corridors and, therefore, no special duty of care applied, only that of a responsible parent. This followed the earlier case of *Smith* v. *Martin and Kingston upon Hull Corporation* (1911) where it was said:

'The Education Acts are intended to provide for education in its truest and widest sense. Such education includes the inculcation of habits of order and obedience and courtesy; such habits are taught by giving orders, and if such orders are reasonable and proper, under the circumstances of the case, they are within the scope of the teacher's authority, even although they are not confined to bidding the child to read or write, to sit down or to stand up in school, or the like. It would be extravagant to say that a teacher has no business to ask a child to perform small acts of courtesy to herself or others such as to fetch her pocket handkerchief from upstairs, to poke the fire in the teachers' room, to open the door for a visitor, or the like: it is said that these are for the teacher's own benefit and to save herself trouble, and not for the child's benefit, but I do not agree: not only is it good for the child to be taught to be unselfish and obliging but the opportunity of running upstairs may often avoid punishment: the wise teacher, who sees the volatile child become fidgety, may well make the excuse of an errand for herself an outlet for the child's exuberance of spirits very much to the benefit of the child. Teachers must use their common sense, and it would be disastrous to hold that they can do nothing but teach.'

Poking the staff room fire indeed!

6.8 The professional

Nevertheless, the teacher's main function is to work with large groups of pupils and to relate his duty of care in such a situation to the action of an ordinary parent is somewhat unrealistic. Parents, the public and pupils have a right to expect that the teacher, as a trained professional, will establish high standards of supervision, care and control when dealing with large groups. In spite of this, accidents will happen and a teacher's standards of care are then those that are reasonable in the light of his knowledge, experience and training.

Ronald Ralph and the glass partition [*Ralph* v. *London County Council* (1947)]

At a London school Ronald and some thirty other boys were having a lesson in a large hall. The section in which they were working was the assembly hall and it was divided from the dining hall by a large partition. Above the level of three feet the partition consisted of panes of glass. The master in charge was allowing the boys to play a game of 'touch'. Ronald, seeking to avoid being caught, ran into the partition. His hand went through a pane of glass and he sustained serious injuries.

The court found that the teacher, and thus the authority, was negligent. No sensible parent would have allowed such a dangerous game to be played and a teacher, dealing with a large group of active boys in such a situation, should have foreseen the possible dangerous consequences. However:

Winifred Butt and the pointed scissors [*Butt* v. *Cambridgeshire & Isle of Ely County Council* (1969)]

Winifred was one of a class of thirty-seven girls in a primary school, aged nine to ten years. They were having a geography lesson and were given pointed scissors with which to cut out illustrations. The use of such scissors was normal practice and the teacher was conducting the lesson in an efficient manner. She turned to comment on the work of one pupil and as she did so another pupil waved her scissors in the air and the point went into Winifred's eye. She lost the sight of that eye.

The action for negligence was dismissed. Here there was a large class but it was being conducted properly and the use of scissors was normal. The risk of such an accident could not have been reasonably foreseen by the teacher. It was an unfortunate accident but such things may happen and the teacher was not at fault.

This case may be contrasted with the recent one of *Black* v. *Kent County Council* (1981). In this case a boy also injured his eye with scissors when his chair was jogged by another pupil. Although the judge criticized the use of pointed scissors the important factor here seemed to be that three members of the staff had examined the boy and had allowed him to walk home without taking proper medical advice. The judge awarded £13,500 damages to James Black.

6.9 Dangerous situations

Not only may the teacher be dealing with large groups of pupils but he may also be dealing with them in potentially dangerous situations which are not likely to be presented to any parent. The most obvious example is a large group in a gymnasium or sports hall.

Roger Wright and the buck [*Wright* v. *Cheshire County Council* (1952)]
A group of forty boys in a Cheshire secondary school were having a PE lesson. They were working in groups at various activities and Roger was in a group vaulting over a buck. The teacher was moving about the gym from group to group. The method used to assist with safe vaulting was for each boy, after he had vaulted the buck, to stop and provide support on landing for the next boy who vaulted. The boys were experienced and proficient at doing this.

Just as Roger was vaulting, the bell went for the end of the lesson and the boy who should have provided support turned and ran for the changing room. Roger fell awkwardly and was seriously injured.

The action by the plaintiff for negligence was lost because the method of support used was a commonly approved one and the teacher was considered to be acting reasonably, having trained the boys to use the method and by moving carefully himself from group to group, but the case illustrates well the potential dangers of such a situation:

> 'There may well be some risk in everything one does or in every step one takes, but in ordinary everyday affairs the test of what is reasonable care may well be answered by experience from which arises a practice adopted generally, and followed successfully over the years so far as the evidence in this case goes.'

In the similar case of *Povey* v. *Rydal School* (1969), the outcome was different. Here the pupil was awarded a large sum in damages after suffering an accident from which he became paralysed and was confined to a wheelchair. In this case the teacher was also moving from one group to another but the exercise the pupil was engaged in was held to be particularly dangerous (exercising on 'rings') and the gymnastic mats being used were of a poor standard. In tragic cases such as this the judge will often look very hard for a way of finding in favour of the plaintiff.

6.10 Dangerous equipment and materials

In a similar way the normal parent is not likely to be faced with pupils in a group using dangerous specialized equipment or materials.

Cyril Shepherd and the phosphorus [*Shepherd* v. *Essex County Council and Linch* (1913)]

Cyril was fifteen and was taking part in a chemistry lesson at a school in Essex. There were twenty-eight boys in the class at the time. They were told to collect pieces of phosphorus to use in an experiment. Cyril put his piece in his pocket for his own use and went back for another piece to use in the experiment. A warning about the dangers of phosphorus had been given to the boys on a previous occasion. The phosphorus in his pocket caught alight, his trousers were burned and so was he.

The court dismissed the claim for negligence. Cyril had been warned that the phosphorus was dangerous and he had no business to take some for his own use. He had done enough chemistry to be aware of the risks he took.

Clearly, the same kind of incident involving younger pupils who had little experience of chemistry and had not been warned of the possible dangers could have lead to a different result.

6.11 Adult pupils

Perhaps 'pupil' is the wrong word. 'Student' might be more appropriate.

When a person reaches the age of eighteen he becomes an adult, under the Family Law Reform Act, 1969. He may make a contract, vote, get married without anyone's consent and make a will. For some strange reason he is still not allowed to stand as a candidate in a local election or for Parliament. For these delights he has to wait until he is twenty-one.

A parent's legal responsibility for his child ceases when the child reaches the age of eighteen. The offspring may then leave home and make his own decisions. The parent may turn him out and refuse to have anything more to do with him.

Once a sixth former reaches the age of eighteen then a teacher cannot be in *loco parentis*. He certainly may not administer corporal punishment, even if the student consents, neither can the student be detained against his will. There may be a moral and professional obligation to consult parents over disciplinary measures, but certainly not a legal one. If a student of eighteen is asked to leave the school then any representation made to the governors or the authority should, strictly speaking, be made by himself.

A student of eighteen is entitled to receive his own school report and this should not be sent to his parents in the first place.

Although the teacher may not be in *loco parentis* he still owes the student a common duty of care. That is, he must act towards him as a sensible person would do towards another. The duty of care is not so onerous as towards a pupil of, say, thirteen but in dealing with an eighteen year old a teacher and his employer may both be liable if they act negligently and the student suffers harm.

7 Negligence and supervision

7.1 'The frosty playground'

It is a cold winter's morning at Everest Secondary School, the morning break has just begun. The playground is covered with frost and ice. Some boys have made a slide in one corner and are enjoying themselves on it.

The staff duty rota indicates that Mr John Moody is the master on break duty. He is a woodwork master and as the bell goes for break he is giving first aid to a pupil who has nicked his finger with a chisel.

Robert Carefree is enjoying himself on the slide. After an especially vigorous effort he falls heavily on the ice. Another pupil tells Mr Moody, who is just on his way to the playground, and Robert is carried into school. He is then sent to hospital.

The injury turns out to be a very serious one indeed and Robert Carefree is never able to walk normally again. On his behalf his father brings an action against the authority. He claims that the school caretaker should have salted the entire playground and that the teaching staff should have prevented the boys from sliding.

1 ____________________

2 ____________________

____

____

3 ____________________

4 ____________________

Questions

1 Is it reasonable to expect a caretaker to salt an entire playground in icy weather?
2 What is your opinion of Mr Moody's part in this affair?
3 Does your school have a staff duty rota, and does it spell out specific duties to be performed?
4 Should sliding be permitted on school playgrounds?

Write your answers in the box on the previous page, they will be discussed later in the chapter.

7.2 Negligence as a tort

In the previous chapter we discussed the role of the teacher as a parent substitute. As such, he had to take the reasonable care of his pupils that the careful parent would do. If he failed to do so then an action against the authority, or the teacher and the authority together, might be brought in negligence. The case study in the last section raises problems of negligence. The word 'negligence' has been used a number of times in this book already. Just what does it imply?

'Negligence' may be used loosely and in general speech it indicates carelessness of some kind. In law, it is a specific tort (civil wrong) which may lead to a suit for damages, the aim of which is to compensate in financial terms (as far as money can so compensate) for the harm that has been done.

Negligence may spring from a positive act or an omission. A hearty, hockey-playing headmistress once described to me how the river near her school had burst its banks and threatened to engulf the single storey building. 'I gathered the girls together and ordered, "Strip girls and swim for it!" Did I do the right thing?' she asked.

Giles (or Ronald Searle perhaps) would have revelled in the spectacle but it raises a serious point. If the girls had swum for it and one had drowned then, if the risk had been unnecessary, and thus unreasonable, it might have constituted an act of negligence. If the headmistress had done nothing and the river had engulfed the school and someone had been drowned then the lack of action might have been negligent. A court faced with all the details would have to decide.

In almost all cases the plaintiff who brings the action must prove the necessary elements to constitute negligence. They are that a legal duty of care was owed to the plaintiff by the defendant, that the duty of care was broken and that damage resulted.

7.3 Duty of care

Broadly speaking, we can say that we all owe a duty of care to anyone whom we can reasonably foresee may be affected by our actions. Lord Atkin in *Donoghue* v. *Stevenson* (1932) gave the classic definition:

'You must take reasonable care to avoid acts or omissions which you can reasonably foresee would be likely to injure your neighbour. Who, then, in law is my neighbour? The answer seems to be – persons who are so closely and directly affected by my act that I ought reasonably to have them in contemplation as being so affected when I am directing my mind to the acts or omissions which are called in question. . . .'

We owe a duty of care to those we meet in the street, on buses or trains, in shops or offices. Teachers owe a duty of care to one another and to parents. Obviously they owe a duty of care to pupils.

The standard of care is that of that elusive legal character – the reasonably prudent man. It must take into account such factors as are relevant and obvious, such as the infirmity of an old man on crutches and the lack of understanding of a small child. The duty of care is more onerous on an infants' teacher in relation to her charges than it is on a teacher taking a group of sixth formers: it is more onerous on a master taking fifteen year old boys in a workshop equipped with lathes and other machines than it is on a mistress teaching English to fifteen year olds in an ordinary classroom.

As explained earlier, no duty of care is owed to trespassers though hazards must not be set deliberately for them. Where it is known that children are trespassing a duty of care is owed, particularly by large bodies such as British Rail, industrial companies and education authorities, who are expected to try to prevent trespassing by children and have a duty to see that hazards are not created for them.

7.4 Breach

The second element that the plaintiff must prove is that the duty of care has been broken. This might be described as doing something that our friend the reasonably prudent man would not do, or failing to do something that that worthy character would have done. If the act or omission was sensible, considering all the circumstances, then there is no breach. Thus in *Beaumont* v. *Surrey County Council*, mentioned in the last chapter, the court felt that a reasonably sensible man would not leave a piece of thick trampette elastic in a waste bin where pupils could get hold of it. In *Butt* v. *Cambridgeshire & Isle of Ely County Council* it was held that a reasonably sensible person would allow ten year olds to use pointed scissors in order to cut out illustrations. While in *Black* v. *Kent County Council* it was held that it was unreasonable to do so with seven year olds.

7.5 Damage

Where there is a breach of duty of care then damage must result before an action may be brought in negligence. The damage may be to the person in the form of injury or nervous shock or to property such as clothing or possessions.

Thus, if a teacher in a primary school allowed pupils aged eight to use dangerous equipment more suited to fourteen year olds and no child was hurt there would be no action in negligence.

The damage must be an outcome of the breach of the duty of care. Let us consider an imaginary situation. A teacher carelessly pushed open a door into the face of a pupil carrying a box of hockey balls. The door struck the pupil on her hand, breaking the little finger. She stepped back and dropped the box. The hockey balls fell out and rolled along the corridor. One ran down some stairs and in front of the school office. The clerical assistant, hearing the noise, came out, stepped on the hockey ball and fell down, breaking her leg.

In this situation the pupil might reasonably sue the teacher in negligence but the clerical assistant would be unlikely to succeed against anyone. The teacher could hardly have foreseen the consequences of his act and the pupil could escape blame also.

7.6 Reasonable foreseeability

It must therefore be shown that a defendant could reasonably have foreseen the possible consequences of his act or omission.

In one case a motor cyclist carelessly overtook a tram and crashed into a car fifty feet further on. He was unaware that a pregnant fishwife was alighting from the tram at the time. In fact, she did not see the accident but heard the impact and saw a pool of blood on the pavement. Later, she had a miscarriage, allegedly because of the nervous shock. She was unsuccessful in suing the motor cyclist in negligence for damages. The judge might have said: 'If you are a motor cyclist riding down the road and you overtake a tram and crash into a car, can you reasonably be expected to foresee that a pregnant fishwife is alighting from the tram at that moment? No you cannot.'

In another case, a man was out shooting rabbits. He saw a rustling movement in the long grass and let fly with both barrels. An angry couple then rose from the undergrowth peppered with shot and adjusting their clothes. Could the marksman have reasonably foreseen such a possibility? The court said not.

In *Wright* v. *Cheshire County Council*, mentioned in Chapter 6, could a teacher reasonably have foreseen that the pupil supporting at the buck would turn and run for the changing room as soon as the bell went? Hardly.

7.7 *Res ipsa loquitur*

The reader will have gathered that it is not easy to bring an action in negligence and succeed. A duty of care always exists towards pupils but there is no breach if the teacher acted as a reasonably prudent person and, even if there was breach, the plaintiff must prove that some damage occurred.

This is the general rule. The exceptions are known as *res ipsa loquitur* situations (where the facts speak for themselves). Where the circumstances are such that the only answer appears to be the negligence of the defendant, then the court may require him to show that he has not been negligent.

In one school a pupil discovered an electric cable sticking out of the ground at some distance from the main building. A mobile classroom had once stood on this spot but had been removed some months earlier. The pupil touched the end of the wire. It was alive and he received a severe electric shock. The negligence appeared to be obvious. No action was brought but if there had been an action the education authority, or more likely the independent contractors carrying out the electrical work, would have been placed in the position of showing that they had not been negligent. In *res ipsa loquitur* situations the defendant must have had control over the happening, possessed knowledge which was not readily available to the plaintiff, i.e. in the incident mentioned the details of the electrical work carried out and there must be a lack of any other reasonable explanation for what has occurred.

7.8 Defences

Not only in most cases does the plaintiff have to prove the three elements of negligence mentioned but it is open to the defendant to put up various defences. The obvious ones are that no duty of care was owed, there was no breach, no damage occurred or that the damage was not reasonably foreseeable.

Other defences to an action in negligence are:

Consent

Where a person consents freely to run a risk then, providing that the harm which occurs was reasonably foreseeable for such a risk, he will not succeed in an action in negligence. If he enters a hospital for an operation he cannot then claim damages for a trespass to the person because he has been cut open. If he attends a cricket match and the ball is hit from the wicket and strikes him on the head he cannot claim damages. By attending the match he consents to run such a risk.

Since pupils are forced to engage in games and other activities in school, it might be asked whether in fact they have consented to run the risks that are involved. By sending a child to school the parents, on the child's behalf, accept by implication such risks as might reasonably have been foreseen. These would include such incidents as hurting an arm or leg in the gymnasium or on the sports field, minor injuries such as a small cut in a craft room or a minor burn in a domestic science room – but only, of course, where these could not have been avoided by reasonable care on the part of the education authority and its staff.

If, therefore, a pupil brings a note from home saying that he is not to take part in physical education lessons, it is unwise to force him to do so. If an accident should occur then consent might not then apply. There are other ways of dealing with this problem through the school medical officer, or even by exclusion. Readers may remember the teacher who forced a boy with a hole in the heart condition to go on a cross country run and the pupil dropped dead.

Pupils may be assumed to have consented to run the normal risks that exist in the everyday school curriculum. Where extra curricular activities are concerned, it is always wise to obtain written consent from parents since they cannot then say that they were unaware of the possible risks that might have been involved. School journeys themselves will be discussed in detail later in this chapter.

Inevitable accident

The incident is a rare occurrence and could not have been prevented by ordinary care. A boy fielder being killed by a hit on the head from the ball during a cricket match might be a good example.

Act of God

Something beyond humanity to prevent. A freak storm floods the school overnight ruining pupils' property legitimately left in lockers.

Necessity

A small harm was done to prevent a worse one occurring. A science master throws a bucket of water over a pupil whose clothes have caught fire.

Contributory negligence

This is not so much a defence as a mitigating factor. It suggests that the plaintiff contributed to his own suffering by his own lack of care. It often figures prominently in motoring cases. It has been held that a passenger who fails to wear a seat belt may have his damages reduced because of his contributory negligence.

In school situations contributory negligence could well be important where older pupils are concerned. If bright fifteen year olds were told not to touch certain chemicals because they were dangerous or not to use certain defective pieces of apparatus then it could well be contributory negligence if they disobeyed. Contributory negligence is unlikely to succeed though in cases involving very young children who cannot be expected to understand the full implications of their actions.

7.9 'The frosty playground' – comments

This case study was based on *Mays* v. *Essex County Council* (1975) with variations. Having read sections 7.2 to 7.8 the reader is asked to look back at his answers in 7.1 and see if he wishes to change them in any way before reading the comments that follow.

Question 1

It is obvious that schools should take reasonable care for the safety of pupils. A common duty of care is owed to all on the premises under the Occupiers

Liability Act of 1957. There is also a statutory duty under the Health and Safety at Work Act to provide safe conditions for those who work in or visit a school but these provisions have to be viewed in the light of what is reasonably practicable. While it may be reasonable to expect main paths to be salted in icy weather, it would be unreasonable to expect all areas where children might slide to be so treated. That was what the case decided.

Question 2

Mr Moody is aware that he is on duty but he is faced with another problem just as he is about to carry out his patrol. Should he see to the boy whose finger has been cut or should he rush off to carry out his supervision duty? *Carmarthenshire County Council* v. *Lewis* (1955) will help us.

Miss Morgan and the straying child

Miss Morgan taught pupils in a nursery class. One lunch-time she decided to take two of them for a walk. She got them ready and left them in a classroom to wait for her. She, herself, then went to the lavatory. On her way back she met a child who had fallen down and cut himself so she washed and bandaged him. In all, she was away about ten minutes but when she returned to the cloakroom the two four year olds had disappeared. They had gone into the playground and through the school gates. One attempted to cross the road and a lorry-driver, Mr Lewis, swerving to avoid the child crashed into a telegraph pole and was killed.

The court held that the education authority was negligent because it was possible for a four year old child to escape easily through its gates and into a busy road. However, the teacher was not negligent. Faced with two choices she had taken the reasonable course that any parent would have taken. The judge said:

> 'Her duty was that of a careful parent. I cannot think that it could be considered negligent in a mother to leave a child dressed ready to go out with her for a few moments and then, if she found another of her children hurt and in need of immediate attention, she could be blamed for giving it, without thinking that the child who was waiting to go out with her might wander off into the street. It is very easy to be wise after the event and argue that she might have done this or that; but it seems to me that she acted just as one would expect her to do, that is to attend to the injured child first, never thinking that the one waiting for her would go off on his own.'

A person faced with two choices must take the one that commonsense dictates at the time, even if in the long run the choice should prove to have been the wrong one. In the case study, if the cut was only a slight one, Mr Moody should have referred the boy to another person or seen to him later. If the cut was a bad one, then he should have seen to it that it was attended to immediately, preferably by someone with first aid experience. Another member of staff might have been requested to carry out the supervision until Mr Moody was free.

Question 3

The answer should be 'yes'. If it is not, then something needs to be done, and quickly! A section below will give specimen duty lists for both small and large schools.

Question 4

The cases in the previous chapter make it clear that schools are not expected to molly-coddle children unnecessarily. A balance must be struck between the need for safety and the need to allow scope for a child's independence and high spirits. This may involve the playing of rough games, climbing trees and taking other risks. In the Mays case itself the judge remarked that people have been sliding on the ice for centuries, it is an innocent and healthy amusement. There was hardly a game or activity where a child might not hurt himself: 'Life is full of physical dangers which children must learn to recognize and develop the ability to avoid. The playground is one of the places in which to learn.'

Most of us would agree. It is, of course, open to any school to ban an activity such as sliding if it wishes. An alternative solution might be to restrict sliding to one clearly defined area.

7.10 Supervision generally

Whilst pupils are at school – or out of school on visits organized by the school – their teachers must supervise them as a careful parent would. By now readers will have understood that this is a complex statement and each case that reaches the courts differs from others in some respects. When deciding what a careful parent would have done or would not have done there are many factors to be considered. One is the age of the child.

Sandra Barnes and five minutes

Sandra, aged five, was a pupil at an infant school in Hampshire. Normally school was dismissed at 3.30 p.m. and mothers waited at the gates to take their children home. The children had been told that if their mothers were not waiting at the gate they must report back to their teacher. One day Sandra's class was dismissed five minutes early. She went to the gate. Her mother was on the way but had not yet arrived. Sandra walked out of the gate, up a short lane and attempted to cross a busy main road. She was knocked down by a lorry and severely injured. The lorry-driver was in no way to blame. The House of Lords held that the education authority and its teacher had been negligent, *Barnes* v. *Hampshire County Council* (1969).

The test was really whether a reasonable parent would allow her five year old child to make her own way home across a busy main road. Of course she would not. Suppose, however, that a sixth former of seventeen was released early and was run over by a car. Could such a pupil be expected to make her own way home through traffic and busy streets? Of course she could, but where should the line be drawn?

7.11 Early release

The Barnes case illustrates other factors that may need to be considered over early release. Is the school on or near a busy main road? A careful parent would be much more cautious in such a situation. In court it came out that Sandra was a rather unpredictable little girl. The known behaviour of a child could be important.

It is always inadvisable to allow any pupils out of school except at the specified times, though obviously the risk of negligence decreases with older children. Certainly, no primary school child should be allowed to leave the premises during normal school hours without a clear authorization from the parent or in a dire emergency, and the same would be true of pupils in middle schools and the first year or two of secondary schools.

There will be times when children ask to be released during the day – to go to the doctor, dentist, funeral, to return home for books or kit or to take a music exam, sing in the church choir and so on. I remember a persistent and ingenious lad who came up with a request to leave school early about once a week. He once requested early release as he needed to place some violets on his granny's grave and it would be too dark to do so after school had closed. This in mid December!

To release a child early will only become actionable in negligence if damage occurs, of course, but there is always the element of risk about it. Here are some suggestions for dealing with the problems:

Early release from school

1 You need the parent's authorization, preferably in writing. If you have this, then unless you create some hazard that the parent could not have reasonably foreseen the defence of consent may be put forward.
2 Have a system for booking out. In very small schools the head should know of each child who leaves. In larger schools it should be made clear to all which senior staff may give such permission. The school office is a good place in which to keep a record, say in the form of a book which notes the name, form, reason for leaving, time of departure and time of return. The same book can be used to note late-comers. Thus a check can be kept on pupils who leave the premises and return during school hours. It will also provide a useful check when fire drills are held.
3 Keep the written requests for early release for a few weeks at least.
4 Senior staff should check the 'booking-out' record from time to time to spot any habitual 'fiddlers'.
5 If a sweet shop or chip shop is near there is a temptation to pupils to escape during breaks and lunch hours. A head in the Manchester area once described to me how a lollipop factory was situated on the other side of one of his school walls. His problems of supervision were abnormal!

   An effort must be made to prevent such excursions. A school could well be liable if a child were injured and no effort of restraint had been attempted. Staff, whether teachers or ancillaries, should pay special attention to the likely escape routes. In secondary schools guarding exits seems a good duty for prefects or sixth formers.

6 The rules should be indicated in the school prospectus and stated clearly to pupils, say at assemblies, at frequent intervals.

Teachers are not gaolers. No matter how hard they try to see that no one leaves the premises, the odd child will manage to escape. An action against the school will only succeed if it can be shown that reasonable care was not taken. If it is discovered that a child has escaped and does not return within a short time, then an effort should be made to notify the parents (a school record should be kept of both home and work telephone numbers for both father and mother). It may well be a good idea in some cases to notify the school welfare officer and the police. Being picked up by a police car and taken back to school or to the police station can be quite frightening for a young truant.

Where a child in a secondary school takes to disappearing at frequent intervals a useful method is to put him on a report card to be signed at the commencement of each lesson by his teachers, or to have him reporting to a senior member of staff at regular intervals during a school day.

Should a school never release children early, then, without direct parental authority? What of power cuts, snow-storms, fires, a breakdown in the heating system in winter and so on?

When a person is faced with two risks he must, in the light of common sense, take the one less likely to cause harm to those with whom he is concerned.

A head once arrived at his school to find the gates secured with a steel chain and padlocked. A threatening picket line of groundsmen and caretakers from various schools and centres in the area stood across the gateway. They said they would forcibly prevent anyone entering as part of their union protest. Pupils began to arrive on foot and school buses began to choke the approach road to the school. An enthusiastic group of fifth and sixth form boys offered to fight it out with the pickets and storm the gates. The head sent all the pupils home who had arrived on foot and instructed the buses to turn round and take all pupils back to the surrounding areas.

It was a difficult decision. The parents in this case did not know that the children were coming home. Some pupils might not have been able to get into their homes. There might have been risks in the home from fires or other equipment. The head had to balance the risks of children struggling with angry pickets against the risks of sending them home. Luckily in this situation no pupil was hurt in any way, so the matter did not reach the courts. But was his decision the right one?

7.12 Supervision during lessons

The basic reason for which any teacher is employed under his contract is to teach groups of pupils, to supervise them, to act in a professional manner throughout and behave towards his pupils as a conscientious parent would. In the light of this he may be expected to arrive at his lessons on time, to preserve class discipline, to give pupils suitable work, to behave reasonably towards them and take care for their safety and welfare. These general duties need to be qualified in relation to the age of pupils, the nature of the tasks they are engaged in and the equipment they may be using.

7.13 Age

It would not be negligent to leave a group of fifth formers alone in an ordinary classroom for a short time, or perhaps for an entire period engaged in private study in the library. It might well be negligent to leave a nursery class unsupervised even for a few minutes. It would probably be negligent to leave a class of thirteen year olds alone for an entire period but not for a few moments while the teacher went to fetch a book. Where a particular class is known to be troublesome particular care should be taken over their supervision.

7.14 Craft subjects

When pupils are engaged in specialist activities the kind of supervision must be related to the nature of the activity. Where a group is using planes, chisels and saws in a craftroom then not only should the teacher be present at all times but he should see that clear instructions and warnings are given, that general rules of safety are known to the class and that he pays close attention to what each pupil is doing. Teachers sometimes think that there is a legal limit of twenty to the number of pupils that may be taught in such a group. There is no such legal limit. The limit should be fixed according to the size of the room, the equipment available, the age of the pupils and any special local problems. An individual authority may recommend its own limits of course. The final test is what is reasonable in the circumstances and this limit may well be less than twenty.

Attention should also be paid to the problems caused by individual pupils. Should a pupil who is subject to mild bouts of epilepsy be allowed to use dangerous tools in a handicraft room? I would not think so. It might also be advisable, on grounds of safety, to ban a child with excessively long hair from using certain machines.

7.15 Home economics

The same might be said of activities in cookery, needlecraft and child care classes. Clear rules and instructions, safety measures regarding irons, stoves, utensils, cutlery, scissors and needles are necessary. There should again be a reasonable limit in numbers. Hair style could also be a factor and proper clothing certainly would be so.

7.16 Physical education

It is not surprising that the subject leading to most accidents is physical education. Not only may dangerous apparatus be used but the physical effort and bodily contact involved always present dangers. The law recognizes that accidents will happen and that risks must be taken but teachers must be able to show that reasonable care has been taken to prevent such accidents. During PE lessons the teacher must be present throughout. Again, clear instructions must be given and safe routines for the handling of dangerous equipment must be established. Defective equipment must be placed where it cannot be reached by pupils and care must be taken to see that younger children do not get the use of equipment that is only suitable for older pupils. When a class works in groups the teacher should see that the groups are at a safe distance from each other and each group should be visited regularly during the progress of the lesson. The local authority's instructions, if there are any, should be observed since these may be taken as evidence of what is reasonable. If, for example, an authority bars javelin throwing during normal lessons and stipulates that this must only take place at other times in a small group under the direct control of a teacher then such a rule must be strictly followed, even if a particular school or teacher considers the rule to be unreasonable. There have been several deaths on school playing fields from javelin throwing.

PE teachers should not allow pupils to participate if they are not suitably dressed. In one instance a school was found negligent for allowing a pupil to do PE in a gymnasium in stockinged-feet. No pupil should be allowed to take part in physical activities (or in craft work for that matter) wearing potentially dangerous jewellery such as rings, brooches or ear-rings.

Swimming presents a particular hazard. Most authorities have strict rules over this activity, usually stipulating that qualified life-savers must be present. It is not always necessary that this should be the teacher since swimming bath attendants may be especially well qualified in this respect but teaching staff should always be present to take overall responsibility for discipline.

Apart from religious instruction, parents do not have a right to withdraw pupils from any part of the curriculum. This includes physical education, which most would agree is essential for any child. However, it would be quite wrong to force a child to take part if he or she was medically unfit. Where a certificate from a genuine medical practitioner is produced the pupil must be excused. Notes from parents are a different matter. If a parent states that his child is ill, then the child should be excused. If this practice continues or recurs at frequent intervals then the school should demand a medical note from the child's own doctor. If this is not forthcoming, even after a written request and a visit from the Education Welfare Officer, then the school medical officer should be contacted. He has the power to insist on a medical examination.

What if the child does not bring a note but says that he is unfit? It is always dangerous to insist on his participation. It is suggested that the correct solution is an immediate letter to the parent requesting information or, in suspicious cases, a visit from the Education Welfare Officer.

Sometimes the opposite can happen. A child who should not participate demands to do so.

Jane Moore's hand stand

Jane was a pupil at a Portsmouth school. She had a medical history of congenital dislocation of the hips as well as a limp. The PE mistress had been told from two sources that she was not to take part in physical education lessons. Jane, no doubt from the best of motives, persuaded the teacher that she was allowed to take part. She attempted a hand stand, collapsed and broke an ankle.

The court found the mistress, and thus the authority, negligent. Jane was awarded £500 damages, *Moore* v. *Hampshire County Council* (1981).

In every staffroom there should be on display an up-to-date list of pupils who have physical defects which prevent them from taking part, or a full part, in various school activities. Staff should familiarize themselves with those pupils who are affected. PE staff need to pay special attention to such lists and would be well advised to keep their own lists in staff changing rooms.

7.17 Science laboratories

Laboratories are dangerous places. They contain substances, liquids and gases which are dangerous in themselves and some which are dangerous when mixed with other materials. Special care is needed over the supervision of pupils in these rooms and should be given by trained science teachers wherever possible. Unless the school is in a difficult situation over accommodation, science laboratories should never be used for lessons other than those taken by the science staff. Care is needed over the storage of dangerous chemicals. They should be kept in special cabinets and access to them by pupils should be severely restricted. Pupils should be warned clearly of the dangers.

A case that illustrates these dangers is *Hamp* v. *St Joseph's Hospital, Alderley Edge* (1972). Here a girl was grinding chemicals for a teacher. An explosion took place and she was virtually blinded. This was tragic for the girl and disastrous for the school. It was an independent school, run by a convent. The school's insurance cover only ran to about a quarter of the total damages and the rest had to be raised elsewhere.

7.18 The DES and safety

It is not the purpose of this book to deal with complicated and technical problems in various school departments. There are a number of excellent publications by the DES on such matters. Those at present available cover:

Safety in Outdoor Pursuits
Safety in Science Laboratories

Safety in Practical Studies
Safety in Physical Education
Safety in Colleges of Further Education
Safety at School – General Advice

Copies of these publications are available from HMSO.

In November of 1981 the DES produced its first bulletin *Safety in Education*. This will be an occasional series and gives good practical advice to schools on various topics relating to safety.

7.19 Breaks and lunch-hours

While pupils are outside the classroom but still on school premises they are in the care of the teaching staff, who must continue to act as careful parents.

The morning and afternoon breaks and lunch-hours are all part of the normal school day. There must be proper arrangements for supervision. Does this mean that all pupils must be watched all of the time?

Anne Ricketts and the bamboo bow

Anne attended the Roman Catholic Primary School in Erith. She remained at school for lunch and one day, after lunch, together with other pupils she went to play in the school yard. There were teachers present in the school and from time to time one or other of them patrolled the premises, including the yard, to see that all was in order. There was no teacher supervising the yard continuously.

The gates were closed but not locked and it was possible for a child to get out. In fact, children were allowed out if they asked permission and could visit the nearby sweet shop.

On the day in question a ten year old boy left the yard without permission and went to the shop. He came back with a toy bow and arrow, both made of bamboo. By accident he fired the arrow into Anne's face. Her spectacles splintered and a piece of glass entered her eye, causing serious damage.

The alleged negligence was on the ground that the pupils should have been supervised continuously and if this had taken place the accident would not have happened, *Rickets* v. *Erith Borough Council* (1943).

The court ruled that the duty of the teachers was to act as reasonable parents but that did not imply continuous supervision. No parent supervised his children continuously and teachers could not be expected to do so.

Some doubt may have been thrown on this case regarding lunch-time supervision by the recent case of *Blasdale* v. *Coventry District Council* (1981). In this case, during a wet lunch-hour, after primary school pupils had taken their meal they went to their classrooms. The pupil concerned was in one room with thirty or so other children and there were about the same number of pupils in a room next door. Supervision was being carried out by the midday supervisor who moved from one classroom to another. While she was away from one room a pupil fired a paper clip from an elastic band which struck the pupil concerned in the right eye and damage resulted.

The distinguishing factors here are that the pupil was only eight years of age and the children were crowded together in ordinary classrooms. The judge found that the supervision provided was not adequate and he awarded damages.

It remains to be seen what attitude will be taken in future cases, but, whatever is decided, there must be 'adequate' supervision and it is necessary to examine factors that ought to be considered when deciding if a system is adequate or not.

There must be nominated staff available to deal with a problem that arises. This means a duty rota, made clear to those affected by it. There should be an arrangement for a senior member of staff to check the system from time to time to see that the rota is being followed.

The area to be supervised and the routine to be followed by each supervisor must be spelt out. So must the times at which the duty commences and ends.

The system must cover broad general supervision of corridors, cloakrooms, toilets, and areas outside the school building, including the playground. Obviously, this means a kind of roving commission. At a break-time it would be impossible to supervise all parts of the school continuously but there must be staff on the move to prevent potential problems arising and to deal with any that have occurred.

Special attention should be paid to any difficult area – toilets, of course, corners of cloakrooms, narrow spaces behind mobile classrooms, known 'smokers' corners', rear exits from the premises, porches where there is likely to be crowding, the school tuck-shop and areas such as laboratories or craft rooms where there could be special hazards. Staff working in such specialist rooms should, of course, lock their rooms securely before going to staffrooms at break, but it is wise for patrolling staff to ensure that this has been done.

Supervision during the lunch-hour presents a rather different problem. Teachers cannot be forced to supervise the school meal and, other supervision during the lunch-hour being an area of dispute, heads would be wise not to insist on supervision by teaching staff, though many schools have no problems in obtaining voluntary help. Nevertheless, pupils remaining on the premises do have to be supervised and it is right that the ultimate responsibility should be in the hands of the professionals. All teaching staff involved in supervision of pupils during the lunch-hour in any way – duty, clubs, extra lessons etc. – are entitled to a free meal.

It is suggested that the best way of dealing with lunch-time supervision is for volunteer teaching staff to be available on call in the staffroom to deal with emergencies or serious misconduct and to make occasional patrols, with the routine continuous patrolling carried out by ancillaries, who may stand in *loco parentis* in the same way as a teacher does. Lunch-time patrolling should take account of all the factors mentioned for breaks and should pay special attention to playgrounds and possible exits from the school (official and unofficial).

Pupils sometimes leave the school without permission during the break but this is much more likely to happen during a lunch-hour. While a school cannot be expected to produce a foolproof system it must be able to show that reasonable precautions have been taken to prevent unauthorized exit from the premises during the lunch-hour. All or some of the following may help to show that reasonable precautions have been taken.

Exit from school at lunch-time

1 If possible restrict exits to one or two places only.
2 Have a pass-out system. Station prefects on the gates to check the passes of those leaving the premises and re-entering. Anyone trying to leave the premises without a pass is not allowed to leave but has to report to duty staff who have discretion to issue temporary passes for one day so that the issue can be dealt with later by senior staff. Pupils who come back without passes are allowed in but their names are taken and passed on to senior staff for investigation.
3 If some pupils are allowed out regularly at lunch-time as a privilege, e.g. fifth formers, then obtain signed parental consent, otherwise do not grant the privilege.
4 Only allow certain senior staff to give permission to leave the premises. In doubtful cases insist on a written request from parents.
5 State the rules over leaving school clearly in the school prospectus. If there is no prospectus inform parents in writing of the arrangements. Do this annually.
6 At intervals remind pupils at assemblies of the rules over leaving school.
7 Inform parents in writing where their children are causing disciplinary problems by leaving the premises at lunch-time without permission.
8 See that gaps in fences and hedges are repaired as quickly as possible.
9 See that ancillaries or teaching staff on patrol pay special attention to known 'escape routes'.

These arrangements are, of course, only suitable for secondary schools.

The special arrangements to take place during wet lunch-hours should be made clear to all, with designated areas to be used by pupils.

The Blasdale case raises again the question of a school where the supervision is inadequate, usually because of the poor provision of ancillary staff. If the head of a school believes that he is unable to provide adequate supervision with the volunteer teachers at his command and the provision of ancillary staff then he should inform the authority to that effect and also see that the matter is brought before his school governors. He may then continue to operate the system as best he can and, if an accident occurs, it will then be the authority that is negligent and not the teaching staff. An alternative is for the head to inform the authority that he will not operate the system because it is not safe to do so with the inadequate amount of supervisory help that he has been given – though this is an extreme measure to take.

Problems may sometimes be caused by pupils congregating at particular establishments, such as chip shops or cafés, near the school premises and causing disciplinary problems. It would be advisable not to name individual establishments if possible since this could be interpreted as some kind of personal vendetta against the proprietor, but it is well established that a school may make rules that extend beyond its gates in the interests of good behaviour and discipline.

Where a difficulty of this kind arises a letter to parents will help. This should give the rule, explain the reason behind it and stress the nature of the problem – fighting and bullying, criminal damage, likely involvement with the police, dangerous strangers lurking in the vicinity, perhaps even vague hints of drug peddling. One is sure that parents will approve because of their concern for Johnny's safety and, of course, the school would not be responsible for the terrible consequences that might ensue.

7.20 Before and after school

Under their contracts teachers must supervise children during breaks. The authority must provide adequate supervision during lunch-times, with or without the assistance of teachers. What is the position before school sessions commence and after they are over?

This is another difficult area to discuss since teachers' contracts do not usually contain express terms that require a teacher to supervise before or after normal sessions. Since it is obvious that there ought to be some kind of supervision of pupils for a short time before school commences and after it has closed, it might well be that the court would infer that there was an implied term that teachers would carry out a reasonable amount of supervision at these times.

The teachers' associations seem to accept that teachers should carry out such duties, providing they are not too lengthy. The head, who is of course responsible for laying down a safe and adequate system of supervision to cover the entire use of the premises by pupils, should see that responsible and reasonable supervision is provided before school, when children enter the building at the appropriate time and when they leave. A member of staff should go through the building at the end of the day and check that all pupils have left the building, unless they are under the direct supervision of a teacher, e.g. at choir practice, play rehearsal or games activity.

Special care must be taken where pupils board contract vehicles on school premises at the end of the day. There should be arrangements to see that they are properly marshalled in recognized waiting areas. They should be supervised while proceeding in an orderly fashion to their buses and watched while they board the vehicles.

Once pupils are on the bus they become the responsibility of the bus-driver or conductor as the representative of his company. Since the school's authority does not end at its gates, disciplinary measures may be taken against pupils who misbehave on buses on the way to school or on the way home. Since teaching staff do not usually travel on school buses, and certainly cannot be required to do so, the bus company must bear the brunt of responsibility for order and safety – they may always refuse to carry a pupil who is putting others at risk through his misbehaviour. Distracting the attention of the driver could always lead to an accident. The school also may ban a pupil from using the school bus if he presents serious disciplinary problems.

Can teachers be asked to supervise pupils who are boarding buses off the school premises? If the bus draws up just outside the school gates it would seem reasonable to say so but if the supervision is at some distance from the school teachers should not be asked to supervise and would be unwise to agree to do so.

A problem sometimes met by infant schools is one where a child remains on school premises waiting for a parent who comes late to collect him. It would be dangerous, as well as callous, for the teacher to simply abandon the child on the premises. If a parent persists in such behaviour then before a teacher decides not to remain and supervise the child a clear warning should be given to the parent. It is suggested that this should be in writing, delivered by the Education Welfare Officer and explained clearly by him. The risk would then be that of the parent and might well amount to neglect.

7.21 Accidents

All schools have to deal with accidents and it is essential to show that where they occur the school has taken the action that would have been taken by a good parent. Not to do so would be a breach of the common law duty of care and could also be an offence under the Children and Young Persons Act of 1933. This means that a clear statement of the school's policy should be made to staff and parents and a routine established to be followed by all concerned.

What does your school do in the event of:

1 Nose bleed?
2 Suspected fracture on the games field?
3 Epileptic fit?
4 Child coming to school with severe bruising or injury?

Although schools are not required by law to have someone on the staff with first aid training it is always advisable to do so wherever possible. Certainly, there should be one or more teachers nominated to administer first aid and someone very senior to make decisions over the final action to be taken. Usually, this will be the head teacher. In large schools it might be appropriate for someone such as the senior mistress to undertake this responsibility.

The school should have a sick-room where children may be removed from the hustle and bustle of general activity. This may seem a pipe dream to small primary schools but with accommodation problems being eased as a result of falling rolls this is just the kind of improvement that could be brought about in schools of even moderate size. In any case, an effort should be made to find some area where a sick or injured child can have peace and quiet until some further action may be taken.

The school should have records for each child that include home and work telephone numbers, or in some cases details of a close relative such as a grandmother, who could be contacted in case of emergency. These details can be obtained when a child first enters the school and should be updated regularly. There should also be a record of each child's own doctor and details of any unusual health problems relating to particular children.

It is essential to keep a record of accidents that occur and the action taken. The Health and Safety at Work Act requires the filling in of a special (rather complicated) form when a serious accident occurs and this rule now applies to schools. A copy of the report should be filed at school. Accidents at school may reveal defects in the equipment or buildings that are dangerous and when this happens remedial action in the form of a repair or withdrawal of equipment from use should be taken. When such action is not within the head's power then the report should be made to the authority immediately.

The four questions raised above illustrate the different aspects of medical problems in relation to schools. Here are my comments:

1 A nose bleed might be quite trivial but it needs attention anyway. A reference should always be made to the person responsible for first aid and if the bleeding does not stop within a short time then further action should be taken to check that there is no serious injury.
2 Usually the pupil may be mobile and the question of a fracture does not arise until he has been brought inside for treatment or complains later of severe pain. Again, the person responsible for first aid must be informed and a decision must be made as to whether the pupil should be sent to hospital for examination and X-ray or not. If there is any doubt, such a course should always be taken – a responsible parent would certainly do so. When it is decided to send a pupil to hospital an effort should be made to contact a parent. If possible the parent should be allowed to accompany the pupil to hospital or arrangements made for the child to be met at hospital. In any event the parent should be informed either by telephone or a note that the child has been sent to hospital and should be given clear details of what has happened.

   What if the sufferer is writhing with pain on the ground?

   This may well be the situation where a 999 call for an ambulance is required, the pupil being made as comfortable and warm as possible in the meanwhile without moving him.
3 This illustrates the need for schools to be aware of any special medical conditions that may relate to particular pupils and to act accordingly. If a pupil is known to have fits of some kind then the action to be taken should have been discussed with the parents and the child's own doctor. It is preferable to have this in writing from the doctor since a verbal message

from the parent may be very unreliable. If there is any doubt over a particular case the school medical officer should be contacted. I well remember a boy who used to have fits or black-outs about once a week. The medical advice was that these were not dangerous as he invariably came round after a minute or two and then resumed his normal existence. When a fit occurred his collar was loosened, a check was made to see that he had not swallowed his tongue, and he was watched until he recovered. All staff who taught him were briefed accordingly. It was agreed that if he had not recovered after five minutes then the ambulance would be called. The school did not allow him to take part in physical education activities, to have lessons in the workshops, or to handle any dangerous equipment or substances in the laboratories. The risk of hurting himself by any other means was accepted in writing by his parents and approval given by his own doctor and a school medical officer.

Where, in all the circumstances, it is felt that pupils with some disability may be best educated in a normal school, the decision whether to admit them or not rests with the head teacher and governors. The head on his own account and on behalf of his staff should not be afraid to say that he cannot accept responsibility for a pupil who presents abnormal risks.

The administering of drugs can raise problems. It may be reasonable to ask teachers to give drugs to children during school-time. This should only be undertaken on the clear written instructions of the doctor and the drugs should be kept in a safe place in school, preferably under lock and key. Again, if there is any doubt the school medical officer should be contacted.

If a child has what appears to be a fit and there is no known medical history then clearly an ambulance should be called and the child sent to hospital.

4 This raises the problem of a medical condition that has arisen outside the school but is such that it cannot be ignored by a teacher who has real concern for his pupils. A tactful and friendly enquiry may discover that there has been a fall or a scuffle with other children. If the teacher is dissatisfied with this explanation or if the child says that he has been struck by a parent, then the conversation should end there. The teacher's next move should be to give the facts to the head. He will need to make whatever enquiries he can and may involve the Education Welfare Officer, the Social Services Department or possibly the NSPCC or the police.

No person has a right to use unlawful force against another. Parents and teachers may administer corporal punishment but it must be reasonable. A parent who strikes his children in an unreasonable way is committing a criminal offence and the amount of child battering that takes place in our society is alarmingly high. Schools can help in serious cases but intrusion on normal family discipline is a delicate matter.

In order to deal adequately with accidents, a school should have certain basic items of equipment and these are recommended in the booklet on first aid in the

DES safety series. The suggestions are basic and a first aid box containing these requirements should be in every school. In schools with specialist rooms such as workshops, laboratories and gymnasia it is suggested that each room should have its own supply. The contents should be checked regularly.

There is no recommendation as to the keeping of such simple materials as aspirin, antiseptic cream and eye lotion. It would seem reasonable to do so but some authorities ban the keeping of any drugs whatsoever which means that schools in such situations cannot even give an aspirin to a child with a headache. Even aspirins may be dangerous, of course, and there is at least one incident on record where a girl pupil took an overdose by taking aspirins from a school medical cupboard. Where simple drugs are kept on the premises they should always be locked securely away.

7.22 Staff duties

All that has been said so far in this chapter makes it clear that every school, no matter how small, must have a system to ensure that supervision is adequate and in line with the doctrine of reasonable care. As the agent of the authority, it is the head's responsibility to decide on the system, taking into account any regulations that his authority may have issued. A sensible head will have consulted his staff over the arrangements but the responsibility of staff is to carry out duties as laid down by the head, even if they do not agree with his decisions. They can only be challenged on grounds that they are unreasonable. If a teacher carries out duties as laid down by the head and the court considers them to be inadequate then it is the head who is negligent, not the teacher.

In all but very small schools there should be a duty list. This should make clear who is on duty and what that duty entails. It should be specific as to times as far as possible. This should be displayed prominently and staff reminded and checked regularly.

What aspects of school routine should duties cover? Many of these are obvious for most schools but it is important to take into account any special circumstances peculiar to an individual school. Here are two duty lists – one for a small primary school, the other for a large secondary school.

Little Coker Primary School

This is a school in a large village. The main building dates from the 1920s. There are two large classrooms and a hall, which is partitioned. One half is used as a classroom, the other for school meals and for PE if the weather is wet. There is a head's office and a small staffroom. A mobile classroom stands on the side of the playground. On the other side is a low wall which makes a boundary with the churchyard. There is a head teacher and four members of staff. Morning school extends from 9 a.m. to 12.15 p.m. and afternoon school from 1.30 to 3.45. There are morning and afternoon breaks, one from 10.40 to 11 a.m. the other from 2.30 to 2.45 in the afternoon. Staff duties are on a weekly basis and the head takes part.

STAFF DUTIES

Duty Teacher 1

8.15 a.m.	Patrol premises, including playground. Ensure that no pupils enter classrooms (which should be locked) before the bell goes or the main building. If the weather is wet or extremely cold pupils may be allowed into the cloakroom. Check mobile classroom.
9.00 a.m.	Blow whistle in yard. Marshal pupils into school and classrooms for registration. Send pupils to mobile.
10.40 a.m.	See that school is cleared for morning break. Check that playground gates are closed. Patrol premises and playground. Check rear of mobile classroom and playground wall next to churchyard. Patrol until relieved by Duty Teacher 2 at 10.50 a.m.
12.15 p.m.	Disperse own class and see that premises are cleared of pupils who go home to lunch. Check that school gates are closed. Check that all classrooms are locked and empty, unless the class teacher is present. Remain on call during lunch-hour if help required by midday assistant. Make several visits to playground and all other areas.
2.40 p.m.	Relieve Duty Teacher 2 on patrol duty. Patrol playground and premises.
2.45 p.m.	Blow whistle in playground and marshal pupils to classrooms.

Duty Teacher 2

10.50 a.m.	Relieve Duty Teacher 1 of supervision duty. Patrol playground and buildings. Pay special attention to mobile classroom area and churchyard wall.
11.00 a.m.	Blow whistle and marshal pupils to classrooms.
1.30 p.m.	Blow whistle and marshal pupils to classrooms.
2.30 p.m.	See that school is cleared for break, and patrol playground.
3.45 p.m.	Dismiss own class. As soon as playground appears to be clear check that all classrooms are empty unless pupils are under supervision from the teacher.

Wet Days

The head will decide when a break or lunch-hour is to be officially 'wet'. In the case of a wet break pupils will remain in own classrooms with their teacher. They should be allowed to go to the toilets in small groups. The head will patrol the premises. In the case of a wet lunch-hour the partition will be drawn back and pupils will go to Room 4 after their meal or sandwiches. The midday assistant will supervise. Duty Teacher 1 will patrol the premises at intervals and will be on call to deal with any emergencies.

This duty list tries to ensure that supervision is present throughout the school-day. It pays attention to the most difficult times – before and after school and during break and lunch-hours. It also recognizes the particular problems the school has. One is the mobile classroom, the other seems to be the churchyard wall. This is perhaps a recognized escape route for the more adventurous boys!

The J. Alfred Prufrock School

This is a large secondary school which draws pupils from the immediate vicinity and also from a number of surrounding villages. There are two main blocks which were built in the 1950s. The further large block was added in the 1970s when the school went comprehensive. One block contains classrooms, offices and the main hall. A second block contains technology rooms and the new block contains science laboratories, language laboratory and other specialist rooms. There is a sports hall as a separate block and the grounds at the rear of the main school contain several clusters of mobile classrooms. There is one large playground and an extensive playing field. The front of the school is rather restricted and the main entrance is a narrow one. All contract vehicles have to load and unload in this restricted space at the front of the school.

There are 73 members of staff and a number of ancillaries including four midday assistants.

Morning school extends from 8.55 a.m. to 12.40 p.m. and afternoon school from 1.50 to 3.45. There is a morning break from 10.35 to 10.55. There is no afternoon break.

Staff duties are on a weekly basis and the staff operate in house teams.

STAFF DUTIES

A list of staff on duty is posted on the staff noticeboard each week, on the Friday preceding the week of duty. No alteration may be made to this list without prior consultation with the deputy head (Admin).

8.45 a.m. A member of staff to be on duty in the girls' porch crush hall area, to supervise pupils entering hall.

8.45 a.m. A senior member of staff, on a daily rota, is on duty to deal with any emergencies. He/she will patrol the school during assembly/registration period, moving pupils to the appropriate areas.

8.55 a.m. Assemblies. Staff will sit with pupils. Assemblies will begin promptly at 9.00 a.m. Afterwards, staff should accompany their forms to registration. Before assembly, one member of staff should be on duty to maintain order and quiet. This member of staff should be in the hall not later than 8.55 a.m. Afterwards, he/she should see to the dismissal of pupils and the stacking of chairs. During assembly two staff will patrol the school.

10.35 a.m.- 10.50 a.m. Three members of staff will be on patrol outside the building, each in one of the designated areas: the school yard and areas around E. room; the side of the school from the front gate to the end of the workshop block; the areas around the sports hall, the tennis courts and all mobiles.

10.40 a.m.- 10.55 a.m. Three members of staff will be on duty inside the school in one of three areas: upper 'C' block, link block and boys' porch; lower 'C' block and link block porch; 'A' block and girls' porch. Their duty is to clear pupils from school wherever possible and at 10.50 a.m.

to move pupils from porches and other areas so that lessons may begin promptly at 10.55 a.m.
On wet days, when most pupils are sheltering inside the school, staff on outside duty should assist staff on inside patrol.

12.40 a.m. Lunch. The member of staff on sandwich duty checks the rooms and ensures that they are left in good order. Two members of staff (1 & 2) are 'on call' in the staffroom. At least two tours of the school, inside and outside, should be made by these staff during the lunch-period, with toilets checked, and note taken of prefects on duty. The third member of staff 'on call' (3) is also responsible for moving pupils in to school at 1.50 p.m., clearing porches and locker areas. Problems encountered by ancillary supervisors will be referred to the staff 'on call'.
On wet days, lunch-time patrol staff should go to the hall and remain there to supervise pupils only after the senior member of staff on duty has declared it a wet day. The senior member of staff will carry out the patrol duty on such occasions.

A staff dining rota is displayed on the staff notice board, nominating staff on a weekly basis to dine with their year.

3.45 p.m. Bus duty. Six members of staff are on bus duty. Two should control pupils on the main yard or in the school hall, making sure that they move in an orderly manner when their bus is called. Two staff should control pupils waiting in the boys' and girls' porches, or on the grass bank opposite the girls' porch. Two staff supervise the boarding of the buses in the forecourt of the school. Bus duty staff should ensure that no pupil who misses a coach is left without arrangements having been made for him/her to reach home.

Here again there is an attempt to provide supervision throughout the school day and to pay special care to vulnerable points where crowding may occur and problems arise. It is obvious that this school is greatly concerned over its bus arrangements, which present a particular hazard.

7.23 Fire drills

Though fires while the school is in session are comparatively rare events, the risk of fire is a very grave one and must be taken seriously even in the smallest schools. The basic aim should be one of swift orderly escape. Never mind about closing windows and doors or gathering personal possessions. Property can be replaced, lives cannot.

Irish fire drill

The head had been having trouble. The fire bells were defective and it was taking too long to clear the school. Finally, all repairs were complete. The school was harangued. A fire drill was held and this was to be the perfect one, with a speedy clearance of the building.

The bells rang. Dutifully the school filed out to the playground in less than a minute. The head walked through the empty building and, as he did so, a door opened and a class walked out, shepherded by the Irish teacher.

The head exploded. He raved at the pupils and, quite unprofessionally, at the teacher for ruining the escape.

Later the teacher came to apologize: 'I am sorry they were late for the fire drill. When the bell went they all rushed for the door. I told them to sit down. I wouldn't let them go to the fire drill until they were behaving themselves properly. It took some time!'

Here is a check list to be used when drawing up arrangements for fire drills:

1 See that there are enough fire appliances and that they are inspected regularly. Authorities usually have a contract with a specialist firm to do this or checks are carried out by the local Fire Service.
2 See that sufficient extinguishers are available at points of special danger such as science laboratories, workshops, home economics rooms.
3 See that inflammable liquids and substances are stored in the safest places available.
4 See that fire alarms are checked regularly, not just before a fire drill takes place.
5 Arrange for someone to be responsible for dialling 999 if the fire alarm goes.
6 Hold fire drills regularly, at least once a term. Do not always give warning and from time to time hold the practice with an escape route blocked.
7 Time fire drills. If they are slow, find out why and review the arrangements. They should be revised periodically anyway, especially where changes in the buildings have taken place.
8 Have an assembly point well away from the main buildings.
9 Arrange for registers to be taken to the assembly point, say by a school secretary. Form teachers should then check their own classes.
10 Have the general arrangements for escape posted clearly in each room. In each case give details of the route to be taken and the particular exit to be used. Have these notices checked regularly.
11 Do not forget arrangements for ancillaries such as laboratory technicians and school meals staff.
12 Ask the Fire Service to send an officer in from time to time to observe fire drills and offer criticism. Refer any particular problems to him for advice and then submit a report to the authority if there does not seem to be a ready solution – the Fire Officer will also submit a report if he is not satisfied.

7.24 Bomb scares

When a fire is suspected teachers must take the measures to protect pupils that a careful parent would take and the same applies to a situation where it is alleged that a bomb has been placed in a school. The publicity given to bombings in the press and on television has led inevitably to an increase in hoax calls being made to schools. It is a criminal offence to make such a call and imprisonment or a fine may be imposed on an offender.

If a call is made to the police or to the operator, there is a method of tracing its origin very quickly, especially if it is made from a private number. Usually, the police will then visit the school and discuss the problem with the head. If the police instruct him to clear the building then he must do so but often the police will give advice but leave the final decision to the head.

If the call is made to the school the head must make the decision and, if in doubt, should always contact the police. If there are authority regulations then they must be followed. The decision can be a very difficult one, especially when pupils are in the middle of taking public examinations. If the school is cleared then the examining board should be telephoned, given details and asked for instructions.

Where a school is cleared because of a bomb scare the obvious method to use is the fire drill.

7.25 Supervision outside school

When pupils are taken from school on organized visits the problems of supervision become even more acute. Consider the following episode.

Ludlow Castle

Miss Jenkins is a young teacher at the Buffalo School. With the consent of the headmaster, Mr Roberts, she has arranged a day's outing for her class of thirty children aged twelve plus. The intention is to visit the museum at Ludlow Castle. A coach leaves the school at 9 a.m. and is due to return at 6 p.m.

In the afternoon Miss Jenkins allows the children to walk through the Castle in small groups. A few moments later there is a loud scream from a girl, Amy Nicholson, who has fallen from one of the battlements. When Miss Jenkins reaches her, the child is unconscious. Miss Jenkins rings for an ambulance and the child is taken to Ludlow hospital. Miss Jenkins contacts the school. Mr Roberts is out but the secretary, Mrs Wilson, promises to give all the details to the deputy head. Unfortunately, she forgets to do so.

Miss Jenkins is determined that the children shall see the Castle so the tour is completed, though somewhat late. On the way home, at about 6 p.m., the bus breaks down. Miss Jenkins, who is a comparative newcomer to the school and the area, does not know the address or telephone number of anyone to contact and she cannot get an answer from the school.

By 7 p.m. parents are becoming anxious and Mr Roberts has received several telephone calls at home, including one from Mr Nicholson. By contacting the bus company he is able to discover that there has been a breakdown and he rings each parent back to say that all is under control.

A relief bus is sent out and the party arrives back at about 9 o'clock. Miss Jenkins allows some of the children to get off at various places before reaching school. Mr Nicholson, waiting at school, is shocked and angry to find his daughter missing. The next day he writes a strongly worded letter to Mr Roberts, threatening legal action.

Do you find any aspects of the visit disturbing? Write your comments in the box opposite.

Comments

No doubt you were horrified. What was a young inexperienced teacher doing on her own with thirty young children away from school? Why, in such circumstances, was she allowed to visit a castle with dangerous ramparts for young children to play about on and perhaps fall over? Why was there no efficient back-up service at school to help in her emergency? Hadn't she been told the home telephone number of Mr Roberts or a senior member of staff whom she could contact? And wasn't she taking risks in dropping off young pupils from the bus at various points rather than taking them back to school?

The head of a school is responsible for organizing a system of supervision, the staff for carrying it out. If there is negligence here then it is more likely to be the head's than that of Miss Jenkins. What is missing is adequate supervision, preparation, procedures to deal with emergencies and proper arrangements for getting children home.

In spite of all this there will not necessarily be a successful action for damages here. Readers will remember that Mr Nicholson will have to prove a duty of care, breach and damage. Children do have accidents. Mr Nicholson will have to show that the accident happened because of the lack of reasonable supervision by Miss Jenkins and, considering all the circumstances, he has a good chance of success. However, Miss Jenkins certainly seems to have done all she could to deal with the injury after it had occurred. No other parent has an action because no other child has suffered damage.

Now let us examine the problems raised by school visits and journeys generally.

7.26 School journeys

These may vary from taking a class into the local area for an elementary geographical survey to taking a party on a visit to Russia via Germany and

Finland. In all cases, however, there must be adequate preparation, good supervision, parental contact, methods of dealing with emergencies that may arise, arrangements for return and a compliance with any regulations that particular authorities may have. The problem of insurance should also be considered.

Preparation

The school must have some method of deciding which visits shall take place. In a small school the head will be well aware of these but in a large school with various active departments control can be difficult. The head, of course, must authorize all visits in some way. If he deals with them on his own he is quite likely to be unaware of the repercussions they may have on academic work and on other school activities. In such circumstances it is sometimes a good idea to put requests for visits to a cabinet of senior staff who meet regularly anyway and who will be aware of the likely problems each visit may create. It may be necessary to obtain the authority's approval or that of the governors and this is, of course, the head's responsibility.

In schools of some size, it is probably worth having a form to be completed by the organizer and signed by the head. This can provide a check list for preparation by the teacher and also a record for the head. It can also highlight any problems at an early stage.

A sample form that might be used is shown opposite.

The teacher's preparation must be thorough. He must make an accurate estimate of the cost involved and ensure that pupils are charged enough. Refunds are always gratefully accepted – it is always hard to ask pupils to pay extra after a trip has been completed. The method of collecting and recording payments must be clear, well organized and in accordance with the school policy. Preferably, it should be undertaken by a member of staff other than the organizer. Receipts should be given where any considerable amount is involved. The school should make no financial commitment over tickets and other matters unless money has been received or a firm commitment to pay has been made in writing by parents.

Where appropriate, the visit should be confirmed in writing by the school and by the establishment to which the visit is being made. Thus a fifty mile trip to find the museum closed can be avoided.

The transport arrangements must be clear with the bus company, say, confirming in writing that the vehicle is booked to depart and return at certain times.

Before any firm arrangements are made pupils who are interested should be brought together and given a realistic picture of what is planned. If the trip will involve walking long distances, hill climbing or a long time in a bus, these should be made clear. Pupils should be told the total likely cost and given the exact dates on which the visit is to take place.

Once the visit is firm and details have been finalized, arrangements should be

SCHOOL VISIT FORM

PART I

VISIT TO: ____________________

FOR: ____________________

DATES AND TIMES

LEAVING SCHOOL ON __________ AT __________ a.m./p.m.

RETURNING TO SCHOOL ON __________ AT __________ a.m./p.m.

STAFF ____________________

____

PUPILS NO. __________

FORMS __________

TRANSPORT ____________________

COST PER PUPIL __________

CONTRIBUTIONS FOR MINIBUS __________

HEADMASTER'S APPROVAL __________

DATE ____________________

PART II

Tick each item when completed

a) Dates filled in on staffroom calendar ☐

b) Information to parents ☐

c) Canteen informed of number of pupils NOT taking lunch (Minumum notice 1 week) ☐

d) List of pupils/forms concerned placed on staff board (Minimum one week's notice) ☐

e) Mrs X informed - for staff cover (Minimum three days' notice) ☐

f) Year Tutor/Head of School informed ☐

made to see that others in the school have been informed, perhaps by use of a form like the one on page 139, or lists of pupils placed on a notice board.

Parental contact

It is always advisable to have parental consent for pupils to go away from school premises, even during normal sessions. The younger the children the more important it is to do so. The consent should always be in writing. Where pupils doing project work for an examination course or undertaking community service on a regular basis are concerned the parental permission might be obtained for a whole year. Here is a sample letter that might be sent out in such circumstances.

Dear Parents,

As you know, your son/daughter .... is taking a CSE Mode III examination course in social studies. As a part of the course a plan has to be made of the area surrounding the school and some personal investigation has to be carried out into traffic flow, housing provision, occupations of residents and so on. Thus it will be necessary for .... to leave school premises to carry out such work. Normally, this will be carried out in the double period he/she has on Thursday mornings between 10.30 and 12 o'clock but it may occasionally be necessary at other times.

At such times the teacher .... will be in charge and will make arrangements for reasonable supervision. However, you will appreciate that the very nature of the exercise will not allow close personal supervision at all times.

This individual practical work is an essential component of the course and I hope you will give permission for .... to leave school premises to take part in it by signing the slip below and returning it to the school.

Please contact me if you have any queries.

Yours sincerely,

Headmaster

....

In accordance with your letter regarding CSE project work, I give permission for my son/daughter .... to be away from school premises during normal school sessions in the academic year ....

Signed: ....

When day trips are planned, or visits of a longer duration to school camps, holiday centres or destinations abroad are contemplated, a letter to parents giving full details is a minimum requirement. For longer visits it may be useful to call a meeting of parents and pupils to explain the arrangements and answer questions. Here is a check list of items that should be included:

Destination, with full address and telephone number
Dates and times of departure and return
Method of travel and name of coach or travel company
Cost
Suggested pocket money
Arrangements for taking pocket money – cash, travellers' cheques
Staff responsible for money
Staff contact at home
Insurance cover provided
Optional additional insurance suggested
Inoculations necessary
Children with any known health problems
Staff accompanying the party
Any potentially dangerous activities that will be included e.g. skating, climbing or canoeing
Date after which deposit cannot be returned
List of pupils, with home addresses and telephone numbers

Here is how the Buffalo School might have written to parents before the trip to Ludlow took place:

The Buffalo School,
18th September

Dear Parents,

Visit to Ludlow

On Friday, the 5th October, we shall be taking a party of pupils to Ludlow. The purpose of the visit is to make a tour of the town, the ruined castle and the local museum in order that the children may collect material to use in the projects they are preparing on towns and castles in medieval times.

The party will leave school at 9.30 a.m. and will return to school by 6 p.m., the coach being provided by Omnibus Tours. Parents are asked to collect pupils direct from school on return. If any parents are in difficulty over this they are asked to contact Mr Reece who will be in charge of the party, together with Miss Jenkins.

The cost will be £1.80 per pupil and this will include entry to the castle and museum. This amount must be paid to Mr Reece by Monday, 1st October. Pupils who book a place and then do not travel can only be given a refund if a substitute is found.

Strong shoes should be worn and a raincoat brought as the castle and surrounds are open and possibly damp. Pupils should bring a packed lunch and there will be an opportunity to buy soft drinks.

If you wish your child to take part, please sign the tear-off slip below and return to the school by Monday, 1st October, together with £1.80.

Yours sincerely

E. L. Roberts

Headmaster

....

I consent to my son/daughter .... taking part in the school visit to Ludlow on ....
I understand that pupils will be returned direct to the school and I undertake to collect my child from there. I also understand that the charge of £1.80 may not be returnable.

Signed .... Parent/Guardian

The parent should always be asked to sign that he understands the arrangements and any risks that might be expected – in this case losing his money. The signature is also evidence that his son or daughter has actually shown him the letter.

Emergencies

When parties are taken on a visit organized entirely by the school itself, such as a camping trip, then plans must be made to deal with emergencies. A supply of first aid equipment should be taken and it should be decided which member of staff will administer first aid and take decisions if necessary. Naturally, any teacher with the party can give first aid that a parent would if circumstances required it. The address and telephone number of the nearest hospital and doctor should be obtained. A record of the home addresses of all pupils in the party should also be taken.

When parties travel by coach or aeroplane then first aid kits should be to hand and, if staying in a hotel or holiday centre, then reasonable facilities for dealing with emergencies can be expected. Nevertheless, the accompanying staff should always make enquiries over first aid provision, hospital treatment and fire escapes. The last should be explained clearly to pupils by their own teachers.

Where an emergency does occur over a particular child the parents should be informed if possible, either directly or through the school contact at home.

Authority regulations

Some authorities leave it to schools to make arrangements for visits, others require permission to be obtained either from the authority or the school governors. If the authority has issued instructions over school visits then these must be complied with. Not to do so could be evidence of unreasonable conduct. Authorities often lay down some rules or guide lines over standards of supervision.

Supervision

Throughout a visit the teacher is in *loco parentis*, possibly for twenty-four hours of the day. He must provide the reasonable supervision that a careful parent would do.

There is no standard ratio of staff to pupils for external visits. Schools must be guided by common sense in such matters. A ratio of one to twenty-five might well be adequate for groups of fifth formers going from door to door by bus to a careers convention. For a rock climbing expedition one to five might be adequate. Younger children need closer supervision. Dangerous activities need closer supervision and of a specialist nature. The rules of the authority should be followed but, if there are none, then the supervision should be more than adequate in the light of all the circumstances.

Where a mixed party is taken a lady member of staff should be included. If this is impossible then the wife of a member of staff would do or even a lady parent. If someone who is not a member of the teaching staff is travelling with the party and helping to supervise then the authority's consent should be obtained.

Insurance

Teachers and parents often assume that if a pupil suffers an accident while on a school visit then he is covered by the education authority's insurance. This is not so. Normally, the authority will have insured its teachers and itself against liability to third parties. A pupil may only recover damages if he can show that the harm was caused by the authority's negligence, i.e. through that of the teaching staff.

Parents should always be informed of the position regarding insurance if some dangerous activity such as climbing is involved. They should be invited to take out personal accidence insurance for their children if they wish to do so. It may be advisable to take out personal accident cover for the entire party and add this to the total cost.

Dangerous activities

From what has already been said, it is clear that extra care should be taken when visits involve dangerous activities. Particular risks should be made clear to parents, the authority's regulations should be followed to the letter and the utmost care should be taken over supervision. Unfortunately, each winter one reads of disasters, or near disasters, befalling groups of young people in such areas as the Cairngorms, Lake District or Dartmoor. Expeditions in such areas need a rigorous insistence on the right equipment which is in good condition. Sound tents and sleeping bags, special footwear, warm clothing, first aid kit and plentiful rations are all necessary. The leader should be properly trained and experienced and, where appropriate, should hold a mountain leadership certificate. Youngsters should never take part in a really tough exercise unless they have taken part in other introductory training exercises. Before setting out, weather forecasts should be obtained and messages left at base as to the route to be taken and the estimated time of arrival at the destination.

Where the exercise involves small groups of older pupils without an adult leader, clear instructions must be given as to the course of action to be taken in an emergency.

The chief dangers seem to occur in hill walking or climbing but pot-holing and canoeing may also come into the same category and the special dangers of each should be provided for. In canoeing, for example, no pupil should participate who is not a proficient swimmer and he should always wear a life-jacket of an approved design.

Insurance cover should be checked carefully for expeditions involving dangerous activities. Many companies issuing policies to cover personal accidents exclude certain activities – usually climbing, canoeing, pot-holing and sometimes horse-riding and cycling. These may usually be covered by the payment of an additional premium.

Readers should consult the appropriate DES safety booklet.

Statements of indemnity

Sometimes schools ask parents, when agreeing to pupils taking part in a journey, to sign a statement accepting that the school cannot be held responsible for any accident that may occur. Such statements have only a limited value in law.

Since the Unfair Contracts (Terms) Act of 1977 it is illegal in an agreement to exclude liability for negligence in relation to death or personal injuries or for any other factor that the court may consider unreasonable. Teachers, pupils and parents are not in a contractual situation but indemnities seeking to exclude such liability would almost certainly be void.

The limited value of an indemnity from a parent is that it establishes that the parent was aware of the likely risks to be run and therefore the defence of consent might be successful to an action for negligence.

The form of the indemnity suggested by some professional associations and other bodies is apt to be longwinded and full of legal terms. This may well deter parents from allowing pupils to participate. In some circumstances it may be necessary for the school's protection to issue such a form but it is suggested that something simpler will achieve virtually the same result and would certainly be more acceptable to parents.

If you were taking a party to North Wales and the stay included hill walking then the parent might be asked to sign a slip something like this:

TRIP TO SNOWDONIA

I consent to .... taking part in this trip. I understand that the stay will involve some hill walking and will include the climbing of Snowdon itself. I consent to the risks involved.

Signed .... Parent/Guardian

If the pupil slips on a mountain path and is injured or twists his ankle badly in walking up rough scree then the parent will be unlikely to succeed in an action. These are always risks in hill climbing but if the teacher takes the group to the top of the mountain and then orders a sprint race down a steep slope which ends in physical damage to the pupil then the parent will be likely to succeed in an action because that is a risk that he could not have been expected to have foreseen. A victim may consent to hazards, but he does not consent to those dealing with the hazardous situation doing so in a negligent fashion.

Visits abroad

The number of schools participating in such visits has increased considerably over the years and so has the number of travel companies providing services. Most of these firms are reliable enough but if they seem to offer bargain rates then the terms and facilities should be looked at critically. One useful check is to find a local school that has used the same firm and put some frank questions to the staff who were involved.

All that has been said of other visits applies to parties going abroad. The need for close parental contact and methods of dealing with emergency situations are even more important. Large sums of money will be involved so proper procedures for receipts and payments must be organized and teachers need to remember that they will be in *loco parentis* throughout the entire visit. Allowing pupils to roam at will in Montmartre while the staff live it up in a night-club is just not on.

Most parties going abroad make arrangements through a travel firm which also offers insurance facilities. These will usually include cover for cancellation, delay, medical expenses, injury or death and theft or loss of luggage or money. Many policies do offer good value. However, each needs to be examined closely because some offer only minimal cover and others have a number of exclusions. It may be more convenient to take out insurance through the travel firm but this is not essential. The insurance company handling the education authority's business will usually offer an excellent alternative which is possibly cheaper.

Schools may be tempted to make their own arrangements and will usually have to do so when school exchanges take place. Such arrangements should only be handled by a leader of considerable experience who is well aware of the problems involved and who has visited the destinations himself beforehand. It helps considerably if one member of the party at least is fluent in the language of the country to be visited. Also, someone in the party will need to understand how banking arrangements work in the particular country and will need to make arrangements over bank drafts or travellers' cheques.

Passports

There are some particular matters to be considered. Passports, for example, may raise problems. There are two kinds – the full British Passport and the British Visitors' Passport. Each adult or pupil member of the party may travel with either of these passports. It should be noted that while a full passport is valid for ten years for an adult it is only valid for five years for a person under sixteen. The Visitors' Passport is only valid for twelve months and is not valid for all countries. The most convenient method for a school party to use is a Collective Passport, which helps considerably in avoiding the loss of individual documents.

An application for a collective passport must be made by the head of the school or the education authority. The named leader and deputy leader of the party must hold full British Passports. The Collective Passport may only cover pupils under the age of eighteen on the day of departure and there is a minimum of five and a maximum of fifty. The test for inclusion is that of nationality. Only pupils who would be entitled to a full British Passport may be included on a Collective Passport. Pupils who do not qualify may, of course, travel under their own individual passports. Any problems over passports need to be checked at an early stage and those relating to non-British pupils should be referred to the appropriate Embassy, Consulate or High Commission.

When an application is made for a collective passport then a card must be completed for each pupil. The card must carry a photograph of the pupil and each card must be signed by the headteacher. The card will then be carried as an individual's identity card.

Parties travelling on a Collective Passport must travel together and remain together. The countries to be visited must be named and it is wise, therefore, to include any country that may be visited, even for a day. Should an individual be separated from the party, perhaps because of injury or illness, then the nearest British Consul must be informed so that individual travel documents may be obtained.

The regulations regarding collective passports for each country must be checked. For example, in Austria each pupil must carry his own identity card. In France, while Collective Passports are acceptable for school parties, they are not accepted where a group travels together for a school exchange and then separates to stay with individual French families.

Applications and queries regarding passports should be addressed to the appropriate passport office.

Addresses

London Clive House, Petty France, London, SW1H 9HD

Liverpool	5th Floor, India Buildings, Water St, Liverpool, L2 0QZ
Newport	Olympia House, Upper Dock St, Newport (Gwent), NPT 1XA
Peterborough	55 Westfield Road, Peterborough, PE3 6TG
Glasgow	First Floor, Empire House, 131 West Nile St, Glasgow, G1 2RY

Health abroad

For most European countries there is no need for inoculations to be given, except for smallpox, but if trips are planned further afield then medical advice should be sought from the District Health Officer. If there is any doubt as to whether a certain inoculation has been given, or indeed if there is any health query, then parents should be required to produce a certificate from the child's own doctor of fitness to travel. Schools should not hesitate to refuse to take pupils abroad where they are not fully satisfied on such matters.

This country has reciprocal agreements with some other European countries for the payment of expenses for medical treatment under the National Health Service. To benefit from this an application should be made well in advance by individual parents to the local office of the Department of Health and Social Security on the special form provided. Self-employed parents are not eligible. The difficulty is that matters covered vary from one country to another and the bureaucratic process involved is often formidable. Usually, the fees have to be paid and then reclaimed later.

Many hospitals and doctors abroad require payment before treatment is given and parties would do well to have enough ready cash available to cope with such emergencies. A reputable travel firm will, of course, assist in such situations.

Travel firms and the law

An agreement between the school and the travel firm forms a binding contract and is subject to the law relating to contract. Since in most cases a school is not a legal entity the contract is likely to be between the travel firm and the teacher making the booking. Either party may sue or be sued. In one case a man took a winter sports holiday. In his second week he was the only holiday-maker in residence and because of language barriers he was unable to hold a conversation with any of the staff. The holiday atmosphere was lacking! He won his case for damages. If a holiday does not reasonably come up to expectations then that can be breach of contract. Similarly, if a travel firm was faced with a bill for damages caused by pupils and the staff concerned had not made reasonable efforts to control them, an action might be brought for a breach of an implied term of the contract.

The Trade Descriptions Act makes it a criminal offence to describe goods or services falsely whether the description is in writing or speech or by illustration.

As far as services are concerned, a firm commits an offence if it knows that the description of the service it is providing is wrong or if it is reckless as to whether the description is true or not. Thus, if a travel firm stated that the hotel was five kilometres from the centre of Paris and in fact it was twenty kilometres from the city centre then that would be an offence. It would not be an offence on the part of the travel firm, however, if the hotel had overbooked and the travel firm itself was not aware of this.

7.27 Work experience

The Education (Work Experience) Act 1973, allows pupils in their last year of compulsory schooling to be involved in work experience schemes under regulations made by the local authority. Work experience may be organized on an area basis, usually through the Careers Service, but it may also be organized by individual schools.

The aim is to allow pupils to gain real experience of working conditions by becoming involved in the actual day-to-day routine, rather than taking a casual look on fleeting visits. The pupil may be involved on one day a week over a period of time or may be engaged in work experience for a week or fortnight at a stretch.

The procedure laid down by the authority must always be followed. This will certainly include the obtaining of parental permission and a letter from the authority to the employer authorizing the arrangement. Usually, the authority will tell the employer that an indemnity is given for damage through negligence caused by pupils on work experience but that the firm itself must be liable for negligence caused by its own staff or defects in its own equipment or premises.

Work experience is not allowed on ships, neither may any young person be engaged in it if he would be banned from doing so by any other statutory provision or by-law, for example those dealing with the employment of children.

7.28 The school's own transport

Today, many schools provide their own form of transport. Some possess a large coach. This may be very useful but it can bring serious problems. Such vehicles tend to be old and their maintenance can be expensive. A school cannot afford to run vehicles which present safety risks. Also, if the coach carries more than sixteen passengers, and the school wishes to make charges for the use of the bus, then it becomes a public service vehicle and this causes complications over drivers, equipment, escape routes and so on.

Most large schools have now acquired that other transport of delight the school minibus. Before the Minibus Act of 1977 there were difficulties over charging pupils for riding in school minibuses and all sorts of questionable schemes were devised to get round the law. After all, petrol and repairs had to be paid for somehow.

The 1977 Act, now replaced by the Public Passenger Vehicle Act, 1981, which applies to minibuses seating eight to sixteen passengers, allows educational, religious and social welfare organizations to charge passengers for riding, without being bound by the regulations relating to public service vehicles.

Schools wishing to charge pupils for riding in their minibuses may now do so under certain conditions.

The act allows the Traffic Commissioners to set up a system of permits. LEAs are authorized to issue such permits to schools so the first step is to apply to the authority for a permit and a copy of its own regulations. The permit identifies the organization, the vehicle and the classes of passenger that may be carried, together with any other conditions. A disc is issued with the permit and this must be displayed on the windscreen, together with the driver's instructions. Since a permit is issued to an individual organization and relates to a particular vehicle then if two schools share a minibus there must be two permits and if a school has two minibuses there must be a permit for each one.

The permit holder is required to see that the vehicle is in safe condition, that routine maintenance is carried out regularly, that defects are dealt with promptly, that the vehicle is properly taxed and insured and MOT tests are carried out as required.

The driver of a minibus under these regulations must have a full licence, be over twenty-one and have some experience. When the LEA becomes the owner of the vehicle it will usually insist on a potential driver completing a declaration form which will be passed to the insurance company for approval. When the school PTA or governors own the vehicle, then approval should be obtained direct from the insurance company before a teacher is allowed to drive. All staff should practise driving minibuses before they are allowed to take pupils on visits in them.

The owner of the minibus may make other restrictions over use. He may restrict drivers to those who have been driving for a certain minimum period. He may lay down rules as to the passengers to be carried. In schools this will usually include staff, pupils, members of a parents' association and other nominated persons.

Other rules have been laid down by means of statutory instruments, the Minibus (conditions of fitness, equipment and use) Regulations, 1977 and the Minibus (conditions of fitness, equipment and use) (Amendment) Regulations, 1980 and these conditions must be observed. All new minibuses must comply, existing ones have until the end of January 1983 to do so. The regulations relate to signs indicating the maximum number of passengers to be carried, fire extinguishers, first aid kit, exits and entrances, the position of the petrol filler cap, carriage of dangerous substances, the use of a trailer and other matters.

Where a minibus has seats for fourteen or more passengers, EEC regulations also apply. For journeys abroad the regulations apply when there are seats for more than eight passengers.

Where a school does not charge pupils for riding in a minibus then, of course, none of the regulations apply since it is treated as a privately owned vehicle. A failure to keep such a vehicle in good condition could always, however, lead to an action of negligence if an accident occurred.

Schools which have minibuses are often asked by other groups such as Scouts, Guides and charitable organizations if the minibuses may be borrowed. When a vehicle is the property of the authority the decision must be referred to it. If the vehicle is owned by the governors or, say, some representative of the PTA as permit holder, then the decision should be referred to the appropriate person. If the school is willing to lend the vehicle it is suggested that the body concerned be left to make its own arrangement with the insurance company.

7.29 Staff cars

Teachers cannot be compelled to use their private cars for activities connected with the school, whether these are for travelling between split sites, to convey sick children home or to hospital, or to carry pupils to a match or to the theatre. Many do so and while there is usually no problem the position is not always as straightforward as it may seem.

Most insurance policies restrict the use of a private vehicle to social and recreational purposes and use by the policy holder in person for business or professional purposes. The receipt of payment for what is known as 'hire or reward' could render the policy invalid.

Most major insurance companies will agree that the receipt of a mileage allowance by such employees as teachers will not count as hire or reward but practice varies. There is little doubt that receiving a payment from pupils or parents could constitute hire or reward. Teachers should contact their own insurance company and explain frankly what they intend to do and obtain the company's agreement.

To accept a 'fare' could also contravene the Road Traffic Act and payment to a school fund for the purpose could also be in breach of the Act. If there is no suggestion of a compulsion to contribute, if no more than four passengers are carried and if the journeys take place only occasionally then the teacher may well be on safe ground.

Providing the teacher's insurance company has agreed, there is no reason why teachers should not carry pupils in their private vehicles but to be absolutely safe it is best not to charge pupils in any way for doing so.

It should be remembered that if an accident occurs while the teacher is carrying pupils the loss of no claims bonus would come from the teacher's own policy, though some authorities do make *ex gratia* payments in such situations.

Most teachers park private cars on school property. An employer is not responsible for the personal property of his employees brought to the place of work. So the general principle is that an authority is not liable for damage to school cars by pupils. A civil action for damages would lie against a pupil, of course, but as parents cannot be forced to pay there would be little point in bringing one. If a criminal action were brought, then in some circumstances it is possible for parents to be made to pay compensation.

Membership of some teacher associations carries the right to limited compensation for malicious damage to members' cars by pupils on school premises.

8 The school's authority

8.1 The letter and the law

I keep a small collection of letters that have taken my fancy over the years. This one, reproduced with its original lack of address and punctuation, has brightened many a gloomy wet November day in school. It came some years ago written on a scruffy piece of paper torn from Paul's maths book:

Mr Adams
Paul has been sick and please would you give him his lighter and fags back I know Paul smokes what happens after school is nothing to do with school hours

Mrs F

Mrs F's short note raises a number of legal problems in relation to school discipline and authority. The school had made rules banning the bringing of lighters and cigarettes to school. Paul had not been smoking on the premises – he had been doing so outside the school gates and was reported. He had been warned that if he smoked again on the way to or from school he would be punished. His lighter and cigarettes had been confiscated.

What kind of rules may be made by the school? To what extent are they enforceable?

Much of this chapter will be spent in dealing with the implications of these two questions and matters arising from them. Paul's rights to his property will also be examined.

8.2 School rules

Any community or organization needs rules for order, safety and the convenience of all. Such rules do not necessarily have to be set out in black and white, they may be of a customary nature where everyone follows them because there is the long tradition of doing so. Some rules do have to be set out clearly so that newcomers may adjust quickly to routines and standards of behaviour and it is necessary to state some rules precisely and publicly so that offenders are unable to deny knowledge of them.

Schools and teachers seem obsessed by rules. If a school staff is asked to come up with a set of rules the result will usually be a long list of 'thou shalt nots' which presents an interesting challenge to the more adventurous and rebellious spirits.

If the old platitude that true discipline comes from within is correct then it would seem that rules should be positive rather than negative: 'Pupils are expected to be courteous and act with common sense and responsibility at all times.' Such rules are difficult to observe but rarely lead to confrontation. It is rules of the negative kind that lead to trouble and though, of course, it will be necessary to have some of them, if they can be kept to a minimum then some unnecessary battles may be avoided. Schools usually win such battles but the attendant arguments, bad feeling and rough handling by the media do considerable harm to the image and morale of the school in the process.

8.3 Legal force

Parliament has decreed that a parent has a duty to educate his child, either by regular attendance at school or otherwise. The responsibility for providing sufficient schools that give efficient education is delegated by Parliament to local authorities. Local authorities in their turn delegate the responsibility for individual schools to the governors and the headteachers. The Articles of Government set out by an LEA for a school will give the head responsibility for the internal organization, management and discipline of the school. It is difficult to see how this could be achieved without the making of rules of some kind both for staff and pupils.

There is a good case, therefore, for saying that the head may make school rules and that these have the force of law, that is providing they are reasonable. If they are unreasonable then that would be *ultra vires*, beyond the powers that Parliament and the local authority intended the head to exercise. It is not even essential for all rules to be communicated to parents, though some information must be given to them under the 1980 Act. It is always wise to make rules clear to parents, however, since if the parent is aware of them and sends his child to the school then by implication he accepts them.

One or two cases have dealt with problems relating to school rules but it was in Warrington in 1954 that a case occurred which was to become a leading authority on the subject.

8.4 Eva Spiers and the trousers

Eva, who was thirteen, attended a girls' secondary modern school in Warrington. After she had suffered several attacks of rheumatic fever, in 1952 her mother began to send her to school in slacks in order to keep her warm. The headmistress was not prepared to allow this as a practice for girls in the school but she agreed to do so in Eva's case if the parent would produce a medical certificate or would allow her to be examined by the School Medical Officer. The parents would not agree.

Each time that Eva came to school wearing trousers the headmistress refused to admit her and she was sent home. The Magistrates' Court fined Mr Spiers for not sending his child to school but the court of Quarter Sessions (now replaced by the Crown Court) reversed the decision. An appeal was made to the QBD on case stated (that is on a point of law). The court again reversed the decision in favour of Warrington Corporation.

In giving judgement, Lord Goddard said: 'Obviously a headteacher must be responsible for the discipline of the school and, indeed, in this particular case the articles provide that the headmistress "shall control the internal organization, management and discipline of the school . . . shall exercise supervision over the teaching and non-teaching staff, and shall have the power of suspending pupils from attendance for any cause which she considers adequate, but on suspending any pupil she shall forthwith report the case to the governors, who shall consult the local education authority." I quote the last part about the time of suspension simply because Quarter Sessions seem to have thought that the headmistress in this case was suspending the girl and ought to have reported it to the governors, who should then consult the local education authority. In point of fact, I think that that is a false point. The headmistress did not suspend this child at all. She was always perfectly willing to take her in; all that she wanted was that she should be properly dressed. Suspending is refusing to admit to the school; in this case the headmistress was perfectly willing to admit the girl but was insisting that she be properly dressed.'

Later the judge went on: 'The headmistress obviously has the right and the power to prescribe the discipline for the school, and in saying that a girl must come to school not wearing a particular costume unless there is a compelling reason of health, surely she is only acting in a matter of discipline, and a matter which must be within the competence of the headmaster or headmistress of any school, whether it is one of the great public schools or a county secondary or a county primary school. There must be somebody to keep discipline, and of course that person is the headmistress.'

This case establishes quite clearly that the head of a school is in the position of having the power to make reasonable rules that are necessary for school discipline and that banning the wearing of certain articles of clothing constitutes a reasonable exercise of that power. This does not mean that uniform can be insisted on but the head has a discretion to ban items that he considers to be unsuitable.

The case also deals with exclusion and suspension which will be discussed later in this chapter.

8.5 The power of the head

The Spiers case makes it clear that the ultimate responsibility for making rules lies with the headteacher. This is his right and his duty under his contract. Since his contract requires him to obey the regulations of the authority, to make a school rule that is in breach of such regulations would be a breach of contract. Authority regulations are far from comprehensive and are often so vague that they will give the head little help in formulating rules. Unless the rules made by the head are in direct breach of the authority's regulations, or they are unreasonable, they will have legal force.

8.6 Drawing up the rules

It is possible, of course, for the head to sit down in his office and draw up a set of rules. He would be foolish to do so unless he had at least first consulted his staff. They have to implement the rules and may well see snags, difficulties and eventualities that the head may have missed.

In the majority of schools it is suggested that a good method of drawing up a code of rules is for a small working party of staff to draw up a suggested scheme which is brought back to the entire staff for discussion. It is a good idea to involve pupils at some stage – though the extreme sanctions they will wish to impose on offenders will need to be avoided. Where the head has their trust and confidence, it may well be useful to ask the views of a body like the PTA committee. The governors should be asked for their views and the list of rules should be presented to them, the head making special reference to any problem areas where he would expect difficulty. He will need the backing of his governors if confrontation comes.

The final responsibility for rules lies with the head. He would do well to see that the rules that are produced are simple, direct and positive, as far as this is possible.

Here is a set of rules used in one school:

Instructions for pupils
At all times, both in school and on the way to and from school you are expected to behave well.

A Uniform
You are expected to wear the correct school uniform.

B Use of school and grounds
- (i) You may enter and leave school only by the gate opposite the girls' porch.
- (ii) You may bring cycles, motorcycles and cars to school when you have obtained permission from Mr .... Cycling in the school grounds is forbidden.
- (iii) Out of bounds:
  - (a) The youth centre, except for 5th/6th years at lunch-time.
  - (b) The front of school.
  - (c) The village library, except for pupils entering on rota via the school library.
  - (d) Area around and behind all mobiles, ES room, greenhouse and sheds.
  - (e) The playing fields and all grassbanks and verges at appropriate times.
  - (f) The areas where staff cars are parked.
  - (g) The school grounds and buildings after 4.15 p.m. (unless a member of staff is in charge).

(h) The churchyard at lunch-time.

(iv) Years 1–4 are not allowed inside the building at break or lunch-time unless they have a pass or are going to the school library on the rota. On wet days, pupils are allowed inside the school.

(v) Locker areas may be used only before morning school, at break and lunch-hour and between 3.45 p.m. and 4.00 p.m.

C Arrival and departure

(i) Morning school starts at 8.55 a.m., afternoon school at 1.50 p.m. You must be punctual.

(ii) Once you have arrived on the premises, you may not leave school without permission from year tutors, heads of school, deputies or head, although 5th year pupils may go into the village at lunch-time if they have passes.

(iii) If you have been given permission to leave school at times other than lunch-time, you must sign out in the school office and sign in on return. If you arrive at school after the registration period, you must sign in at the school office.

D Behaviour

(i) You must not interfere with electrical fire appliances, apparatus in workshops and laboratories, or blinds.

(ii) You must not bring to school knives, matches, lighters, cigarettes, radios, cassette recorders and cards. For reasons of security and safety, jewellery should not be worn.

(iii) You must not eat sweets, etc. during lesson times; you must not eat packed lunches anywhere else other than in sandwich rooms.

These rules set out to give some positive directions and do not consist entirely of a list of prohibitions. There is an attempt to cover important areas such as safety, the parts of the school that may be used by pupils (this will aid efficient supervision), routines for arriving at school and leaving the premises, behaviour problems and particular difficulties that the individual school has.

The use of one exit will aid supervision and probably prevent masses of pupils spilling out on to a busy road. Control has been kept over the dangers presented by cars, motor-cycles and cycles. A clear warning exists over meddling with dangerous equipment and bringing potentially dangerous items, such as knives and jewellery, to school.

Areas where pupils may not go are clearly identified and the trouble spots are revealed. It is clear that the smokers' lairs are behind mobile classrooms and sheds and probably the local churchyard (a recent complaint from the vicar?). The school has obvious difficulties with a public library which is accommodated next to the school building. The Rule B (iii) shows the hand of the staff in drawing up the list!

Times of arrival are stated clearly. Routines for leaving school during sessions and the action to be taken by late-comers is made clear.

The rules do not give the uniform list though that must be presented somewhere. It may be in the form of a separate sheet though the best place will be in the school prospectus that amplifies all rules and which will be given to all parents when the pupil joins the school.

The list shows certain other problems that this particular school has. The locker areas provide good hiding places and perhaps invite theft. As with most schools, there are problems over smoking but this school has an affluent clientele that will bring transistors and cassette recorders to school, thereby encouraging theft and making the establishment even noisier than usual. There seems to be a particular problem of chewing in class (there must be a good tuck-shop!).

School rules have to be read and understood by pupils. The merits of this list are simplicity and directness. An attempt to go beyond the simple list will inevitably mean more and more items in an unsuccessful attempt to cover everything. The way to expand on rules is through the school prospectus issued to parents and more detailed explanation to pupils at assemblies or in the classrooms.

The list above is short enough to be placed on a class notice-board for all to read. The court would be unimpressed by a long list of complicated rules that were not readily available to pupils and could not easily be understood by them.

8.7 Discipline

The head has the duty to see that reasonable rules are made. He also has the responsibility for discipline and that means the control of sanctions that are to be used against those who break the rules. Here, again, his actions and those of the staff must be reasonable – reasonable in the sense of the kind of action that a conscientious and sensible parent might take. How to relate what such a parent would do in relation to thirty or a thousand children is difficult. Let us examine the various sanctions currently in use in schools.

8.8 Corporal punishment

This can often be an emotive issue and some teachers and organizations, such as STOPP, are completely opposed to its use in school at all. The majority of teachers and the majority of parents still seem to believe that it should be available if required.

Until the use of corporal punishment is banned by an Act of Parliament or in particular areas by an LEA the school may continue to use it, though the head would certainly be within his rights to restrict its use to certain trusted senior members of staff.

Decisions of the European Court of Human Rights could well change this situation in the near future. The Scottish 'tawse' case has meant that a parent has the right to request that his child is not beaten but the court has not yet declared that corporal punishment in schools is actually a breach of the

Convention. It could be argued that if parents are told clearly that corporal punishment is used in a school and they make no request concerning their own child, then the school is entitled to inflict such punishment.

No person has the right to use unlawful force against another. That is a basic rule of English law. Such application of force is usually known as assault and battery, though the terms are often used incorrectly. An assault is a movement which puts a person into fear of being physically harmed. A battery is the application of the unlawful force. The two often go together but a fist raised to a child could be an assault alone, the hit on the head from behind would be a battery alone if the victim was unaware of what was coming. If the physical harm done was considerable, such as a fracture or very severe bruising, then this could amount to grievous bodily harm and if the skin was broken and blood drawn this could be a wounding.

Assault and battery are criminal offences but they are also forms of trespass to the person in the law of tort. Thus, if a teacher strikes a pupil and the matter is reported to the police an attempt is being made to bring a criminal charge. If the police refuse to prosecute then a private prosecution may be brought. An alternative, however, would be to bring a civil action for assault and battery in the county court where the remedy would be one of damages.

A parent who strikes his child is open to prosecution in a criminal court or an action for damages in a civil court by the child, unlikely though that might be. Both the parent and the teacher, however, have the defence of discipline or as it is sometimes described 'lawful chastisement of a child'. The defence will only hold if the punishment was reasonable in the opinion of the court.

Most secondary schools still have the power to administer corporal punishment, though a number of authorities have removed this right from primary and special schools. Nationally, the only rule relating to corporal punishment is that of the DES which requires every school to keep a punishment book and enter details of corporal punishment given. This book is open to inspection by the governors and by inspectors. Local authorities may make their own rules such as a restriction on who may administer corporal punishment (usually the head or his deputies) or specify the instrument that must be used (usually the cane). Where the matter is left to the head, as it often is, then he needs to make reasonable rules. It would be quite wrong not to make a clear statement and allow any member of staff to administer corporal punishment at will.

Where the head has to lay down rules then it would be wise to take staff opinions, but something like this might be a sensible arrangement:

1 Corporal punishment only to be administered by Mr A, Mr B and Mrs C.
2 All corporal punishment to be given by the cane and to be recorded in the punishment book.
3 An adult witness always to be present when corporal punishment is given.
4 A check to be made on a pupil's medical record before corporal punishment is given.
5 A letter to be sent to the parents by first class mail explaining what has

happened, why the punishment was given and inviting them to visit the school to discuss the problem.

No. 3 is useful because it provides a witness in case of an action being brought, though no doubt the view might be taken that one teacher is likely to support a colleague. Rule 4 is essential – it would be wrong to cane a child with a heart condition or, as in one instance, a child with large scars on his bottom as a result of burns. No. 5 ensures that the parents receive the facts of the situation and not just Johnny's one-sided account of the fearful thrashing he has received for nothing at all.

A fifth form boy once raised his fist and threatened to strike a woman teacher. He was reported to the head, who felt that he had no option but to cane him (though privately he felt that the lad might have suffered some provocation). The boy drew himself upright and said, quite politely, 'I am afraid I'm not prepared to accept your punishment, sir'.

What should be done in a situation like this? Should the head attempt to use brute-force or have the pupil held down? This was what happened in *R.* v. *the Newport Justices* mentioned earlier.

That kind of physical confrontation seems unreasonable and undignified. A better course would be exclusion until the punishment was accepted or an alternative agreed between the head and the parents. In the case mentioned, the boy was excluded. The parents agreed with the punishment but could not persuade the boy to accept it. He had only one month left of his school career and he never returned.

8.9 Detention

Letter to parent:

Highwalls Comprehensive School,
Fetter Lane,
London.
23rd May, 1982

Dear Mrs Magwitch,

Your son Abel has been neglecting his homework and in spite of several warnings there has been no improvement. I am sure you would wish to support the school in ensuring that he keeps up-to-date with his studies. I am writing to let you know that he has been placed in detention on Wednesday, 25th May. This will mean that he will leave school at 4.30 p.m. instead of 3.45 p.m.

Yours sincerely,

E. Havisham (English mistress)

Letter from parent:

Tuesday

Don't you dare keep my Abel in. It's a teacher's job to get through the work in school time, not outside. Besides he does my shopping at 4 o'clock and then there's his papers. I shall be waiting at the school gate.

Mrs Magwitch

Detention is a recognized form of punishment. The school has done the decent thing and given the parent reasonable warning and the justification for the punishment. In the light of Miss Havisham's letter and the reply she has received may Abel now be kept in?

No person has the right to restrict the liberty of another without a lawful reason – to do so is false imprisonment, a form of trespass to the person. There are acceptable reasons, lawful arrest being one. Another is the right of a parent to restrict the liberty of his child while he is under the age of eighteen. Since the teacher in *loco parentis* assumes the rights and duties of the parents then he also may restrict the movement of a child, for example by preventing him from running away from school premises during school hours. But what if parents and teachers clash over the restriction of a child's liberty?

It has been asserted by at least one education authority that a parent cannot demand the release of his child until the end of a school session. This cannot be so. A parent has the ultimate right to control and custody of his child at all times, unless a court has decreed otherwise. Since a parent does not have to send his child to school then it is maintained that he may gain control at any time. Similarly, if a parent arrives at school at 3.45 p.m. and demands his child then the teacher must give him up. Not to do so would be false imprisonment.

This does not mean that the pupil can escape reasonable punishment. Once again, the solution would be exclusion until the punishment was accepted or some alternative agreed between school and parent.

When detention is used then it must be reasonable. Anything longer than half an hour might well be unreasonable. Even fifteen minutes might be unreasonable for a primary school child in December or January who might then have to make his way home through dark streets. When detention takes place there must be reasonable supervision.

A particular problem is created where pupils are entitled to free transport. To keep a child in does not remove the parents' right to have such transport provided, so if a child misses the school bus because of detention the teacher, as the agent of the authority, might well be obliged to see that the pupil gets home. The sting of the punishment would certainly have been removed!

8.10 Exclusion

There seems to be some sort of confusion in the thinking of many authorities in relation to exclusion and suspension.

Exclusion is not a term mentioned in the Articles of Government for schools. Most local authorities seem to assume that excluding a child from school is only a term to be used in relation to children who have head lice or some highly infectious disease.

The intention here is that for the sake of other pupils, and in the case of head lice ensuring that some action is taken by parents, a child is not allowed to return to school until a certain condition has been fulfilled i.e. that the period of infection has passed or that the head has been cleared of lice.

The booklet *Control of Communicable Diseases in School* should be available from education authorities. In recent times the tendency has been to reduce the number of diseases for which a child should be excluded and to ease the conditions on which pupils may be re-admitted.

The minimum periods of exclusion for common complaints are usually as follows:

chicken pox	6 days from onset of rash (scabs need not have all disappeared)
german measles	4 days from onset of rash
measles	7 days from onset of rash
mumps	until swelling has subsided
whooping cough	21 days from onset of paromysmal cough
impetigo	until spots have healed, unless lesions can be covered
athletes foot	exclusion from bare-foot activities and swimming until treatment is effective
ringworm	until treatment is given and lesions are covered
pediculosis	until treatment is given

There are certain serious complaints which should be notified to the District Community Physician and pupils excluded on his advice. These include bacilliary dysentery, diphtheria, food poisoning, infective jaundice, acute meningitis, poliomyelitis, small pox and tuberculosis. In any other cases schools should not hesitate to contact the Child Health Service for advice over exclusion. The final decision should be the head's and in the unlikely event of a disagreement he would be entitled to exclude the child if, in his judgement, there was an unreasonable risk to other pupils. In doubtful cases the child's own doctor might be asked to certify that he or she was fit to return to school.

Where in rare cases an epidemic breaks out, such as food poisoning in a school kitchen, then both the District Community Physician and the Public Health Authorities will be involved and the head may be required to close the school.

Exclusion is included in this section on disciplinary measures because, it is maintained, that it may also be used in reference to breakers of school rules and disruptive pupils. The judge in *Spiers* v. *Warrington Corporation* said that in his view Eva Spiers was not suspended and there was no need to go through suspension procedures (see 8.4 above). He did not use the term 'exclusion' but it is clear that that was what he meant.

Exclusion, in the sense of a disciplinary measure, does not mean that a pupil is prevented from coming to school but that he prevents himself from being admitted by the breach of some rule or condition laid down by the school. Since the head may only make rules that are reasonable then the rule in question must pass the test of reasonableness if tested in court. Thus, if a pupil is excluded from attending school because his parent insists on his wearing a kilt then as soon as he appears wearing a normal pair of trousers he must be admitted. The same can be said of a pupil wearing jeans or a leather jacket where these are banned. The same could be said of long hair, shaved heads or some of the weird varieties of dyed hair or unusual cuts, such as the 'tomahawk' which leaves one strip of hair down the middle of the head.

Where a decision is made to punish a child by setting him extra work or by administering corporal punishment and the child will not accept such punishment, or the parent forbids such acceptance, then exclusion seems the right method of dealing with the situation. The matter is then open to negotiation between the head and parent and usually an amicable solution is found. No responsible parent wishes his child to miss school and no sensible head wishes to have bad feeling between the school and parents. If, however, no solution is found and the pupil and parents will not give in then the right course of action is a prosecution for non-attendance, as in the Spiers case. Naturally, the parent may test the reasonableness of the school's action in the courts.

8.11 Suspension

Here there is a clear intention to ban pupils from attendance at school either for a specified period or for an indefinite period until an investigation has been carried out, recommendations put forward, or alternative arrangements made for the education of the pupil.

The Articles of Government will always make a general statement regarding the powers of the head in relation to the suspension of pupils. In some cases he has to consult the authority before suspending a pupil, in some he has to consult his chairman of governors. In others he may suspend and then consult. Some authorities, like Staffordshire, give the head the power to suspend for a short period, say three days, entirely on his own initiative though he must then inform both the authority and the chairman of governors.

No matter what form the Articles of Government take, the head would do well to consult both the authority and the chairman of governors at all stages even if the case is a clear-cut one such as a violent attack upon a teacher or fellow pupil. Where the suspension results from disruption over a period, as it often does, then there must be clear evidence of the involvement of parents and such agencies as the Education Welfare Officer, Educational Psychologist, Child Health Service, as appropriate, and any other body that might be of assistance in particular cases. There must also be evidence that the school has made every effort to solve the problem through its own systems. This may be attempted in various ways, such as class changes or subject changes, or the involvement of individual staff who may have a special relationship with the pupils. It may be in more negative ways through the use of whatever minor forms of punishment the school uses, such as the removal of privileges or the use of report or record card systems, warnings and corporal punishment if appropriate.

In a number of schools there appears to have been an increased amount of disruptive behaviour in recent years, particularly with older pupils. When all reasonable efforts have failed and traditional punishments have been discarded then the number of suspensions seems likely to increase.

Many authorities realize this and have made attempts to deal with the problem by setting up working parties with teachers and producing documents giving advice and procedures to be followed. The Staffordshire authority produced such a booklet in 1977 entitled *Disruptive Pupils, Guide-lines for dealing with disruptive behaviour in Schools*. This discusses the problems and lays down procedures to be followed within the authority's own schools but it also contains a check list over suspension which any school would do well to follow in the absence of specific guidance from its own authority:

CHECK LIST (for heads and teachers in dealing with disruptive behaviour in schools)

Stage 1

Preventive Action whilst retaining the pupil within the school:–

Staff consultation, including consideration of suitability of the curriculum to the needs of the pupil; adequacy of pastoral care; appropriate disciplinary measures; records, case histories, documentation.

Effective liaison with parents.

Consultation with Education Welfare Officer.

Seeking help from support agencies – social services, remedial advisory service, school psychological service, school nurse or school medical service, probation officer where child already under supervision.

Consultation, if necessary, with Education Department to co-ordinate help.

Stage 2

Formal Interview with parents – the Education Department being asked to help in arranging meetings if parents do not co-operate with the Head.

Stage 3

Short-term suspension – up to 3 days on not more than 3 occasions.

Immediate notification to:–

Parent(s) Chairman of Managers/Governors

Chief or Area Education Officer for details of information required by the Education Department)

Invite parents for discussion

Liaison with Education Department as necessary

Pupil returns to school or longer term suspension confirmed.

Stage 4

Longer-term suspension resulting from an initial decision after consultation with the Chief/Area Education Officer, or an agreed extension of a short-term suspension:–

Notify parents

Notify Chairman of Managers/Governors
Continue consultation with Chief/Area Education Officer
Invite parents for discussion
Chief Education Officer will convene Managers/Governors meeting if necessary
Head and Chief Education Officer will consult on action to be taken in seeking appropriate help from support agencies and in securing continued education for the pupil temporarily by means of home tuition/part-time schooling or possibly in a special unit with objective of securing return to full-time schooling.
Case conference in appropriate cases.

Stage 5
Return to original or alternative school
Subject to
Consultation between Chief Education Officer and Heads
Discussion with teaching staff and professional associations if required.

Most authorities have no regulations over the return of a pupil to a school where an indefinite suspension has been imposed. Usually, it is assumed that if the head is willing to accept a pupil back then that will be an end of the matter and in practice this is what often happens. However, the Articles of Government give the head the power to suspend – it is most unusual for them to say anything about the power to re-admit. It could be held that a meeting of the governors would be necessary to endorse such a decision. It could also be that the governors have the power to overrule the head and order re-admittance.

Suspension should be the last resort but when a pupil is violent towards others, either staff or pupils, or is so disruptive that others cannot make progress and staff cannot carry out teaching effectively, or when the pupil makes the orderly running of the school impossible, then the head has a duty to suspend for the sake of the school as a community. What is then to happen to the pupil if there is a decision not to re-admit?

In law the parent has a duty to educate his child by regular attendance at school or otherwise. Education authorities have a legal duty to provide sufficient schools which give efficient education. If the parent is willing to send his child to school regularly but the school will not accept him then this places the education authority in some difficulty. It is not complying with the law. The following options seem to be open:

1 Find another school which will accept the child. In some cases this may be the answer – a fresh start. Naturally, most schools are reluctant to accept trouble-makers from other establishments since it is likely that they will have been suspended only as a last desperate measure.
2 Send the pupil to a centre for disruptive pupils or to a special residential school dealing with problem children. There are very few of the latter and many are independent, which involves the local authority in heavy bills for fees. More and more authorities have set up centres for disruptive pupils as one answer to the problems raised by suspension. The centres have very few pupils and specially appointed staff so that much individual attention is

possible and the organization can be arranged to deal with pupils who are abnormal (not sub-normal) in some way. Some very real achievements have been made in some instances, in others it has to be admitted that what is taking place is a containing exercise. At least the authority can be said to be carrying out its legal obligations.

3 Provide home tuition. This is likely to be inadequate and very expensive but it is a way of showing that the authority is doing its best in a difficult situation.

4 Seek a care order from a court. This could happen in a case where parents were co-operative but unable to control a child. A case that springs to mind is where a divorced mother was left with the custody of a large and very rebellious boy of thirteen, who not only caused serious problems in his school but subjected his mother to violent physical attacks as well.

8.12 Expulsion

Where a pupil is suspended his name must not be removed from the registers until he is in attendance at some other institution. To do so would signify expulsion. Very few Articles of Government allow a head to expel a pupil. Again, if a pupil were expelled and the education authority did not provide an alternative school or some other means of education, then a parent would have grounds for complaint that the authority was not carrying out its statutory duty. If the governors expel a pupil then the parent may have an appeal to the Secretary of State under Section 68 of the 1944 Act on the grounds that the governors are acting unreasonably. The Secretary of State may overrule the governors and the pupil would then have to be taken back.

Once a pupil reaches the end of compulsory schooling then both the school and the authority are in an easier position, since the availability of courses at further education establishments offer another way out of a difficult situation.

It is clear from all that has been said above that the word expulsion needs to be avoided if at all possible, since it is fraught with so many difficulties, and heads are advised not to use the word when writing to parents.

8.13 Minor sanctions

All schools must have various methods of dealing with offences in the day-to-day life of the community. These may be stated in the school rules, they may be of a customary nature or they may be *ad hoc* decisions. Like the main rules themselves they must be reasonable. Pupils being kept standing for long periods on one leg; a backward child being locked in a small room alone for several hours; a pupil being forced to wear a notice on his back announcing he was a thief; and a girl pupil who swore being forced to wash her mouth out with soap are all examples of what most of us would consider to be unreasonable punishments.

As with corporal punishment and detention, it is always wise to give details in the school prospectus of punishments commonly used. If the parent knows of the punishment, or could reasonably have discovered it while reading the prospectus, then by sending his child to the school and not raising the issue he can be assumed to have accepted it.

Punishments should be fair, should be seen to be fair and should be useful. Learning a spelling list is much more useful than writing 'I must not talk in class' a hundred times. Punishments of a whole class for the sins of a few are usually considered most unjust by the innocent many.

One useful method used by many schools is a report card system. A pupil is given a card something like the one shown opposite.

The card is taken to each class and completed by each teacher, the pupil reporting back to a senior member of staff at the end of each session or at the end of the day. This enables a close check to be kept on behaviour and will show particular lessons where troubles are occurring. It also helps weaker members of staff to deal with a difficult pupil since later he is going to have to explain himself to a stronger personality. It is a good idea to inform parents when a pupil is placed on report and perhaps send them the card at the end of the week.

Another sanction used is to withdraw a pupil from class and place him in a separate room to work on his own. If so, the responsibility of supervision must not be forgotten.

This is also the problem when teachers send pupils outside the room for misbehaviour. The supervision of the class is the teacher's responsibility and sending a child out of the room does not release a teacher of this responsibility. If the pupil is known to be unreliable, takes to his heels and leaves the premises then if an accident takes place there could certainly be an allegation of negligence.

8.14 How far do school rules extend?

Mrs F gave it as her opinion that 'what happens after school is nothing to do with school hours'. She hadn't studied *Cleary* v. *Booth* (1893), of course. In that case two boys named Booth and Callaway were on their way to school when they met a boy called Godding. A fight took place in which Callaway struck Godding. The head of the school had a complaint from Godding's mother and he caned both Callaway and Booth. Booth's parents, no doubt feeling that their son, who protested his innocence, had been unfairly treated, brought an action. The issue was whether the school's authority extended beyond the school premises. The judge said that it did:

'Can it be reasonably argued that the only right of a schoolmaster to inflict punishment is in respect of acts done in the school, and that it is only while the boys are there that he is to see that they are well-mannered, but that he has exceeded all the authority delegated to him by the parent if he punishes a boy who within a yard of the school is guilty of gross misbehaviour? It is difficult to express in words the extent of the schoolmaster's authority in respect to the punishment of his pupils; but in my opinion his

Parent's signature:

(*The school would be grateful if parents would sign to show that they know their child has been placed on report.*)

Special comments:

REPORT CARD

Name

Form

Week beginning:

Report with this card to your year tutor during morning registration each day. Hand it to your subject teacher to be filled in at the end of each lesson.

Form tutor

Year tutor

Reason for report.

Will staff please indicate subject, put an effort and attitude grade A-E, add a comment if necessary and initial. Grade A-very good; C-satisfactory; E-very poor

Monday	Tuesday	Wednesday	Thursday	Friday

authority extends, not only to acts done in school, but also to cases where a complaint of acts done out of school, at any rate while going to and from school, is made to the schoolmaster.'

The reasoning in this case was followed later in the case of *R.* v. *the Newport Justices* (1929). The same theme has been pursued in other cases, notably in one instance where a pupil ran across the road in front of a teacher's car on the way to school and was nearly run over. The pupil was caned and the court upheld the punishment. *Cook* v. *Attock* (1955).

The judges in these cases all recognized the obvious fact that if schools could not deal with matters occurring outside the school gates then it would be impossible to maintain order and discipline. The classroom lawyer would soon discover that he could take one pace off the premises and then commit whatever breach of rules that he wished. The judges however do not really attempt to define the actual limits of the schools' powers.

From the comments of the judge quoted above it seems reasonable to say that a school is entitled to deal with problems created by pupils on the way to school or on the way home, particularly when the pupil is in uniform and thus closely identifying himself with the establishment and its rules. It would be inadvisable for a school to go further than this.

A problem that is a particular worry to some schools is that of misbehaviour off the premises during the lunch-hour. In the case of the sample rules quoted earlier, it was clear that there were 'goings on' of some kind in the nearby churchyard. Similar problems may be raised by chip shops or amusement arcades, which attract large groups of youngsters and thus create behaviour problems which are bad for the school's image and can lead to fights, throwing of litter and annoyance caused to shopkeepers and members of the public. In one instance a chip shop was discovered to be a regular battle ground for warring factions from a grammar school and a nearby secondary modern school.

May the school place certain establishments or areas out of bounds during the lunch-hour? The matter needs to be handled tactfully since a parent may well feel that if he wishes to give his child permission to be out of school during the lunch-hour to eat his meal at a café or chip shop and he absolves the school of all responsibility, then he has a right to do so. Also, to name particular establishments could well cause offence to the owners.

Nevertheless, it is maintained that where the welfare and safety of pupils is concerned the school has a right to make such rules. A letter to parents explaining the dangers involved and the sensible reasons for the rule will usually gain the necessary co-operation.

It is also maintained, though not all authorities agree, that once a pupil steps on to a contract vehicle provided by the authority, he is in the care of the authority's agents (the bus company and the school) for the rest of the day. Therefore, although at the parent's request a pupil might be allowed to leave the premises, the school has the discretion to refuse and ban him from visiting certain establishments or areas.

As far as supervision is concerned, though, once a pupil is off the premises at the end of a session a school's responsibility may cease. There is a discretion then of whether to take action or not over a pupil's conduct on his way to school or on the way home.

Would this apply to pupils travelling on buses and trains? It would seem so on trains and on public bus services. It would certainly be so on contract vehicles hired by the authority. The bus operator, under his contract, will be responsible for the safety of pupils and would be entitled to refuse to carry a particularly troublesome one. The school would be entitled to deal with trouble-makers on contract vehicles and to ban them from travelling, with the agreement of the operator. Prefects might be put in charge of buses but they must always obey the instructions of the driver or conductor.

In a recent incident a large group of pupils was waiting one morning on a pavement to catch a contract vehicle. The bus approached slowly and the pupils surged excitedly forward, each trying to be first to board. One girl was pushed into the road and the wheel of the bus ran over her foot. Luckily she was unhurt. The incident did not reach the court but it poses a serious problem. A large group of youngsters sky-larking by the roadside create a potentially dangerous situation. The school is not responsible for their supervision, neither is the bus operator, neither under the present law is the local authority.

Now let us examine some particular areas where school rules and sanctions can cause difficulties.

8.15 Uniform and clothing

As the law stands, it is possible for a school to ban almost any article of dress such as jeans, multi-coloured sweaters, high-heeled boots, leather jackets, trousers for girls and so on. It is not possible to insist on the wearing of a particular uniform in maintained schools, unless this can be achieved by some complicated process of elimination. Schools which charge fees can, of course, do so since the wearing of a particular uniform may be considered as a term of the legally binding contract between the parents and the school. There is no contractual relationship between parents and maintained schools.

It should be said, however, that the compulsory wearing of uniform in maintained schools has never been tested in the courts but such an attempt would be unlikely to succeed since most authorities, when pressed by parents, will agree that uniform is not compulsory.

Those schools, mostly secondary, which do have uniform and wish to have all pupils dressed in this way should therefore handle such issues carefully. The best method is to have a clear uniform list presented to all parents when pupils join the school. It helps to have as many items as possible which may reasonably be worn outside school as well as being part of the uniform. It is much easier to persuade parents to buy a grey, black or brown V-neck sweater than a green blazer with red braid round the edges.

A pupil may be expected to come to school reasonably dressed so the more flamboyant and extravagant articles of attire may certainly be banned.

When a pupil attends school, it is reasonable to expect that he will take part in all school activities, except religious education and worship and those from which he is excused on medical grounds. It is certain, therefore, that a parent may be expected to provide suitable clothing for physical education and games, unless the authority is prepared to do so itself. This would include suitable footwear and other items such as shorts but an insistence on a particular pattern of, say, a football shirt would probably not be enforceable. Since pupils may be required to take part in art lessons or instruction in home economics rooms and workshops, it would seem reasonable to ask parents to provide aprons or overalls. If not, the parent would have no complaint against the school if the pupil's clothing was spoilt or damaged.

8.16 Property and confiscation

A school may make rules over property which may not be brought to school. Items which are often forbidden include cigarettes, lighters, watches, jewellery, radios, tape recorders, playing cards and knives. Some are banned on grounds of safety, some because they lead to unacceptable behaviour and some because they are valuable and create problems over loss or theft.

To deprive another of his property is a form of trespass to goods at the very least. To take an object from a pupil and say, 'you're never going to have this back, my lad' could be something worse. The definition of theft in the Theft Act 1968, is: 'A person is guilty of theft if he dishonestly appropriates property belonging to another with the intention of permanently depriving the other of it.'

The taking does not necessarily have to be for gain or for the thief's own benefit. So if a teacher says that property will never be returned that could be theft if a court considered the act to be 'dishonest'. There are, unfortunately, cases of teachers who steal from children, sad though this may seem.

Just as a good parent may take things from his child for reasons of safety or discipline, so a teacher may confiscate items but the pupil should always be told when the property will be returned and it must then be handed back. Schools may sometimes refuse to hand over some items, such as cigarettes or knives, to the pupil but send a letter to the parents asking them to collect the items and stating that they will be destroyed if not claimed within a certain time.

Examples of property confiscated on grounds of safety would be knives, matches and jewellery such as rings or brooches with sharp pins. Property likely to lead to unacceptable behaviour could include cigarettes or playing cards. Where a ban is placed on items of value, such as tape recorders, it is suggested that a warning is sent to parents that if they are brought to school then the school will not accept responsibility for them. This means that the school might do well to ban them but not confiscate them, for confiscation involves a measure of responsibility for the article concerned.

This can often be a problem over confiscation. If a teacher takes over the property of a pupil then he is bound to take reasonable care of it. If he then loses it through negligence, e.g. leaving it lying on a desk in a classroom, then he may be liable. Since, as we saw earlier, an employer is vicariously liable for the torts of his servants, the authority may be liable for such a loss but, as far as I know, the matter has not been tested in court.

The teacher also may become liable if he voluntarily agrees to look after money or other property belonging to a pupil and there is loss. Teachers of physical education in particular are often involved in this situation. The boy who places his watch in a box with other watches and then comes last at the end of the lesson only to find that all the watches have been claimed is not unknown. Various methods have been tried to deal with the problem, such as issuing tickets or sealed envelopes with names on them, but they seem rather burdensome for busy teachers. The obvious precaution of locking changing rooms should, of course, be taken.

While it would be churlish for teachers never to look after the property of pupils a certain reluctance to do so needs to be shown in order to avoid the worst difficulties. Parents should be told clearly in the school prospectus, or by letter, that if valuables are brought to school then responsibility for them will not be accepted. Some attempt should be made to explain what the school means by 'valuables'. It should be made clear that the only cash brought to school should be dinner money or small sums to spend in the tuck shop. At times it will be necessary to bring larger sums for trips, or other reasons, but if a large sum is brought then it should be handed over for safe-keeping. Where the amounts are large, payments by cheque could be encouraged.

Where a teacher does consent to look after the property of pupils he should arrange to put it away securely, preferably in a locked drawer. The school should have some arrangements for special security, such as a strong box in an office or a safe, so that teachers can readily deposit valuable articles and cash given to them for safe-keeping. Valuables should never be left in classrooms overnight, even in locked drawers.

8.17 Lost property

There is no legal compulsion on a school to make specific arrangements over lost property. Under Section 41 of the Local Government (Miscellaneous Provisions) Act of 1982, a local authority, and therefore a school, has certain rights with regard to lost property however. After six months, lost property becomes the rightful possession of the authority who may dispose of it. When the owner is known and fails to collect the property after at least one month's notice has been given, then the property becomes the possession of the authority. Where the property is perishable or to look after it would be inconvenient or expensive then time limits do not apply. Reasonable steps must be taken to find the rightful owner.

Problems of lost property will be assisted greatly if parents can be encouraged to mark all clothing and other articles with the pupil's name. The use of plastic tape can help in marking many items of personal property.

8.18 Theft

Most children are incredibly careless over their possessions, as the display of new anoraks, raincoats, watches and sports gear in any lost property collection will demonstrate. The usual cry is that they have been stolen. Most losses in school turn out to be the result of the owner's carelessness, someone else's carelessness or a practical joke. Of course, theft does occur but the difficulty lies in separating the real cases of theft from the other causes.

To accuse someone of theft is no light matter and teachers should be careful of making wild accusations since pupils are protected by the law of defamation in the same way that adults are.

When there are suspicious circumstances the teacher is entitled to question the child as a parent would if something went wrong at home. Strictly speaking, if theft is discovered then the matter ought to be reported to the police but this would be rather ridiculous if the theft were a very minor one. In such circumstances it is suggested that the school should deal with the situation as a matter of discipline, but parents should always be informed so that the importance of the incident can be emphasized. A child who commences stealing small items at school may soon take to the richer pastures of shop-lifting. It should be emphasized to the parent and to the pupil that further incidents will be reported to the police and that suspension will have to be considered as a protection for other pupils in the school.

Should a teacher search pupils when theft is suspected?

To search a person forcibly would constitute an assault in law and while a reasonable parent might expect to search his child's person, if he wished to do so, a teacher is in a more vulnerable position. The defence of discipline might still be put forward but the best advice to be given to teachers is that they should request pupils to turn out their pockets rather than conduct a forced physical search. The latter should be undertaken only as a last resort in very exceptional circumstances.

When serious theft is involved the matter should be referred to the police anyway. They should be involved once a school becomes aware that theft on any significant scale is taking place and their advice and help sought as to how the culprits may be caught. It should be remembered, however, that once the police are involved the decision as to whether court action will be taken or not may be removed from the school.

Sometimes schools are asked to deal with theft committed off school premises, say by the owner of the sweet shop not far from the school gate. Although at times the motive behind such a request may be to prevent the young child from becoming involved with the police, the frequent reason is that the shopkeeper does not want the embarrassment and unpleasantness of calling the police and becoming involved in a hearing himself. If the theft is being committed on the way to school or on the way home then the school may perhaps consent to be involved. But the school should be reluctant to do so where criminal offences are involved and should only consent where the offence is an isolated and trivial one. Parents should always be informed of what has happened.

8.19 Smoking

Most schools have problems over smoking and ban it on school premises or on the way to and from school, though some schools may allow it in sixth form centres if parents have given permission.

Under the Children and Young Persons Act 1978, the sale of tobacco or cigarette paper to a person apparently under sixteen years of age is an offence, whether the tobacco is for the youngster's own use or not. Tobacco includes cut tobacco, smoking mixtures, cigars, cigarettes and even tobacco substitutes. Apart from cigarettes, a person will not be guilty if he did not know and had no reason to believe that the tobacco was for the use of the person to whom it was sold.

Where a person under sixteen smokes in a public place then the police have power to seize and destroy the tobacco. A school may make a rule banning smoking, for pupils of all ages, but the tobacco should not be destroyed immediately. As suggested earlier, the parents should be contacted and asked to collect the offending items.

When a shop near to the school is causing disciplinary problems by selling cigarettes to pupils a friendly word with the owner may suffice. If not, then the police should be informed.

8.20 Alcohol

Except on medical grounds, it is an offence to give intoxicating liquor to a child under five years of age. Over that age a child may be given such liquor in the home. It is an offence for a person under eighteen to buy, or attempt to buy, intoxicating liquor and an offence to sell such liquor to a minor.

Under the age of fourteen a child may not be in the bar of any licensed premises during the permitted hours, unless he is the child of the licensee or is resident on the premises or the bar is the only access to some other part of the building. He may enter a licensed restaurant. Between the ages of fourteen and eighteen, at the licensee's discretion he may enter the bar but must not consume intoxicating liquor.

While smoking has always been a problem in schools, alcohol has not been so until recent times. Pupils remaining longer at school and the increased ease with which drink may be purchased from supermarkets and off-licences have both helped to present problems of teenage drinking on school premises and the bringing of alcohol into school.

If the source of supply can be traced then appropriate action may be taken. Although normal school sanctions may be used against offenders, including suspension, there is also the possibility of police involvement on the grounds of disorderly conduct or a breach of the peace if pupils become aggressive.

8.21 Drugs

Under the Misuse of Drugs Act 1971, it is an offence to possess what are known as 'controlled' drugs and it is an even more serious offence to possess such drugs with the intent of supplying them to another, unless the person is permitted to do so, as in the case of a doctor or chemist.

'Controlled' drugs include cocaine, LSD, heroin, mescalin, opium, cannabis, cannabis resin and amphetamines.

Where drug-taking is suspected in school it is important that swift action is taken, since not only may the pupil concerned be harmed but the damage to others could be considerable. Parental involvement is clearly advisable but the police should be involved also at an early stage and they have the right of search on grounds of mere suspicion. For the safety of other members of the school community a pupil carrying drugs should be suspended immediately.

8.22 Pregnancy

After the raising of the school leaving age in the 1960s and in the early 1970s many schools were faced each year with the problem of girls becoming pregnant while still at school. The problem remains, though it seems on a lesser scale – perhaps because of the ease with which the pill and other means of contraception may be obtained.

It would be embarrassing for the girl herself, for other pupils and for teachers, if a girl were to remain in school once the signs of pregnancy were obvious. It could also be prejudicial to discipline and a bad example to others, especially as a pregnant girl could become something of a heroine to her classmates.

The school must take some action. The formal suspension procedures may be used, of course, but unless the pregnant pupil insists on attending school, this would hardly seem to be necessary. Under Section 39 of the 1944 Education Act it is a defence to a prosecution for non-attendance that leave of absence has been given by a person authorized to do so by the governors of the school. A resolution by the governing body that the head shall have power to do this will enable him to deal with pregnancy situations by granting leave of absence. The power can be useful in other situations, such as where there is family crisis of some kind and a day's absence would help, though not strictly allowed by the law. The girl's doctor may certify that on medical grounds she is unfit to attend school and this may also be a method of keeping her away.

Usually, where pregnancies occur they are with pupils who are at or near the statutory leaving age so that by the time the child is born the mother will have left school anyway. When a younger girl has a child then there is still the statutory requirement that education be given. In such a case the authority will need to be approached and asked to provide some form of home tuition while the girl is absent from school. Once she is fit to return to school she must do so, though in view of the circumstances it may be necessary to discuss with the pupil, the parents, and the authority the advisability of a change of school.

The situation can produce its surprises. One teacher describes how she had trouble with a fourth year class and told one girl that she was to stay in at the end of the morning session and complete a piece of work.

'I can't, Miss.'

'Why not?'

'Got to go home and breast-feed the baby, Miss.'

8.23 Violent and disruptive pupils

Schools reflect the society they serve so it is hardly surprising that the violence in our society that displays itself in such an ugly fashion at football grounds and on city streets is also to be found in schools. Considering the publicity given to violence in the popular press and on television it is surprising that there is so little violence in the vast majority of our schools.

It is always difficult to draw a dividing line between the rough and tumble of horse-play which is natural to children and the element of calculated or reckless use of physical force that could cause real harm. However, the school has to try to do so.

All unlawful use of physical force is actionable at law but it would be ridiculous to allow a criminal case to develop from two teenage lads scuffling in the playground. It would also be ridiculous not to take very seriously indeed a situation where one pupil threatened another with a knife.

Where there are physical encounters between pupils then the school's routine disciplinary measures must be used to sort out the problems and see that a firm check is kept on such unpleasant activities as bullying. Good supervision by staff will help to prevent most of this from happening. Where an offender persists with a series of minor offences, or where a more serious event occurs, then the parents must be involved and help sought from whatever other agencies may provide it. If all else fails and due warnings have been given then the obvious case is suspension, in the interest of other pupils in the school.

Schools would do well to remember that where minor physical violence is involved the parents of the child who has been the subject of the bullying, or other harm, should also be informed and told of the action that has been taken or will be taken. This will often prevent those parents from storming down to the police station and setting events in motion which may well be regretted later by everyone concerned.

Where a pupil makes a really vicious and unprovoked attack upon another then there is no alternative to immediate suspension and the involvement of the police.

Where physical violence is involved there is a clear case for swift disciplinary action to be taken by a school. Disruptive pupils who are not violent are, in many ways, much more difficult to deal with. They rarely do anything which appears to give good grounds for suspension, but their influence on the work of their class and the nerves of teaching staff can be considerable. Cases that spring to mind are of the boy who had an aversion to women teachers and refused point blank to obey them, but complied meekly when a male teacher was called; the girl who, contrary to the school rule, wore an outside coat to each lesson and needed a brief but unpleasant encounter each time before she would remove it; and the girl who was such an attention-seeker that she could induce herself to faint in lessons at will (usually mathematics).

Most pupils of this type are in need of some kind of psychiatric help and schools must endeavour to gain such assistance for them through the School Medical Service, Educational Psychologist, or the child's own doctor. Early consultation with parents and the involvement of outside agencies are obviously essential but, when all else has been tried, the school may have to face the fact that not only is it unable to cope with the pupil but the welfare of many other pupils is being affected. The answer may lie in some form of special education or recourse to one of the units for disruptive pupils that have been set up by many authorities. Where an education authority will not make an effort to assist, then suspension is the only method by which to force its hand.

No one can be in favour of removing a child from the normal environment of the school but the advantages of centres for disruptive pupils are considerable. They have fewer pupils so that problems can be dealt with on an individual basis by teachers with a special expertise. The mass of ordinary pupils do not suffer from the peculiarities of the few who, in a normal school, will take up a grossly disproportionate part of the teacher's time. Lastly, they relieve the authorities of being in breach of the act by not providing a school for each child.

8.24 Assaults on teachers

Sometimes a violent pupil may assault a teacher and sometimes a teacher may be assaulted by an angry and violent parent.

In one incident a woman teacher found a fifteen year old boy smoking behind the corner of a school building. She told him to report to the deputy head. He refused so she took him by the arm to make him do so. He turned and struck her on the shoulder. She was upset but not hurt. In another incident two senior boys had a grievance against a science master. They attacked him, punched him and wrecked apparatus in the science laboratory. The master suffered a fractured skull.

In the first incident the boy's parents were sent for. He was caned, made to apologize and warned clearly in front of his parents that a further similar incident would result in immediate suspension. In the second incident the two boys were tried by a court and sent to a detention centre. Thus, assaults on teachers may range from those which may be dealt with by the school to those which clearly need a criminal trial. If school discipline is to be maintained then swift and decisive action needs to be taken if a pupil attacks a teacher.

The teacher, of course, has a right to take action, whether the school does so or not. If the woman teacher mentioned above had wished to bring an action, since there was no actual bodily harm the police would not do so on her behalf.

She would have to commence proceedings herself in the Magistrates' Court for common assault under Section 42 of the Offences Against the Person Act 1861. If successful she would not then be able to bring a further action for damages in a civil court.

In the second case the police would bring the action, which would be at least a charge of causing grievous bodily harm. Here the teacher could claim compensation from the Criminal Injuries Compensation Board and would also have the right to sue the pupil for damages in a civil court though as the pupil is unlikely to be able to pay that would usually be pointless.

It was reported recently in a newspaper that in one school a parent marched into the building, along the corridor, burst into a classroom and attacked a teacher in front of a class of pupils. This, of course, constituted a criminal offence and the police took action. Although some allowance might be made for a parent who says things when under great stress, a serious threat to do physical harm to a teacher, or an attempt to do so, should be reported to the police. Some local authorities provide advice and assistance to teachers who are assaulted whilst carrying out their duties by parents or members of the public – but this is somewhat rare.

Any person who is attacked is entitled to use reasonable force to defend himself, though he must also make reasonable efforts to avoid the confrontation. Another option open to a teacher who has been threatened is a warning letter written by a solicitor. Where a parent threatens violence, then the head can declare him to be a trespasser and forbid him entering the premises. The effect of this is to make the offence, if one is committed, even more serious.

Of course, a prosecution is now also possible under Section 40 of the Local Government (Miscellaneous Provisions) Act of 1982.

9 The daily round

In this chapter we shall look at extracts from the diaries of three teachers. Each raises routine matters that affect such teachers quite frequently but which have not been dealt with thoroughly in this book as yet. Each also raises some points which have been dealt with earlier and give an opportunity for testing whether they have been understood.

9.1 Diary of Elizabeth Bennet (Assistant Mistress at the Edward Darcy County Primary School)

Monday

The day began badly with Charlie Wickham coming back after a week's absence. Says he's had 'flu. No note from mother. Told him to bring one or else, so he began to cry and his nose began to run. He says she won't give him one but if he doesn't produce one, you-know-who will be breathing down my neck.

May Bingley also came back. She brought a note saying she had been kept away for just one day to help with her sister who was sick. That means to let Mrs B go to work as usual!

Josephine Collins late – again. What am I supposed to put in the register for this child and why doesn't someone do something about this lateness of hers? It's almost every morning!

Gave her a good telling off so she disappeared at break. Ran home, I suppose, so I reported this to you-know-who and left him to deal with it. Also presented him with Mrs B's letter.

Wet lunch-hour. In the afternoon Charlie Wickham (it would be) writing 'Miss Bennet is a bastard' on the back of his exercise book. Lost my temper and smacked him across the face. Charlie crying again but class beautifully quiet for remainder of day. Mrs W will be up tomorrow no doubt.

Thankfully home at 4 o'clock.

9.2 School sessions – registers and attendance

The Education Act of 1944 requires a parent to educate his child, either by regular attendance at school or otherwise. If a child attends a school then he must do so regularly, as we saw in Chapter 5.

Under the Education (Schools and Further Education Regulations) 1981 Section 10 the requirements are as follows:

10. Duration of school year and day (1) Subject to paragraph (5), every day on which a school meets shall be divided into two sessions which shall be separated by a break in the middle of the day unless exceptional circumstances make this undesirable.

(2) In each year a school shall meet for at least 400 sessions reduced, where occasional holidays are granted in term-time, by not more than 20 sessions in respect of such holidays so, however, that nothing in this paragraph shall require a nursery class to meet for that number of sessions:
Provided that where at any time a school is prevented from meeting, for one or more sessions for which it was intended that it should meet and it is not reasonably practicable for arrangements to be made for it to meet at an alternative time for those sessions, the school shall be treated for the purposes hereof as if it had met as intended.

(3) Subject to paragraphs (5) and (6), on every day on which a school, other than a nursery school, meets there shall be provided—
- (*a*) in classes mainly for pupils under the age of 8 years, other than nursery classes, at least 3 hours of secular instruction, and
- (*b*) in classes for pupils of or above that age, at least 4 hours secular instruction.

(4) Subject to paragraphs (5) and (6), on every day on which a nursery school or nursery class meets there shall be provided at least 3 hours of suitable activities:
Provided that on a day on which a pupil—
- (*a*) attends a nursery class which meets for only a single session; or
- (*b*) attends a nursery school or class for one only of two sessions,

it shall be sufficient to provide him with 1½ hours of suitable activities.

(5) In a school which meets on 6 days a week there may on 2 of those days be only a single session and, in relation to a day on which there is only a single session, paragraphs (3) and (4) shall have effect as if the periods of 3 hours and of 4 hours there mentioned were, respectively, periods of 1½ hours and of 2 hours.

(6) The marking of registers shall be carried out outside the minimum periods of instruction or activities referred to in paragraphs (3) and (4) but there shall count towards those periods, as if it were time spent upon secular instruction or suitable activities—
- (*a*) any time allowed for recreation;
- (*b*) time occupied by medical or dental examinations, or treatment;
- (*c*) time required in a voluntary school for the inspection of religious education in pursuance of the proviso to section 77(5) of the Education Act 1944.

To comply with the law a child must be present for each session unless there is a 'good cause'. The cause must be one to do with the child and not with others.

Under the Pupils Registration Regulations 1956, each school must keep an admission register. This register must contain a list in alphabetical order of all the pupils of the school. The following information must be available for each pupil:

1 Name in full
2 Sex
3 Name and address of parent
4 Day, month and year of birth
5 Day, month and year of admission or re-admission

6 Name and address of school last attended, if any

A pupil's name may only be removed from the admission register for certain reasons. These include his death; his registration as a pupil at another school; that he has been absent for a period of 4 weeks and that efforts to trace him have failed; that he has moved to a place from which access to the school at which he is registered is unreasonable; that his parents have satisfied the authority that he is receiving efficient education otherwise than by attendance at school; that the medical authorities have certified that he will not be fit to attend school until he is legally exempt from doing so; that he will be over the compulsory leaving age by the time the school next meets; or that he has been excluded permanently from the school by the authority or the governors.

The last named means expulsion and this is a dangerous step to take since the regulations give the parent the right of appeal to the Secretary of State. If he decides that the pupil has been excluded on unreasonable grounds then he may order his name to be reinstated on the admission register.

In order to establish whether a child is present or not there needs to be an official record kept and this is the reason for having school attendance registers, which are legal documents and may be required as evidence in court. Clearly, there has to be a system of marking registers to show children who are present and have attended at the correct time, pupils who are absent, pupils who come too late to be counted as present officially but who are nevertheless physically present on the premises, and pupils who have a right to be absent for some good cause. It should be noted that a pupil who comes after the register has been closed is absent as far as legal school attendance is concerned.

The registers themselves should be marked at the commencement of each session. Not to do so leaves open questions as to when a certain pupil was or was not present.

Attendance registers should be marked in ink and alterations should be made so that the original entry and the correction are clearly distinguishable. Registers must be preserved for a minimum of three years. Both HMI and representatives of the local authority have the right to inspect the registers of maintained schools and may make extracts from them.

Some authorities include a code to be used in the printed registers. Others do not, so in their cases the school will need to devise a scheme of its own. Opposite are the instructions given to the staff in one comprehensive school. They are pasted into the inside cover of each form register.

This system emphasizes the importance of keeping registers properly. It gives a clear system of recording essential information and of checking on absentees. It is a complicated one because the school is a large one. Smaller schools will be able to devise a simpler system.

The form teacher will know his charges best and should be the most suitable person initially to spot truants and difficult cases. He might send home a form like the one on page 182. If he cannot obtain satisfaction, then the system tells him what further action to take.

REGISTERS AND ATTENDANCE

A. Registers are documents which must be kept by law, and may be given in evidence in court. They must be filled in only by members of staff. Accuracy and promptness in dealing with them will be of particular help to office staff, year tutors and the Welfare Officer.

B. The register should be completed in ink at the end of the registration period, absences also being recorded. It helps to have uniformity so staff are asked to adhere to the following code:-

1.	If a pupil is present	/ in red
2.	If a pupil is absent	O in black
3.	If a pupil arrives after the registration period (Note: This counts as an absence)	Ⓛ in black
4.	An authorized absence for dental or medical treatment, to attend an interview or go on an organized visit, this counts as an attendance)	A in red
5.	If a pupil has leave of absence or an annual family holiday, or some other reason authorized by the headmaster (this counts as an absence).	V in black

C.

1.	If a child is marked absent and is subsequently found to be present, the letter P should be inserted within the absence mark. This includes pupils who miss registration because their bus is late. It does not apply to other children coming late.	Ⓟ red P in black
2.	If a child is marked present and is subsequently found to be absent, the present mark must be cancelled by placing a black ring round it.	(/) red stroke in black

D. Absence must be explained by the parent or guardian. When this has taken place either by letter or telephone, the form teacher should pencil a dot within the last absence mark. Letters should be dated and placed in the front of the register. Those involving particularly difficult cases or raising important issues should be passed to the year tutor or head of school, as soon as possible. When the reason for absence is given over the telephone, a note is unnecessary as a slip will be put in the register by the secretary for the information of the form tutor.

E. Registers should be sent to the collection point in the vestibule at 9.20 a.m. and 2 p.m.

F. Pupils arriving after 9.20 a.m. or 2 p.m. must report to the school office and have their names recorded.

Pupils leaving the building during the morning or afternoon sessions (unless with a member of staff) must have their names recorded at the office and must report again to the office on their return.

G. When you are informed of a change of address or of parentage (e.g. on death or remarriage of a parent) please:-

1. Change the information at the front of the register.
2. Inform your year tutor so that the change is recorded on the pupil's record.
3. Inform the school office.

N.B. When a pupil has been away for THREE days with no explanation, or if a pupil is away for even just one day and you suspect truancy, a form (obtainable from the year tutor) should be sent home asking for an explanation. The same form should be used for pupils returning after less than three days' absence who do not provide a satisfactory explanation.

If the parent does not respond within three days to the form sent, then the matter should be referred to the year tutor who will contact the Education Welfare Officer.

NAME ______________________ TUTOR GROUP __________ DATE ___________

Dear

I note from my register that your son/daughter

____________________________ has not been at school since

____

To help with my records, please return the slip below - or telephone the school if you prefer.

____

Form Tutor

NAME ___________________________TUTOR GROUP _______________________

My son/daughter is away from school because

____

____

and will return on ____

Date: _________________________ Signed ____________________________

Parent

Once the school has decided that absence is unreasonable or that no explanations are forthcoming, then the Education Welfare Officer must be involved. His job is to visit the home and discover why the child has been absent. In consultation with the school, he may then involve medical services, the Educational Psychologist, Social Services, or other outside agencies. He may recommend prosecution, it is often the Welfare Officer who acts as prosecutor on behalf of the authority.

A parent who is found guilty of not educating his child (either by sending him to school regularly or otherwise) under Sections 37 or 39 of the 1944 Act is liable to a fine not exceeding £200 on a first or subsequent offence. In the case of a third or subsequent offence then a month's imprisonment may be given with or without a fine.

Only an education authority may prosecute in these circumstances and instead of prosecuting the parents they may bring the child before the Juvenile Court, which may well then involve care proceedings. The Magistrates Court may, when faced with the prosecution of parents, direct the education authority to bring the child before the Juvenile Court and the authority must comply. This may well happen where it is clear to the magistrates that fining the parents is unlikely to have any effect because they are unable to control the child and thus secure attendance.

Where a child is not attending a school at all, and is not being educated satisfactorily at home, then the education authority must serve a notice upon the parents. This requires them to satisfy the authority within fourteen days that the child is receiving efficient full-time education suitable to his age, ability and aptitude either by regular attendance at school or otherwise. If the authority is not so satisfied then it will issue an attendance order but first it must inform the parents of its intention to do so, and must name the school, or possibly alternative schools, which it intends to name in the order. Within fourteen days the parent must agree to one of the schools offered or name another school under another authority which will accept the child, or name a non-maintained school which will accept the child. That school must then be named in the attendance order. These rules do not apply to children in need of special educational treatment.

These new arrangements for school attendance orders are laid down by the Education Act 1980, Sections 10 and 11. Some of the provisions did not come into force until 1 July 1982.

Failure to comply with a school attendance order may result in prosecution.

9.3 Test yourself

a) Was Mary Bingley's absence permissible?

b) What can be done about lateness?

c) To what extent is the school responsible for Josephine Collins' truancy?

d) Is Miss Bennet in desperate trouble if Mrs Wickham decides to cut up rough?

Answers

a) No it was not. Education is for the benefit of the child and there is a statutory obligation on the parent to see that she gets it. Absence must be to do with the child's own illness or welfare, not that of others. If you-know-who was authorized by the governors to give leave of absence he might do so at Mrs Bingley's request.

b) A pupil who arrives at school after the register has been closed is not receiving 'full-time education' as required by the Act and is technically absent. Therefore an action may be brought against the parent. When is the register closed? This has never been defined precisely but it is suggested that it is when all the strokes, circles and totals have been entered. There is an obvious advantage in fixing a time when registers should be closed if the school wishes to put pressure on late-comers, but schools which have pupils who travel on contract vehicles are in some difficulty. Once a pupil steps on a bus chartered by the education authority he is in its charge and if the bus arrives late at the school he cannot then be said to be absent because of unpunctuality.

c) The school and its teachers owe a duty of care to pupils and that entails the reasonable supervision that would be given by a careful parent. Parents cannot be expected to watch their children all the time, neither can teachers. Miss Bennet must supervise her class and the school must provide adequate supervision at break. If Josephine is determined to run away then it is almost impossible to stop her from doing so.

Miss Bennet was right to alert you-know-who. He should then make an effort to contact the parents, and, if they agree, the police. If the parents cannot be contacted then the police should certainly be informed. If the school has taken all reasonable steps to supervise a child and keep her on the premises, and has taken reasonable steps to trace her after disappearance then there will be no breach of the duty of care.

d) Possibly. A teacher is only entitled to administer reasonable punishment and in most schools corporal punishment may only be administered by certain senior staff. There may also be rules as to the method to be used, e.g. the cane.

It is likely that Miss Bennet does not have the right to administer corporal punishment. It is possible that a court may consider the punishment unreasonable. In one case a civil court awarded damages where a child was hit on the head by a teacher and became deaf. However, in another, a criminal court found a teacher not guilty when, under extreme provocation, he struck a boy on the face and broke his jaw bone.

To strike a pupil in an unauthorized way is always risky. While Mrs Wickham may not succeed in an action she can cause a great deal of worry and embarrassment to Miss Bennet.

Most reasonable parents, if shown the evidence of Charles' offence, would understand the justified anger of the teacher but is Mrs Wickham a reasonable parent?

9.4 Diary of Cyril Boldwood (Head of English department at Mellstock Upper School)

Friday

Hectic as usual. This huge 'O' level set of thirty-six is quite impossible. How can one cope? And a triple on a Friday to boot! Does anyone think about the effects of a timetable? Does God even care?

Problems over exam entries. Tom Hardy's mother sent a rather rude letter demanding that Tom be entered for 'O' level English Literature rather than CSE and suggesting that it is my job to get him up to scratch. Somewhat unreasonable since he is in set 6. Passed the problem to the Director of Studies, who says the matter will have to be referred to God if Mrs Hardy will not see sense.

Visit from Fiona Robin, also set 6. She does not wish to be entered for any examination. As she is now sixteen she intends leaving at Christmas. Exams and job unimportant, as she intends marrying at the first opportunity. Very likely.

Also from Jason Troy, 4th Year set 1, reported for not completing several homework assignments. Tried to explain that he is a bright lad and must work for his future. He replies, politely but firmly, that he has joined some way-out religious sect which does not believe in an earthly future, so no point in working for same.

Departmental meeting. Asked to see staff record books. Obvious that Mr Oak hasn't been keeping his as he puts forward a strong argument for not bothering with such useless paperwork. Since everyone fabricates records, he says, why be dishonest about it. Explain that God, moving in his mysterious way, requires them to be completed.

Just as I'm about to settle down to some free writing exercises with that illiterate but highly articulate 3D, God ushers in an inspector – specialist English, if you please. Spends a whole lesson with 3D and asks why I don't do some basic grammar with them. Is the pendulum beginning to swing again?

9.5 The timetable, curriculum and examinations

The law is very vague as to what the curriculum of the school should contain. In many countries this is laid down precisely, even including the exact text books that are to be used. In this country there must be efficient instruction which is appropriate to the needs of the pupils. Religious instruction is a statutory requirement, though parents have a right to withdraw their children from it if they wish. No other subject is a compulsory part of the curriculum, though no doubt if English and mathematics were not included this could be challenged on grounds that the education provided was inefficient and inappropriate to the needs of pupils. On the other hand, a school may introduce whatever subjects it likes and these can be made compulsory for its pupils.

There is no absolute right for a pupil to be entered for external examinations. The entry forms have to be signed by the head, or someone to whom he has delegated that duty, so the final responsibility for entries lies with the school, though, since the authority pays the bill, then it may impose restrictions e.g. making a parent pay the fee for one examination where the candidate is entered for both 'O' level and CSE in the same subject, or requiring the parent to re-pay the examination fee where the pupil does not appear to take the examination and no acceptable reason is given. Some authorities require a medical certificate where illness is claimed as the reason for absence. One or two authorities impose a charge where a pupil enters for more than a stated number of subjects.

While the administrative procedures vary from board to board all entries require absolute accuracy over names and dates of birth. In doubtful cases the school is perfectly entitled to require the production of a birth certificate in order to ensure that entries are correct.

The school also needs to take great care over the communication of results. The practice of displaying all examination results prominently in school and allowing pupils to discover their own results may relieve the school of responsibility but it can be very embarrassing for those who have not done well. It may also be a breach of confidence which publication in newspapers will not be as specific grades are not then mentioned. Where examination boards issue individual slips for pupils the school has no responsibility for errors. However, if the school takes results from a master sheet and then transmits them to pupils it may well be negligence if mistakes are made. In a case in Canterbury a student was awarded £50 damages for shock when she discovered after some months that she had failed in four subjects after the local technical college had informed her that she had passed.

Normally, examination certificates should only be handed to the pupil concerned or his parents. In the case of an eighteen year old the school would be acting strictly within its rights even to withhold the certificate from parents. Most examining boards will not replace certificates if they have been lost but will only issue a letter certifying that certain results have been obtained. The certificates are valuable documents which may be required as evidence in the future and should be handled very carefully.

Sometimes employers require evidence of examination passes before certificates are issued. The school should then issue a letter certifying that certain results have been obtained but checking carefully on the accuracy of the statement.

The actual conduct of examinations also needs careful attention. Each board produces its own regulations which will usually specify arrangements over seating, timing, distribution, collection of papers and scripts and invigilation. Representatives of the board will visit the school from time to time and make spot checks. Where the school is in breach of the regulations this will have to be remedied and, if the breach is a serious one, then a report may be asked for and an enquiry held. Under such circumstances the board may cancel the papers of all the candidates involved. Candidates should be told clearly beforehand of all the rules and it is a requirement for these to be displayed prominently in the examination room.

Opposite is the notice issued by the Joint Matriculation Board.

In fairness to all candidates and to employers, examinations should be conducted according to strict rules. Nevertheless, in spite of all precautions malpractices do occur (pupils cheating, staff giving help) and unfortunate but innocent errors made. The board has to consider all such occurrences and take whatever action it considers to be fair in the circumstances. This may include cancellation of a candidate's paper, cancellation of all papers in a subject (as where a printer revealed the contents to some candidates beforehand), banning a candidate from taking any further examinations of the board, or even cancelling the right of a school to be an examination centre for that particular board.

Take the case of Susan.

Susan and the two biology papers

It was the custom of the school to lay out the question papers and answer books on individual desks in the examination room before candidates were allowed to enter. On each desk there should have been placed a question paper and an answer book. In error, two answer books were placed on the desk that Susan was to occupy.

She commenced writing and completed four or five pages. Realizing that she had made a disastrous start, she left one answer book and started afresh in the second one. She did not cross out the work in the first book. At the end of the

Joint Matriculation Board G 8

Examination for the
General Certificate of Education

Notice to candidates

1. Every candidate is forbidden to introduce any unauthorised material into the examination room, or to communicate in any way with another candidate, or to indulge in any other form of unfair practice. Candidates are also forbidden to indulge in any unfair practice in the preparation of course work or project work required for assessment as part of the examination. Any candidate who uses, or is suspected of using or attempting to use any unfair means will be reported immediately to the Secretary. If the Board is satisfied that an offence has been committed, the candidate will be liable to be disqualified in the whole of the current examination for the General Certificate of Education, including all work completed before and after the offence was committed, as the Board in the exercise of its discretion may decide.

2. Except in emergencies or other mitigating circumstances no candidate may be permitted to enter the examination room later than half an hour after the beginning of a session. No candidate may be permitted to leave the examination room, and normally no copy of any question paper may be taken out of the examination room, until after one hour from the beginning of a session as given in the official timetable.

Manchester M15 6EU

JMB 12.77

examination she left both answer books on the desk and left the building. The invigilator who collected the answer books picked up the book containing her first efforts and somehow the other book was left in a pile of additional sheets in the examination room.

This was on a Friday. On the Monday Susan's second answer book was discovered. It was assumed that the invigilator had not collected it, though he was convinced that the correct number of scripts had been collected and despatched. The board was contacted and the script sent to the examiner in the hope that it could still be marked.

The examiner thus had two scripts for Susan. The obvious suspicion was that she had re-written the paper in her own time and had somehow introduced the second copy into the examination room – though the school kept this locked, except when an examination was taking place.

Susan could not be questioned as, in the meantime, she had gone to Canada with her parents for a holiday and no one knew how to contact her. The problem hung over the school until she returned at the end of August. An investigation was held and a report made to the board's committee which finally agreed to allow Susan's better script to be marked. She failed.

The incident illustrates how easily things can go wrong and emphasizes the need for great care in the administration of external examinations.

May a school or individual pupil appeal against an examination result? Most boards have arrangements to deal with such requests, though fees are usually payable. A request may be made to check for clerical errors and for a script to be re-marked. It is possible for a report to be obtained on a school's performance by all its candidates in a particular subject. However, appeals are rarely successful. Take the case of Joanna.

Joanna and the art exam

She was a talented artist. She completed her 'O' level examination and the head of art, a very experienced teacher, saw her work before it was sent to the board. She obtained a Grade D.

No one could believe this and a fee was paid for the work to be re-marked. Even though there is obviously a subjective element in marking artistic work, the art staff felt that her work was so good that the low grade could not possibly be correct. The D grade was confirmed however.

Joanna re-sat the examination at Christmas and obtained a Grade A. She passed 'A' level art with a high grade and later obtained a diploma from a college of art.

However, if appeals frequently succeeded then most candidates who failed would wish to try their luck! The general impression is that the examining boards try to be scrupulously fair and make great efforts to avoid mistakes. One wishes that they would acknowledge the presence of human error and not tend to use the computer as a scapegoat!

9.6 Class sizes

The School's Regulations of 1959 limited the numbers of pupils in classes to thirty for a nursery class, forty for a primary school class and thirty for a class of secondary pupils but that section of the Regulations was revoked in 1963.

There are now no limits as to class sizes but anything over the figures quoted above would certainly be considered unreasonable. The concern nowadays is with teacher–pupil ratios and there are no regulations concerning these.

Specialist teachers sometimes claim that only a certain number should be permitted to work in their rooms at any one time, e.g. twenty as a maximum in a workshop. The maximum permitted to work in such areas should be based on the equipment available and the safety of all concerned. DES pamphlets and authority inspectors may give guidance but there are no strict legal requirements.

9.7 Homework

The only case dealing with homework is a very old one, *Hunter* v. *Johnson* (1884). This case held that homework could not be made compulsory. Schools have changed so much since those days, particularly over the widespread preparation for public examinations and the raising of the school leaving age (twice since the last war), that one can say with some confidence that it would not be followed today. The use of homework is so common and so well established in modern schools that it would be held to be a necessary part of education.

Nevertheless, it is important for schools to make their policy over homework clear to parents, preferably by including a statement in the school prospectus. If the parent is aware of this policy and sends his child to the school, then there is an implied acceptance of the rule. It is best if the homework set has a clear value and purpose and can be well justified on educational grounds.

9.8 Leaving dates

Education is compulsory for pupils between the ages of five and sixteen. A child must attend school as from his fifth birthday but most authorities have a policy of admitting 'rising fives'. There are now two dates on which a pupil may leave school. Those reaching the age of sixteen between 1 September and 31 January inclusive may leave on the last day of the spring term. Those reaching sixteen after 31 January and by 31 August, both dates inclusive, may leave on the Friday before the last Monday in May so that some pupils are eligible to leave before they attain their sixteenth birthday.

A pupil who remains at school after the date on which he was eligible to leave may then leave school at any time. Once he has done so there is no obligation on the school to re-admit him.

9.9 Test yourself

a) Does Mrs Hardy have the right to demand that Tom is taught English literature or, indeed, any particular set of subjects?

b) May Cyril Boldwood call departmental meetings as and when he wishes?

c) Is the keeping of records a part of a teacher's contract?

d) What is the legal position of teachers in relation to HMI or an authority's inspectors?

Answers

a) Mrs Hardy has the right for Tom to receive 'efficient instruction'. If this term could be held to include English literature then Tom must be taught it. Apart from religious instruction no subject is required specifically by law to be placed on the timetable. 'God', in the person of the head, may decide. The courts have held that a school may force pupils to follow subjects against the wishes of parents and that parents do not have the right for their children to take certain groupings of subjects from a range of options (see 5.17). As a result of the Sex Discrimination Act a school may not, however, restrict subjects to either boys or girls but does not have to devise a system where boys and girls take identical subjects.

b) Definitely not. It may be an implied term of a teacher's contract that he should attend meetings to discuss organization and policy, though this has never been tested in court. Even if it were to be an implied term, then such meetings should only be held at reasonable intervals and fair notice given.

c) Again, this is a grey area. Can a teacher carry out his duties efficiently under his contract without keeping records of the work and progress of his classes? It seems unlikely. There is a strong case for saying that some form of recordkeeping is an implied term of a teacher's contract. The same could be said of the preparation of a syllabus and the planning of lessons.

d) HMI are servants of the Crown and have a right of entry to all schools, maintained or otherwise. They may inspect premises, check on teaching and the curriculum, indeed on all aspects of the functioning of the school – except that they may not inspect the denominational teaching of religion carried on in voluntary schools. However, they cannot compel a school to implement curriculum changes. They may make reports and recommendations to the authority which obviously will carry considerable weight.

Officers of the LEA may be in an even stronger position. They represent the employer and may, therefore, relay his reasonable instructions to the head and staff. If the curriculum is in the hands of the authority, as it is in some cases, and not in the hands of the head and governors then an authority inspector may be able to dictate to a school over curriculum matters. In relation to such problems the articles of government for the particular school will need to be studied carefully.

To obstruct HMI or authority inspectors is an offence. 'God' and his staff must not prevent them from entering the premises but in most situations will not be bound to follow their suggestions.

9.10 Diary of James Polly (Headmaster of the Potwell County High School)

Spent an hour with deputy 1 going over the new prefect system and the arrangements for our school council. He emphasized that the school council was not to become just a talking shop and then made it clear, in a roundabout sort of way, that my presence would not be welcome.

Letter from Mrs Larkins pointing out that her daughter Miriam plays full-back in the local ladies soccer team. Why can't she play soccer at school instead of netball? She doesn't mention the Sex Discrimination Act, but I wonder. . . .

Letter from Mr Parsons refusing to pay the termly contribution of 25p to school funds. What is he getting for it? Since his daughter is in the hockey team and rides free in the minibus every week the answer's obvious.

Also, letter from Mr Garvace complaining because boys are allowed to wear open neck shirts in the summer term. If a school has a tie then the wearing of it should be enforced at all times, he says. You have no right to change the rules, he says. Telephone call from the chairman of governors who has received a copy of Mr G's letter and a phone call from the same saying that the matter will be referred to the CEO, if not resolved.

Fire drill. School cleared in two minutes flat, recorded in Log Book.

Tussle with caretaker over writing on lavatory wall. Unsightly and indecent, he says, but when it refers to the peculiar habits of deputy 2 and the senior mistress, the limit is reached. His solution – close all lavatories for a week as a punishment. Quickly direct his attention to blocked drain outside art room and faulty socket in room 10.

Make mental note regarding deputy 2 and senior mistress.

9.11 Prefects

Most secondary schools have a prefect system of some sort and many primary schools appoint monitors to carry out various duties. Pupils do not attend school just to engage in academic work, they should also learn to take responsibility, play their part in the life of the school as a community.

In secondary schools prefects may even be used to supervise other pupils, though the practice should be used as little as possible.

Roland Jaques and the paper pellets

Roland was a fourteen year old pupil at an Oxfordshire school. He travelled to and from school on a contract vehicle provided by the authority. As on most vehicles of this kind today, there was a driver and no other adult supervisor. However, as is the custom in most schools, senior prefects were asked to supervise younger pupils on the bus.

On one particular evening there was some larking about on the bus and paper pellets were flying about. There was a suggestion that lead pellets were also being used. Roland was hit in the eye by a pellet, supposedly fired by one John Merry. At first the injury caused seemed trivial but later it developed into a serious condition, almost amounting to loss of sight.

An action was brought against John Merry in negligence and also against the authority for not providing adequate supervision. The action against Merry failed. Other pupils were flicking pellets about and it could not be said with any sureness that Merry had fired the pellet that did the damage. The court also dismissed the action against the local authority. The pupils on the bus were usually well-behaved. It was sufficient and reasonable to ask senior pupils to take charge. The judge said: 'The system of a prefect on the bus was a proper system, both from the point of view that the prefect should learn to exercise control himself but also from the point of view that the other boys and girls should learn to accept that control.' [*Jacques* v. *Oxfordshire County Council and another* (1968).]

This incident took place on a school bus where supervision by teaching staff was impossible. Where a supervision system by prefects operates within a school then there must be overall control by teaching staff. The system should be organized by staff and patrolling staff (or ancillaries during a lunch-hour) who should check regularly on prefects and the way in which they are carrying out their duties.

If prefects are allowed to punish other pupils the best method is some kind of report system so that the final punishment, such as extra work or detention, may actually be imposed by a senior member of staff.

9.12 School (or pupils) council

Some schools have a council on which both pupils and staff are represented but, more commonly, a body is formed of pupils elected by various groups throughout the school, with staff present as advisers.

Such councils may provide good training in the workings of democratic processes (or in the difficulty of getting people interested in such processes) but they can have no legal standing. A head may involve such groups in the process of making decisions but he cannot avoid his final responsibility for decisions regarding the internal organization and management of the school.

9.13 School funds

The local authority will give instructions for the collecting, accounting and banking of money received on its behalf in the school. This will include school meals payments, money paid for materials used in practical lessons, examination fees and so on. Such arrangements will be checked from time to time by auditors from the authority's Treasurer's Department and schools should seek their advice if a problem arises or if changes are proposed in administrative arrangements e.g. changing from a dinner ticket system to a cash over the counter system in connection with school meals.

It is with unofficial school funds that serious problems may arise. Such funds may include the voluntary donations of parents towards a school fund, the money to be spent on items which cannot be obtained through the normal channels of capitation or equipment allowances. They may be profits from a school tuck shop or from the sale of sports equipment, photographs or ball-point pens. They may include donations from the PTA or from well-wishers, or the income from trust funds.

It is common practice for the school fund to be used for money paid in for school visits and camps, for prizes, for subscriptions to sports associations, for payments relating to minibuses, for providing refreshments for speech days and other occasions – in other words for every aspect of school life which cannot be dealt with through the authority's own system of finance.

Some schools set up separate funds for different activities – a school visits account, a minibus account, a visit to Russia account and so on. This also has its dangers since a proliferation of funds leads to too many people being involved and checking becomes difficult.

Financial situations involving frequent payments, whether the sums are large or small, require thorough organization and accounting. Teachers are usually much too busy to handle all the details themselves. Occasionally, the teacher is tempted by the large sums that may be involved, but the usual reason for discrepancies is inefficiency and lack of care. The school needs to have a clear policy to be followed by all dealing with money brought by children. This is necessary to protect pupils and parents and at times to protect teachers from the consequences of their own mistakes.

The first rule should be to insist that all payments are made through only two or three central funds and that the deposits are only to be made by nominated persons. The ideal persons are the school clerical staff, preferably those who deal with the banking of official school funds such as dinner money. They should receive and record all money paid in. Staff should be given a copy receipt for all sums deposited. Accounting will, therefore, be in the hands of persons who will be directly responsible to the head.

The second rule is that no member of staff, including the head, should be authorized to make withdrawals on his or her own initiative. Withdrawals should be authorized on the signatures of those empowered to give approval, at least two being required, one of them being the head.

The third rule is that for every major event, such as a foreign visit, the organizer should produce a balance sheet. This should be checked by the clerical assistant responsible for accounting and passed on for the approval of the head.

The fourth rule is that the head of the school should never be involved in collecting or handling cash that is to be paid into school funds. He is the person who can most easily stoop to dishonesty and escape detection. His role should be that of the person who devises a clear and sensible system, sees that others operate it fairly and checks that all is well and above board. It is difficult for him to do this if he has been personally involved in handling cash himself.

Unless the authority has made special regulations to cover unofficial school funds then these are not subject to audit by the Treasurer's Department. Nevertheless, they should be audited and it is best to find auditors from among parents or other interested parties, if possible, rather than staff. The governors have a right to be told that unofficial funds exist and each time they are audited this should be reported at a governors' meeting. Governors would certainly have the right to examine the accounts of school funds if they wished to do so.

When parents or staff are critical they should be offered the same facility.

It is the apparent secrecy over unofficial school funds that causes resentment among staff, pupils and parents and schools should make every effort to see that details of expenditure or statements of accounts are published. This can often be very difficult since money from school funds is often spent on a hundred and one trivial items that cannot be funded from official sources.

The decision as to the items on which school funds may be spent is that of the head, though he may wish to set up a staff committee to make recommendations. He may hand over the decision making to such a committee but, whether he likes it or not, he will be responsible for the action that is finally taken. He would be well advised to keep a power of veto. The legal position is that unofficial school funds are in the nature of a trust fund with the head as trustee.

To finance a member of staff's holiday in Spain from school funds would be an offence under the Theft Act. To buy the best porcelain teacups for use in the sixth form common room would not be a criminal act but most would feel that it was a misuse of money obtained from pupils, parents and others. To help a child from a poor home who could not go on a valuable educational visit because of lack of money would be considered by most to be an appropriate use of school funds. It should be clear that money from school funds has been spent on items that will benefit all, or a considerable number of, the pupils; on items of obvious use to the school which cannot be purchased by other means; or on charitable uses for those pupils in need.

Many functions are organized to raise funds for specific purposes. In such cases the purpose should always be made clear and the charges for admission. Parents should later be advised of the amount of money raised and how it will be spent.

PTAs often make donations to school funds. It is always advisable for the donation to be used for a specific purpose and better still if the PTA donates equipment purchased by itself rather than cash. There can then be no question of the use to which the money has been put. When PTAs do buy equipment the payment of VAT may be avoided if the purchase can be made through the education authority. Such purchases, of course, then become the property of the authority and the nature of the items is subject to the authority's approval.

9.14 Tuck shops and other money raisers

Profits from school tuck shops are also not liable to VAT providing the annual turnover does not exceed a certain figure and that all the proceeds are used for the benefit of the school. In one school a member of staff was allowed to run a tuck shop taking the profits himself and making regular small donations to unofficial school funds. Most of us would consider it to be morally wrong for teachers to be involved in such activities for personal gain. If the teacher had not been declaring his profits on his income tax return then not only was he committing an offence but the school was assisting him to do so.

The best way to deal with tuck shop finances is to see that profits are paid immediately into school funds that will be used solely for the benefit of pupils. There can then be little difficulty over the payment of tax.

A different kind of warning is necessary over the sale of goods in tuck shops. What if these are in poor condition so as to constitute an offence under the Foods and Drugs Act? The basic rule here is that when goods are sold which are in poor condition or in an unhygienic state then the seller may well be liable, though in some cases the action will lie against the manufacturer. It is essential for schools having tuck shops to check on the freshness and suitability of the goods that they are offering for sale and to store them under hygienic conditions. Since the tuck shop is unofficial and the profits go into unofficial school funds the most likely person to be prosecuted in the event of an offence being committed is the head of the school himself. To the best of my knowledge this has never happened but the risk is always there. Perhaps the best course is to stock only items that are clearly pre-packed by the manufacturer and to have a regular system of close inspection.

When schools sell sports goods, ball-pens etc. as money-raisers, they may be liable under the Trades Descriptions Act or the Sale of Goods Act. The first is a criminal Act, prosecutions being brought by the local Inspector of Weights and Measures. If a school sold sports holdalls where the bags differed substantially from the descriptions circulated to pupils and parents then an offence could have been committed. The second Act is a civil one which gives a plaintiff the right to sue for damages. Such a right can arise under the Act in a number of ways but the most common is where the goods are not of merchantable quality, or not reasonably fit for the purpose for which they have been sold. Thus, a sports holdall which fell to pieces after a week's use could give the buyer the right to sue for damages. While the school could have an action for breach of contract against the supplier it could also be liable to the purchaser. Before a school ventures into selling enterprises it should check the quality of goods very carefully.

Raising money by holding raffles and lotteries is a common method used by schools and PTAs. They are subject to strict control by the law and will be dealt with in Chapter 12.

The sponsored walk is another method used by schools to raise large sums of money with which to purchase items of equipment or to swell unofficial school funds. When such a walk is organized at a weekend, during a holiday or outside normal school hours then clearly it is an extra curricular activity where, if parents' consent is obtained, the education authority cannot prevent the walk taking place – though it could publicly disclaim any responsibility for it. Since the urge for pupils to participate is likely to be stronger in school time, most schools go for that alternative.

Here is a check list for organizing a sponsored walk which is to take place in school time – though many items would apply to any sponsored walk:

1 Prepare details of the area to be used including access, rights of way and parking facilities. The details should be prepared by a small committee

appointed for the purpose who must make a physical examination of the ground to be covered. Try to avoid the crossing of roads open to cars, if at all possible.

2 Approach the education authority for permission to hold the walk. Give full details of the arrangements – dates, times, distances, route maps, supervision, transport, first aid and teaching arrangements for non-walkers. Stress that the walk will be subject to consent by landowners and individual parents. State clearly the object of the walk and justify the exercise on educational grounds if possible, e.g. nature trails, note-taking or map-making.

3 Once permission has been given, approach bodies such as the Forestry Commission, local authorities, the National Trust and police as well as private landowners. The fact that there is a public right of access does not necessarily mean that there is a right to hold a sponsored walk involving large groups of people. Give all the bodies concerned full details, as supplied to the education authority.

4 Send clear basic details to parents and obtain consent. Explain the arrangements at school for those not taking part. Stress the need for suitable clothing and footwear.

5 Issue sponsorship forms stating clearly the name of the pupil and school and the purpose of the walk. Each form should be given a number and this recorded against a roll of pupils participating. There should be a space for the sponsor to enter the amount promised and his signature and a space for one of the organizers to certify the actual amount handed in.

6 Take out a third-party insurance and consider the advisability of a personal accident policy covering all pupils.

7 See that the route to be taken is clearly marked or that check points are so frequent that it is virtually impossible for anyone to become lost. Take special care over likely danger spots. Have a fast runner to go through first to check that supervisors are in position (youngest member of the PE department?). Then start the walk with the youngest forms first. Two or three worn-out, but game, members of staff to bring up the rear and act as 'sweepers' both of pupils and litter. Have several places on the route where the lame, blistered, bootless and disillusioned may drop out and be ferried away by minibus or staff cars to receive attention.

8 Establish at least one first-aid post which can be reached easily by walkers or by transport and have emergency first aid kit carried by 'sweepers' and others.

9 Establish points where hot and cold drinks are available (PTA members with motor caravans?) and toilets if possible. Make the first of these points over half-way as a spur to flagging spirits.

10 Have a thorough system of checking the pupils at the end of the walk. A good method is to collect sponsor forms from each pupil as he or she sets off, tick off the numbers against the roll of those participating and then hand back each form as the pupil reports in at the end. Those who drop out

at earlier stages will need to be ferried to the last check point to receive back their forms or a careful note will need to be made of their names and numbers.

11 The 'sweepers' pick up those at check points as the last pupils go through and then carry on to the final check point. In theory no child should be lost!

12 Write letters of thanks to all bodies and individuals outside school who have helped to stage the walk. When the result is known, circulate details to parents and report to school governors.

If a sponsored walk is undertaken then a school and its staff may be liable in negligence just as for any other activity.

9.15 School annals

Under DES Administrative Memorandum No. 531 of 1956 each maintained school must keep not only an admission register, attendance register and a punishment book but also what are known as school annals – formerly known as the school log book.

The nature of keeping the annals is at the discretion of the head but records must be kept of 'events specially worthy of permanent record in the history of the school'. A log book seems a convenient method. The head may record anything he wishes, though perhaps one of my predecessors was showing an excess of zeal when he entered in the Log Book: 'October 12th. Nothing of note occurred today and there were no visitors.'

The memorandum does suggest some matters which ought to be included. These are significant changes in the character, organization and curriculum of the school; major alterations to premises; the receipt of reports of the functioning of the school; and reasons for temporary closures or unusual variations in attendance. A change from a selective school to a comprehensive school; a change from streaming to mixed ability teaching; the replacement of traditional subjects by integrated studies; the opening of a sports hall; a report issued as a result of a general inspection; or the school being closed because of fire, snow, floods or strikes would be obvious examples.

It is suggested that it would also be useful to record some of the following:

Staff changes at the commencement of each term.

Brief details of staff appointments.

Internal staff promotions.

Absence of staff in unusual circumstances e.g. reporting ill and then bumping into the chairman of governors at the open golf championship, or attending three funerals in a month.

Details of lengthy staff absence because of illness, or frequent short absences for similar reasons.

Reprimands of staff – a note of the warnings referred to in the previous Chapter.

Serious defects in premises and the date reported to the authority.

Exclusion or suspension of pupils.
Serious accidents to pupils or staff.
Fire drills – evidence of reasonable practice.
Plays, concerts and PTA activities.
Any happening likely to lead to argument or criticism at a later date.

Many of these will be recorded in various reports and letters but there is a distinct value in having them collected together in one volume.

9.16 Discrimination against pupils

In an earlier Chapter we saw that to discriminate against teachers on grounds of colour or sex was illegal. The same is true of discriminatory treatment of pupils. Discrimination on grounds of colour in schools seems unlikely. Discrimination on grounds of sex has undoubtedly been practised in our schools for many years.

Recently a court held that it was not discriminatory for a girl to be excluded from a boys' football team (this was not a school team). But another court held that it was discriminatory for a school to close certain craft subjects to girls. The latter case seemed to be brought in an effort to enforce a rule that all boys and girls should follow the same subjects – the courts held, however, that it was sufficient if all options were open to both sexes.

The head of the Potwell School need not feel that Miriam Larkins must be given a chance to play in the school football XI – but she must be given the chance to take woodwork, metalwork or technical drawing if these are available to boys in the school.

9.17 Test yourself

a) How far does the head have the power to make school rules? Does Mr Garvace have any rights over the discarding of ties in hot weather?

b) How far may governors influence the formulation of school rules and the general conduct of the school?

c) Is the caretaker liable under the Health and Safety at Work Act if a child receives a shock from a faulty electrical socket?

Answers

a) Under his contract the head is usually responsible for the internal organization, management and discipline of the school. The judgement of the *Spiers* v. *Warrington Corporation* case makes it clear that pupils must obey reasonable rules when attending a school and the person to make such rules is the head. A rule made by the local authority to apply to all in schools would be binding on the head but an attempt by an authority to impose detailed specific rules upon an individual school might well be a breach of its contract with the head.

Mr Garvace may complain to the governors or the authority. He may remove his child from the school and 'educate him otherwise' but he cannot remove the head's responsibility for decisions affecting the day-to-day running of the school.

b) It is difficult to say. The governors have general oversight of the conduct of a school and significant changes in the curriculum or the way in which the school is organized should be reported to them. But there is no clear legal evidence for saying that they may make or break school rules or, indeed, dictate over matters of organization and curriculum. The head has such responsibility but must keep his governors informed.

Of course, governors do have legal powers – in particular over the appointment and dismissal of staff. Where there is a serious lack of confidence between the head and governors then the ultimate weapon is a resolution recommending the dismissal of the head.

c) The authority will be liable under the Health and Safety at Work Act. It cannot escape liability for defects on the premises, though if the head and caretaker do not respectively take steps to remedy known defects then this may well amount to breach of contract. If the caretaker had been grossly negligent in disobeying instructions over safety requirements then it is just possible that he might himself face a criminal prosecution.

10 External relations

10.1 Johnny Bull

Johnny Bull was a boy from a working-class home where there were a number of other children. Relationships between mother and father were not good and in Johnny's first year at the secondary school the father left home and went to work on an oil rig. He set up a second home with a lady friend in Aberdeen. Occasionally he sent money to Mrs Bull and he also visited her from time to time (usually when he had had a row with the other lady). On these visits he amused himself by giving Mrs Bull a mild beating-up and extending it to any of the children who were around. Eventually Johnny and two of his brothers set about Mr Bull and he disappeared for good.

During his school career Johnny had various medical inspections like everyone else. In the primary school there was a suggestion that his own illness was being used as an excuse for looking after his infant sister and contact was made with his own doctor. He had severe learning problems coming under the broad umbrella of dyslexia and he caused some difficulties by bullying younger pupils, so he was referred to the educational psychologist. When father left home the Social Services department became involved with the family and the question of care proceedings over the children was considered. However, Mrs Bull was doing her best in very difficult circumstances so no action was taken.

Johnny was a good lad at heart with a real concern for his mother. In his second year at the secondary school there was an investigation after Johnny had bouts of falling asleep during lessons. It was discovered that he had illegally taken on two part-time jobs in order to help his mother with money. In his third year he was in court for shop-lifting. He admitted a string of offences and was placed on a supervision order for two years.

The school did what it could to help Johnny. It was in close touch with the social worker, the probation officer and the educational psychologist. It encouraged him to become a member of the youth centre near the school site. He was allowed to take part in a link course with the local college of further education. Johnny's work and behaviour improved. In his final year work experience was arranged for him. He had interviews with the member of staff responsible for careers and also the local careers officer.

Eventually Johnny left school with a reasonable group of CSE passes and obtained a job as an apprentice garage mechanic.

Schools are not isolated communities. We have already discussed the relationships with some outside bodies such as teacher associations, local authorities and the DES. There are, of course, many others with which a school may or must have contact and this chapter will examine them.

Consider the story of Johnny Bull and how he was involved with agencies outside school.

10.2 Medical services

The National Health Service Reorganization Act of 1973 removed the responsibility for the School Health Service from local education authorities and it became part of the National Health Service, as from 1 April 1974. The area health authorities, which were then set up, now run the School Health Service and, apart from London, the boundaries of the area authorities coincide with those of local authorities themselves. Responsibility remains with the education authority for identifying the need for special education and the provision of it, also for education welfare and educational psychology.

Each area health authority is responsible for appointing a senior doctor known as the community physician, who specializes in community medicine and is in charge of a whole range of services for children. It must also appoint a senior dentist and a senior nursing officer. It must also appoint all the staff needed to administer the School Health Service and it is responsible for arranging all medical and dental inspections. The local education authority must provide suitable rooms and facilities in schools for such inspections to be carried out.

Medical inspections are indeed a major part of the work of the School Health Service and under Section 69 of the 1944 Act the Secretary of State has the power to order a pupil to be medically examined if he considers it necessary. Non-compliance by the parent constitutes an offence.

Routine medical examinations usually take place just before or just as a child becomes of compulsory school age. A school can refuse to admit a child who has not been subjected to a medical examination. A further examination takes place somewhere around the usual age of transfer to secondary school. A third takes place during the pupil's last year of compulsory education.

A parent has the right to be present at a medical examination and the first dental inspection, providing it is reasonable and practicable for this to be arranged (School Health Service Regulations 1959). It would seem that the parent has the right to be present but not to dictate as to the time and place of the examination.

In addition to the routine inspections, both the school and parents have the right to ask for a medical examination to be carried out at other times if there is a cause for concern. This might be advisable, for example, if a pupil wished to go on a school camp or visit and had recently suffered from black-outs of some kind.

Under the Regulations, records of medical and dental inspections must be kept for each child. At one time schools kept these records but the current practice is for the area health authorities to undertake responsibility for them. This has the disadvantage for the school that if a crisis occurs it cannot readily refer to the child's medical record. It is important, therefore, to have references on the pupil's school record of any condition such as deafness, diabetes or heart trouble that could be of serious significance.

Routine inspections of hair and feet are carried out by school nurses. Where treatment is needed, say for nits or verrucae, the parents will be informed. Children who have nits, or other infestation, or who are in a dirty condition may be compelled to have a special examination and may be excluded until appropriate action is taken by parents. Parents who refuse to take such action may be prosecuted for not causing their children to be educated and it is possible for the area health authority to order the child to be removed and compulsorily cleansed.

10.3 Child guidance

Provisions for child guidance throughout the country prior to reorganization of the Health Service in 1974 varied from highly specialized units to virtually no provision at all. DES Circular 3 of 1974 recommended that child guidance should be a network of provision ranging over health services, welfare services, psychiatric services and psychological services rather than a provision by small highly specialized units. The result in many areas seems to be more of a jungle than a network. The school has great difficulty in discovering exactly who is the appropriate person to deal with the problem and professional differences between psychiatrists and psychologists have not helped.

Nevertheless, most areas do now have child guidance clinics and the help of psychiatrists, though often only on a part-time basis. Most authorities are now better staffed with educational psychologists who are assisted directly by social workers. Unfortunately, the proportion of clients seems to increase in line with the increase in the number of psychologists, an off-shoot of Parkinson's Law perhaps!

A child may be referred for guidance to the psychiatrist or psychologist, or their ancillary helpers, by the school, the child's own doctor, or the Social Services Department.

Schools are most likely to have contact with the educational psychologist. Usually, this will be a person with teaching experience, a degree in psychology and additional training. It is not necessary for a school to obtain parental consent before a child is referred to the psychologist but it is always advisable to do so, since so often problems that show themselves in school have their root causes in the home. I remember the pupil who used to visit the psychologist regularly. At the latter's request the father always accompanied the boy. The lad once complained to me, 'Sir, he spends all the time with my father'.

The help given by the School Psychological Service may include assistance for pupils who have various forms of learning difficulties, those who have problems of adjustment to school such as 'school phobics' and others who present behaviour problems such as bullying.

10.4 Employment of children

Many pupils in secondary schools take part-time jobs of various kinds and while this may be useful experience for them, and most parents and employers are reasonable over the nature of the work and the amount of time involved, the law lays down certain restrictions. These are created in order to see that children are not exploited and, in particular, that their right to education is not affected.

Before 1973 it was possible under the 1944 Education Act, Sections 58 to 60, for local authorities to make by-laws restricting the employment of children. The Employment of Children Act of 1973 transferred the responsibility of making such regulations to the Secretary of State but leaves the education authority with the responsibility for enforcing them.

The general restrictions on the employment of children below the compulsory school leaving age are, firstly, that no child under the age of thirteen may be employed at all. There must be no employment within normal school hours. No child must work before 7 a.m. or after 7 p.m. on any day. Work on school days and Sundays is limited to two hours and to eight hours on other days. No child may be employed to lift or carry anything so heavy that it might be likely to cause him injury. Any employment may be banned or restricted if it can be shown that it is interfering with the good health or education of the child.

There are also certain specific restrictions. No child may be employed in an industrial undertaking (except where it is a family business and no outsiders are employed). Children may not work underground in mines or quarries, in factories or ships.

It is possible under the regulations, however, for children of parents who have agricultural or horticultural businesses to help even if under the age of thirteen, including one hour before the commencement of school. The Secretary of State may insist on all children who work having a permit to do so issued by the local authority on the application of employers and employers may also be required to keep records of the children they employ. Education Welfare Officers are often asked to deal with checking such matters. It should be noted that employment does not necessarily depend upon the payment of wages. Where a child works for an undertaking designed to make a profit then he is employed as far as the law is concerned.

There are special regulations relating to performances by children of compulsory school age and below – before 1963 there was a barrier at the age of twelve. The situation now is that normally no child under the upper limit of compulsory school age may take part in public performances unless a licence has been granted by the local authority. This applies to performances where a charge is made, to performances in licensed premises or registered clubs and to broadcasts and recordings intended to be used for public exhibition. Licences are issued originally under the Children and Young Persons Act of 1963 and the Act makes clear that a licence will not be granted unless the local authority is satisfied that the child is fit to perform and that his health, welfare and education will not suffer as a result. There are restrictions over the number of days on which performances may take place and over the number of weekly or daily performances. Adequate arrangements must be made for the child's education, e.g. by private tuition.

No licence is required when the number of performances in six months does not exceed three or where the performance is given under arrangements made by the school (thus covering school performances), or by the local authority (thus covering tours by county orchestras and choirs), or by anybody approved by the Secretary of State.

Full details of the law relating to performances by children may be found in the Children (Performers) Regulations 1968 and *The Law on Performances by Children*, published by the Home Office, HMSO, 1968.

The unlawful employment of children is an offence and the local authority has power to prosecute in such cases. Where a school believes that the law has been broken or suspects that, even though the letter of the law is being kept, a child's education or welfare is at risk, then the facts should be reported to the authority. Common instances are the illegal employment of children by newsagents and the overworking of children on farms in country districts.

10.5 The Juvenile Court

It is with this court that the school will have contact when a pupil is involved in crime, in non-attendance at school, or when civil matters such as care proceedings take place.

The Juvenile Court is a separate sitting of the local Magistrates' Court. The magistrates involved are specially appointed for the purpose. Normally, not more than three will sit and one must be a man and one a woman. No sitting of a Juvenile Court may take place if a sitting of any other court (apart from another Juvenile Court) has taken place during the preceding hour or is due to take place during the following hour.

Unlike the sittings of the full Magistrates' Court, juvenile hearings are not open to the public. Only members and officers of the court may be present, together with the parties concerned (including parents), legal representatives, witnesses, newspaper reporters and any other person specifically authorized to attend. It is useful for senior staff in schools to understand Juvenile Court procedure and permission may sometimes be obtained to attend on application to the Clerk to the Justices.

Reports of the proceedings in Juvenile Courts may be published but the names, addresses, details of school and any other particulars of the accused juveniles, or juvenile witnesses, may not be published unless the court, or the Home Secretary, specifically directs that this be done. Neither may any photograph of an accused juvenile or juvenile witness be published without a specific instruction to do so. In relation to juveniles the words 'conviction' and 'sentence' are not used – instead the terms are 'finding of guilt' and 'order made upon a finding of guilt'.

Juvenile courts deal with children and young persons. A child is anyone under fourteen years of age and a young person is fourteen but under the age of seventeen. The law assumes that no child under the age of ten is capable of committing a crime, since he is incapable of forming the necessary *mens rea* (guilty intent). The age of criminal liability is eight in Scotland. The Children and Young Persons Act of 1969 recommended that no child, that is between the ages of ten and fourteen, should be the subject of criminal proceedings but might be brought before the Juvenile Court for other reasons. This recommendation has not been implemented and the opposition to it means that it is unlikely to be so, for some time anyway. At present a child may be prosecuted for a criminal offence but the onus is on the prosecution to prove, not only that the accused committed the offence and intended to do so, but also that he understood the exact nature of his actions and its consequences and he fully realized the wrongfulness that was involved. The older the child the easier it may be to prove this. There is a presumption that a child is incapable of committing certain offences, e.g. a boy under fourteen cannot be accused of rape, though he may be charged with indecent assault. With the exception of homicide or indictable offences where a child is jointly charged with a person of seventeen or over, all cases involving children are dealt with summarily in the Juvenile Court.

Young persons of fourteen and under seventeen are normally tried in a Juvenile Court, except for homicide and offences where they are jointly charged with a person of seventeen or over. When juveniles are tried jointly in the Magistrates' Court and are found guilty they are remitted to the Juvenile Court for sentencing. Where homicide is involved the juvenile must be remitted to the Crown Court for trial. For other serious indictable offences the magistrates may remit the juvenile to the Crown Court if they wish.

Apart from criminal offences, the juvenile may be brought before the court if his health or development are being restricted or impaired; if he is exposed to moral danger; if he is beyond parental control; or if he is not being educated properly.

If a juvenile is arrested on suspicion of homicide or some other serious crime, then he may be detained. Otherwise, unless brought immediately before the court, he must be released on bail, unless to do so would endanger his own safety or would be likely to defeat the ends of justice, or if there is good reason to believe he would not surrender to bail.

In the Juvenile Court in criminal matters the procedure is basically the same as in the full Magistrates' Court but attempts are made to make the proceedings as simple as possible and to explain matters clearly as the trial proceeds.

A juvenile may, of course, have legal representation but where he does not his parent, guardian or some other adult may be allowed to represent him. The court may order the parent not to represent his child if that seems to be in the child's interest and may appoint some other person to do so.

When deciding on the action to be taken in juvenile cases the court will have recourse to reports from various sources. These will usually include one from the school commenting on such matters as behaviour in school, attitude to work, attendance record and the attitude of parents towards schooling. Great care should be taken over the wording of these reports. Parents are entitled to know the contents and it is the practice in some areas to hand the school report to the parent to be read, though most courts restrict themselves to informing the parents of the contents. Such reports are protected by qualified privilege (see Chapter 11) but an ill-judged comment may lead to difficult relationships with parents afterwards. If the school feels that something important needs to be commented on, but it would be wise not to do so on the report form, then a telephone call to the social worker or probation officer in the case may be worth considering.

The options open to a Juvenile Court when deciding on the action to be taken are many.

A number of criminal sanctions that are available in the Magistrates' Court may also be used against juveniles. A child may be fined up to £50 and a young person up to £200 and the parent may be ordered to pay such fines, unless the court is satisfied that he has done all in his power to control the juvenile. New legislation is proposed which will increase the liability of parents in such matters. A juvenile may also be ordered to pay compensation for damage caused by the commission of a criminal offence. There is a limit of £1000 for each offence and the juvenile has a right of appeal.

For an offence which could have led to imprisonment for an adult a juvenile may be ordered to report for a specified number of hours to an attendance centre. Here he is given instruction or useful employment, often some kind of community service. The times should not be within working hours or school hours.

Juveniles may not be sent to prison but they may be sent to detention centres for offences which could have led to imprisonment for an adult. The aim is to give the juvenile a short sharp shock under a regime of strict discipline. The limit is three months for any one offence. A person of fifteen but under twenty-one may be given a youth custody sentence if the court is fully satisfied that there is no other way of dealing with him.

Juveniles, like adults, may be given an absolute discharge or a conditional discharge. An absolute discharge means that a criminal conviction is recorded but no other punishment is given. A conditional discharge records a criminal conviction and discharges a guilty person on certain conditions e.g. that no further offence is committed within a specified period. If a further offence is committed then the offender may be punished for that and for the first offence. The court may also bind the juvenile over to keep the peace and require the parent or guardian to enter into a recognizance, for a sum not exceeding £200, that proper control will be exercised.

The court may defer sentence, if the guilty person agrees, for a period of up to six months.

There are a number of orders that the court may use in dealing with juveniles. The juvenile may be made the subject of a supervision order. This places him under the supervision of the local authority for a period of up to three years. If he is over thirteen then the probation officer may be responsible for the supervision. The order may specify certain requirements such as those of medical or psychiatric treatment and conditions as to residence and other matters. A supervision order may not extend beyond the juvenile's eighteenth birthday and an application may be made for it to be discharged earlier.

A care order may be used where the offence is one for which an adult could have been imprisoned and this has the effect of committing the juvenile into the care of the local authority, which then assumes the rights and duties of the parents. The local authority may then place the juvenile in one of its community homes, may allow him to go to foster parents or it may allow him to live with relatives, or even his own parents, whilst still retaining rights of guardianship. It may transfer those rights to a voluntary organization, such as Dr Barnado's, which will also have actual care of the juvenile.

When a juvenile is brought before the court on a non-criminal matter e.g. that he is beyond control, is in moral or physical danger, or is not receiving efficient full-time education, then a care order may also be issued. In such circumstances the juvenile may be brought before the court by a local authority, a constable or some other authorized person. In such circumstances a juvenile may be removed to 'a place of safety' but he must be brought before a magistrate within seventy-two hours. The magistrate may then order his detention for up to twenty-eight days so that the court may deal properly with the matter. Only the education authority may take proceedings where the juvenile is not receiving efficient full-time education and it is at such times that evidence may be required from the school registers.

At one time parents themselves could ask for a juvenile to be taken into care but now they may only do so through the local authority. They may be ordered to attend the hearing even if they do not wish to do so.

In many school attendance cases it is clear that there is little point in punishing parents who are unable to control their children and make them come to school. Care proceedings or supervision orders involving the child himself present obvious alternatives.

Other alternatives open to the court in both criminal and civil matters are hospital and guardianship orders. Where two doctors certify that a juvenile is suffering from some kind of mental illness or disorder, then the court may order his detention in hospital. By means of a guardianship order an alternative is to commit the juvenile to the care of the local authority or any other suitable person willing to receive him.

10.6 Minors and civil law

It is strange that the criminal law should retain the age of seventeen as the time at which the criminal young person virtually becomes a criminal adult since for almost all purposes of civil law the age at which the great change comes is eighteen. The age of majority was reduced from twenty-one to eighteen by the Family Law Reform Act of 1969. At eighteen a person is able to vote, make a contract, marry without consent of parents, in fact exercise all the privileges of an adult. There are a few exceptions, such as the ineligibility of standing as a candidate at local or Parliamentary elections.

Apart from juvenile courts or courts dealing with matrimonial matters, young people are unlikely to be concerned with courts of law. There are two branches of law which may provide exceptions.

Contract

A contract is a legally binding agreement between two parties. The agreement may be written, spoken or implied and such simple daily occurrences as buying a packet of sweets form a contract just as much as the purchase of a house. The common law remedy for breach of contract is damages, though the equitable remedy of specific performance which forces a person to carry out his contract, may be available in some situations such as the purchase of land. Minors, or infants as they are often called, are those under the age of eighteen. The basic rule is that a contract cannot be enforced against a minor but he can enforce it himself if he wishes. There are two exceptions when contracts may be enforced against minors.

A minor may be liable for payment for 'necessaries'. These are goods which the court considers to be essential to the minor, taking into account his particular needs and other factors such as his social position. Food and clothing are obvious examples. A gold watch would not be a necessary for an ordinary teenager, however it has been held to be so for a minor from a rich family. A motor-cycle has been held to be a necessary for a minor commercial traveller, it was essential for him to have one in order to carry out his work. If a minor orders necessaries but does not take delivery of them then he cannot be forced to pay for them. Indeed, even if he does accept delivery, then he can only be forced to pay what the court considers to be a reasonable price, not necessarily the price demanded by the seller.

A pupil who bought a pair of shorts from the school which he needed for PE lessons could theoretically be sued in the County Court if he did not pay since it is likely that PE shorts would be considered a necessary. The case would be heard under the facility known as the Small Claims Court.

Of course, if a minor ordered goods that were not necessaries, the vendor could seek a court order ensuring that the goods would be returned to him.

Minors are also bound by those agreements known as beneficial contracts of service. These are agreements made for the benefit and training of the minor. The most obvious example is a contract of apprenticeship or any contract of employment. A minor who breaks his contract with his employer is liable to an action for damages in the County Court though the court will not insist on the carrying out of the contract by a decree of specific performance.

Tort

As we said earlier, torts are civil wrongs such as trespass, negligence, nuisance and defamation. There are no age limits in tort and some torts are actionable *per se* – that is no damage has to be proved. Libel and trespass are examples of such torts. If a person's rights have been unlawfully interfered with then the court must give him a remedy. However, a plaintiff would be unlikely to have much success in a tort action if it was clear that the defendant did not have some understanding of the wrong that was alleged. Trespass to land is the infringement of a person's right to enjoy exclusive possession of his land and a mere unauthorized crossing of another's land is a clear infringement of that right, even if no damage occurred. It would be useless however to bring an action for trespass against a toddler of three who had wandered across your front garden.

Minors, however, do have the right to sue in tort just as they may be sued. A minor injured in a car crash may sue for damages either in the County Court or the High Court according to the amount claimed. If the accident was caused by his father's negligence then it is his own father that he will sue, though it is the insurance company that will pay if negligence is proved.

There may be some point in a minor suing but there is little purpose in suing a minor, unless he is covered by insurance. The only common law remedy is compensation in the form of damages and the minor is most unlikely to be able to pay. His parents cannot be made to pay for his torts. If it could be shown, however, that the damage occurred because of the negligence of the parents in not exercising reasonable control over the child, rather than because of the child's own negligence, then an action against the parents might be worth while.

A minor does not usually appear in a civil action. He sues through his 'next friend' and defends through his guardian *ad litem*, usually his father. Thus, if a pupil suffers an injury as a result of the negligence of an education authority or its employees, the pupil will sue through his 'next friend' for damages in the County Court or the Queen's Bench Division of the High Court, according to the amount involved.

10.7 The police

Sociologists, psychiatrists, and criminologists cannot agree on the reasons why, but the statistics shown here indicate that the great majority of petty crimes are committed by young people. The police have a duty to protect life and property, to prevent crime and to apprehend those who commit crimes – in that order. If the amount of juvenile crime is ever to be reduced then, clearly, co-operation between police and the schools is vital.

Some education authorities do not allow police to enter school premises in uniform unless they are engaged in a criminal investigation. This seems a short-sighted and negative attitude. Police fill an important role in the life of the community and their informal visits to school and their involvement in school courses on aspects of law and order, road safety and so on would seem to be

Offenders found guilty at all courts by type of offence, sex and age

England and Wales 1980

Number of offenders (thousands)

Type of offence	Males					Females					Other offenders
	All ages	Aged 10 and under 14	Aged 14 and under 17	Aged 17 and under 21	Aged 21 and over	All ages	Aged 10 and under 14	Aged 14 and under 17	Aged 17 and under 21	Aged 21 and over	
Indictable offences											
Violence against the person	48.1	0.7	5.7	15.2	26.5	4.2	0.1	0.9	1.0	2.2	–
Sexual offences	8.0	0.1	0.6	1.2	6.1	0.1	–	–[1]	–[1]	0.1	–
Burglary	65.4	5.9	18.6	19.6	21.2	2.7	0.3	0.8	0.9	0.8	–
Robbery	3.2	0.2	0.6	1.1	1.4	0.2	–[1]	0.1	0.1	0.1	–
Theft and handling stolen goods	183.5	8.8	32.4	51.1	91.3	50.1	1.5	5.6	10.2	32.8	–[1]
Fraud and forgery	19.3	0.1	0.7	3.8	14.7	5.5	–[1]	0.2	1.4	3.9	–[1]
Criminal damage	10.6	1.0	2.0	3.6	3.9	0.8	–[1]	0.2	0.2	0.4	–[1]
Other (excluding motoring offences)	23.6	–[1]	0.5	4.8	18.4	3.3	–[1]	0.1	0.7	2.4	1.0
Motoring offences	24.8	0.1	2.4	5.8	16.5	0.9	–[1]	0.1	0.1	0.7	0.1
Total	386.6	16.9	63.5	106.1	200.0	67.8	2.0	7.8	14.7	43.3	1.1
Summary offences											
Offences (excluding motoring offences)	390.5	3.0	18.5	76.3	292.7	65.4	0.2	1.7	6.9	56.6	6.3
Motoring offences	1,156.8	0.2	13.6	151.3	991.6	115.6	–[1]	0.5	7.9	107.1	21.7
Total	1,547.3	3.2	32.2	227.7	1,284.3	181.0	0.2	2.2	14.8	163.8	28.0
All offences	1,933.9	20.1	95.7	333.8	1,484.3	248.8	2.2	10.0	29.5	207.0	29.1

[1] Less than 50

(HMSO *Criminal Statistics in England and Wales 1980*, Crown copyright reserved)

valuable and likely to help young people to understand and trust the police more than they seem to do. A school has a duty to safeguard the interests of the vast majority of pupils, who are honest and responsible, and the occasional visits of uniformed police do no harm in letting potential petty thieves see that the school maintains links with the local force.

Apart from such informal visits or involvement in school curricular activities there are other times when the school may call on, or should call on, the police.

The police should always be called where a serious criminal offence has been committed. This would include a violent attack upon another pupil or a teacher leading to serious bodily harm, any attempt at arson or serious criminal damage, serious theft, or the possession of drugs. Where pupils have fights or petty theft occurs then, strictly speaking, criminal offences have been committed but in such situations the school must use its judgement as to whether the matter should be dealt with internally or whether the police should be called. For instance, a pupil who steals a small item might be punished by the school and his parents informed but if he persists in thieving then he might well be suspended and the police informed.

When there is petty theft occurring regularly and the efforts of the school to find the culprit, or culprits, are unsuccessful then the police should be brought in to give advice and help, including the possible setting of traps with marked money or other objects.

The police may be called to give advice on crime prevention. If there is a feeling that certain parts of the school are particularly vulnerable to break-ins then their advice may be sought and any recommendations they make passed on to the authority. The police may be asked to arrange for car or foot patrols to visit the school while on their rounds, especially where there is no caretaker resident on the site. The caretaker should always be encouraged to maintain close and amicable contacts with the police.

Formal visits to schools by the police in the course of their investigations often cause concern. What information should be given in such circumstances? Should the police be allowed to interview pupils? If they insist on doing so what action should the school take?

The police have a duty to investigate crime and use all legitimate means to discover offenders. All members of the public have a duty to assist them and so does the school. To obstruct the police is a criminal offence in itself but the powers of the police are limited by law and they have to observe a code of conduct known as the Judges Rules. These rules are not enforceable at law but if the police do not observe them then not only will they be the subject of criticism but a successful prosecution is far less likely.

It is perfectly in order to give the police the names and addresses of pupils. It may well be acceptable to allow the police to obtain information from pupils themselves, although the Judges Rules advise police not to interview pupils at school at all. If such a request is made then the questioning should only be allowed if the police give an assurance that the pupil is not to be accused of any offence and the pupil must agree freely to giving the information. The head and, if the pupil is a girl, a senior lady member of staff should also be present. Where it is clear that the police visit is not just to obtain information then the school should refuse to allow a pupil to be questioned. The Judges Rules advise police that, as far as possible, children should only be interviewed in the presence of their parents or guardian or, if this is not possible, in the presence of some adult, other than a police officer, who is of the same sex as the child. If it is essential that the child be interviewed, or even arrested, at school, the police are advised that this should only take place in the presence of the headteacher or his nominee and with his consent.

If the head, or senior member of staff present, refuses to produce a pupil or refuses to allow him to be questioned and the police insist then their demand should be acceded to under protest. To do otherwise would be obstructing the police in the execution of their duty. The head should insist on being present throughout the questioning, should make a note of the officer's number, telephone the authority as soon as possible, record the happening in the school log book and follow this up with a detailed report.

If the police have a warrant for the arrest of a pupil or are exercising their statutory powers to remove him to a place of safety then the school cannot prevent them from taking him away but this should only be allowed under protest.

Throughout, it must be remembered that the school is in *loco parentis* and must act as a reasonable parent would to safeguard the rights and liberty of the child.

10.8 Youth and community services

Section 41 of the 1944 Education Act requires local education authorities to provide as part of further education, 'leisure time occupation, in such organized cultural training and recreative activities as are suited to their requirements, for any persons over compulsory school age who are able and willing to profit by the facilities provided for that purpose'. It is under this umbrella that local authorities set up provisions for youth centres and classes and adult education classes, often housed in school premises.

Provision for the youth service varies widely from one authority to another. Some authorities see the service as an integral part of community provision and either house the youth centre in a separate block on a school site or use a wing of the same building. Designated staff are then part of the staff of the host school, which is a great aid to close collaboration, and the overall responsibility for all educational provision on the site is in the hands of a head or warden. Other authorities have a policy of separate provision of youth centres away from school premises with separate staff. The youth service may be run by qualified staff, who have special training in youth leadership, or by those who have followed the teacher/youth leader training courses run at some colleges of education. The employment of part-time unqualified assistant leaders is common.

Community provision also includes evening classes. Again, these may be an integral part of the work of a community school under the head's direction and organized by a member of his staff or they may be run by a person appointed from outside, the centre merely using the school's facilities at night. Adult classes of this type are rarely held during the day-time but such classes are to be found in a few areas.

Most authorities have arrangements whereby the school premises and playing fields may be used by outside bodies. Most allow the free use of school premises by youth organizations, such as scouts or guides; have cheap rates for groups such as Women's Institutes and those raising money entirely for the benefit of charities such as Oxfam, Cancer Research or Muscular Dystrophy; and charge economic rates for other bodies. Many schools are hired out for dances, concerts and other community activities. PTAs normally have the free use of school premises, though one authority has recently commenced charging both PTAs and schools themselves for the use of premises after hours for fund-raising activities.

Responsibility for the use of premises by the community generally is usually in the hands of the governing body, though the local authority will probably have power to overrule them in the case of maintained schools. In practice, it will be the head who deals with applications. He is entitled to refuse an application if, in his view, such a hiring would interfere with the conduct of the school or be likely to lead to misuse of the building or equipment. If he does refuse, an appeal might be made to the governors against his decision.

Payments for the hire of school premises usually consist of two elements, a charge for the premises and facilities and payment for the caretaking and cleaning. Where no charge is made, the caretaker will still be entitled to his payment since security and cleaning will still be involved. Caretakers are not usually well-paid and the fees they receive for lettings, especially for weekend use, are of considerable value to them. The caretaker's responsibility will usually include unlocking and locking the premises and reinstating the accommodation for school use.

Heads would do well to remember that when outsiders use school premises they are owed a common duty of care under the Occupiers Liability Act of 1957. This means that the school must take all reasonable care for their safety and well-being. Ramps without warning signs on a school drive, unreasonably slippery floors or faulty light switches could all possibly lead to an action for damages brought by an aggrieved adult against the education authority.

Similarly, if an outside body damages a school building or school equipment, it could be sued by the education authority for damages in a tort action. Malicious damage, say smashed windows at a disco, could also lead to a criminal prosecution.

Some authorities require outside bodies to take out insurance cover before they will allow school premises to be hired.

10.9 The Careers Service

Some schools have specially trained teaching staff who are responsible not only for giving advice on careers but who also take lessons labelled 'careers' on the school timetable. Other schools have staff designated to give careers advice but their teaching commitment is through general studies courses in the fourth and fifth years. They have non-teaching time allocated for personal interviews. Some schools have a teacher labelled 'careers master' who receives some sort of graded post as a recognition and who acts as a dispenser of booklets and a co-ordinator of form-filling at the appropriate time of the year. Some schools are able to provide separate accommodation for careers work and display, others use the school library and corridors, some have a hole in the corner such as the office of a senior member of staff. Provision varies enormously and is, generally speaking, unsatisfactory.

Full responsibility for the careers service has been with local education authorities since the passing of the Employment and Training Act of 1973. Previously, the Youth Employment Service had been administered by local education authorities on behalf of the Department of Employment. The Careers Service is not restricted to assisting and advising school leavers – it is responsible for helping all full-time or part-time students who attend educational institutions. 'Attend' is taken as a very broad term – for example Open University students are certainly entitled to help if they ask for it.

The Act requires local education authorities to provide a vocational guidance service for those attending education establishments and an employment placing service for all who leave such establishments. Education authorities are not required to provide this service for universities, but those who attend or leave universities have a right to come to the Careers Service for help and receive it. Those who attend part-time evening classes are not entitled to such assistance and the Act makes provision for other part-time students to be excluded if necessary. Properly trained and qualified persons must be appointed to administer the service. The DES has residual powers in relation to the service but the inspectors for the service are provided by the Department of Employment.

Schools may seek active help from the Careers Service at any time. When pupils, usually in their third year of secondary school education, have to choose optional subjects for examination courses then the assistance of careers officers, as well as school staff, can be most valuable – not only for specific career purposes but for providing a broad education and keeping options open.

This expert assistance may be utilized throughout fourth and fifth year courses but the main task of the Careers Service is to interview all pupils in their final year of compulsory education, to give them information and advice and assist them in finding a suitable job. The school co-operates by completing forms which give information and assessments regarding the pupil. The pupil is asked to make his own assessment and parents are asked for their views. Parents have a right to be present at careers interviews. Whether their presence or that of members of the school staff is always beneficial, is open to question.

Sometimes, the wealth of information and advice that is poured upon a youngster can leave him in a state of confusion. I well remember one boy cut through the various and lengthy efforts being made by a lady careers officer with a clear, positive statement: 'Thanks for your trouble, miss, but I think I'll find me own job if you don't mind.' He became a very competent plumber.

It is obvious that for the benefit of the pupil, careers advice should be seen as a part of the broad curriculum of the school and that there should be the closest consultation between teachers, careers officers, parents and pupils themselves.

At the end of the last year of compulsory school education the careers service may help to find a leaver a job but it is under no compulsion to do more than offer advice and assistance. It may give him the specialist advice needed to go on to a specialist course of some kind at a college of further education or advice as to which 'A' levels should be taken with a specific career in mind or provide entry to higher education courses.

When 'A' level results are published a rush begins for leavers from the sixth form to find places on suitable courses at universities, polytechnics or colleges of higher education. This is a veritable jungle with each university, for example, having its own criteria and methods for admission. The Careers Service assists by designating certain officers who will be available during the second half of August and in early September to give advice and to maintain up-to-date details of vacancies at various establishments.

All school staff involved in careers work will at times need to write reports on pupils either for the information of careers officers or for employers. Note should be taken of the comments in the next chapter on the law of defamation and the writing of reports.

10.10 Further and higher education

It seems difficult to decide exactly what is meant by these two terms since the dividing line seems to be at 'A' level and the Ordinary National Diploma, which is now being phased out. Work above this level is usually termed higher education, so that a number of so-called colleges of further education are, in fact, also dealing with some higher education courses.

Some schools have close contacts with their nearest college of further education, often still called the local 'tech'. Other schools tend to see them as competitors for their 'A' level candidates and try to ignore them. Some of the colleges do tout for customers, it is true, but in a time of scarce facilities and even scarcer financial resources co-operation between educational establishments would seem to make good sense.

The first contact between school and college may well be over 'link courses'. These are courses where school pupils visit the college, perhaps for an afternoon a week, to use specialist facilities such as workshops, vehicle maintenance bays and kitchens. Sometimes courses are geared to CSE Mode 3 or other examinations. Usually, the instruction is given by college staff but it may sometimes be given by school staff who accompany pupils on their visits to the college. There is no legal basis for 'link' courses, they are the result of local arrangements being made between the two establishments.

Usually, both school and college are provided by the same education authority. Even so the arrangements should be put to the authority for approval by the governing bodies of both institutions. If the college is maintained by a different authority then governors' approval will ensure that both authorities are aware of what is happening. This is essential since there are likely to be awkward situations over legal liability if a pupil is hurt either by defective machinery or by the negligence of staff.

It is essential that the parents of pupils taking part in link courses should be informed in writing of the proposed arrangements. They have a right to expect that their children will be on school premises, unless they have been told otherwise. It may well be possible for a school to insist on a pupil taking part in a link course, if the school transports him and supervises him, but it is suggested that the wiser course is always to obtain parental permission and not to allow a pupil to participate if that is the wish of the parents.

As a part of their careers programme schools will distribute literature relating to college courses, arrange visits, invite speakers into school and write reports on pupils. This will also apply to entry to other colleges such as colleges of art or colleges of fashion and design. Schools do not have to do any of these things, except perhaps write reports, but they would be failing in their duty to pupils if they did not do so. Again, the law relating to defamation and the writing of reports will be discussed in the next chapter.

Where a school has a sixth form then it will be concerned with pupils entering higher education courses, which may range from those demanding entry of one 'A' level to those, such as the universities, which demand high grades in a number of 'A' level subjects. Usually, the school will have its own programme of talks and visits and its provision of specialist information and literature. Again, the only legal duty upon a school is to supply information, in the form of a report, to the institution concerned or, in the case of university entrants, to UCCA.

The procedure for entry to all institutions, except the universities, is to apply direct and therefore a prospectus from the individual institution is essential. Each will lay down its own criteria for admission, the basic requirement for any degree course now being two passes at 'A' level. It should be noted, however, that all entrants to teacher training courses such as Bachelor of Education courses must not only possess the requisite 'A' levels but must also hold, or obtain, 'O' level passes in English language and mathematics – the aim being to raise the standard of general education of those entering the teaching profession.

Degree awarding bodies include certain institutions of further and higher education, polytechnics and universities, including the Open University. Most degrees require full-time study but it is possible to take external degrees from

London University. The Open University involves part-time study and most universities and polytechnics have facilities for advanced degrees to be taken full-time. Bachelor of Education degrees are often available to serving teachers by part-time study.

Apart from the universities, the only body authorized to grant degrees is the Council for National Academic Awards (CNAA) and this validates degrees of polytechnics and similar institutions.

Although universities receive their finance through the University Grants Committee they are created by Royal Charter and the only control that may be exercised over them is a financial one. As far as courses, standards and methods of entry and degrees awarded are concerned they are a law to themselves. There are fifty-three British universities and practices vary widely from one to another. Some interview students, others do not. Some only offer places to applicants placing them at the top of their list of preferences, others do not. Some offer very low grades to outstanding candidates to encourage an acceptance of a place, others do not.

All British universities, with the exception of Oxford and Cambridge and some Scottish universities, at present take part in the UCCA scheme (Universities Central Council on Admissions). This acts as a sort of clearing house for university applicants though it does not select candidates itself. Annually UCCA publishes details of the pressure of applications on different subjects and faculties which may well be of value to prospective applicants who are unsure as to which course to apply for.

Each university sets its own criteria for admission and the standards will often vary from course to course, according to the places available and the number of applicants. At present it is a great deal easier to obtain a place to read German than it is to read veterinary science. The normal basic requirement for a degree is a number of examination passes at GCE, at least two of which must be at 'A' level. Faculties then lay down further requirements. Most universities have special regulations that enable them to take older students who do not have the formal academic qualifications.

10.11 Examining boards

The two main external examinations taken by schools are GCE and CSE. There are eight boards, all independent bodies, which conduct GCE examinations at ordinary and advanced levels. Mostly, the examinations are held in the summer but a limited range is offered by some boards in the late autumn and January. Over the years there have been a number of changes in the various grades of pass and the form of results and certificates.

The GCE 'O' level is normally taken at the end of a five year course and is no longer a pass/fail examination. Results are given in Grades A, B, C, D, and E. A standard below E is termed 'unclassified' and is not recorded on the certificate. Since it is clearly stated that Grades A, B and C are equivalent to the old Grade of Pass then in the eyes of most people Grades D and E are failures.

GCE 'A' level is usually taken after two years' study and it is not necessary to have taken the subject at 'O' level in order to take it at 'A' level. Indeed, candidates who do not reach the required standard for an 'A' level pass but who reach a lower level of attainment may be granted an 'O' level pass in the subject. Passes themselves are in five grades A (over 70 per cent), B (over 60 per cent), C (over 50 per cent), D (over 45 per cent) and E (over 40 per cent) and confusion in the minds of both parents and pupils often arises since an E Grade at 'A' level is a clear pass and acceptable entry for many courses, whereas an E pass at 'O' level is practically worthless.

GCE has been in existence since just after the last war but CSE came much later, originating in 1965. It was introduced because of the increase in pupils wishing to remain for a fifth year in secondary schools and for whom GCE was not an appropriate examination. No doubt it was introduced also with the raising of the school leaving age in mind.

There are fourteen CSE boards in England and Wales, organized on a regional basis. Schools must take the examination of their particular regional board, though subjects of other boards may be taken if the home board does not offer them.

CSE sets out to provide suitable examinations for the vast majority of pupils of secondary school age and it offers three forms of examination. Mode 1 consists of a syllabus set by the board, the examination also being set and marked by the board; Mode 2 has the syllabus drawn up by the school, the examination being set and marked by the board; and Mode 3 allows the school to draw up the syllabus, set and mark the examination – subject to supervision and moderation by the boards. In Modes 2 and 3 prior approval of the syllabus must be given by the board. In Mode 3 prior approval must be given to the examination paper. Continuous assessment, oral examinations and project work are all freely used in CSE examinations.

CSE passes are graded from 1 to 6 though only grades 1 to 5 are recorded on the certificate. Grade 1 has national recognition as being equivalent to a pass at Grades A, B or C at 'O' level. Other grades may be accepted as evidence of certain standards by individual bodies and employers but, generally speaking, employers have not given CSE the standing and credit it deserves.

One important difference between GCE and CSE boards is that of the involvement of teachers. GCE boards have teacher representation but they tend to be dominated by the universities, representatives of teachers have overall control of CSE boards and can exert a much greater influence over policy changes.

The present dual system is most unsatisfactory. CSE vies with GCE and the various boards often vie with each other. Parents, pupils and employers find it difficult to make their way through what has been aptly described as 'the examination jungle'. Plans have been afoot for a number of years to replace the two examinations with a common system of examining at 16+. The inability of various governments to make firm decisions; the entrenched position of the present boards; the opposition from universities and other bodies; and the tremendous difficulties of devising examinations that will test such a wide spectrum of ability are all factors that have hindered progress

10.12 School transfers

To return to Johnny Bull. Johnny would certainly have begun his school career in an infants' class unless he had been lucky enough to go to a nursery school. His first school might have been a separate infants' school or it might have been a primary school with an infants' department. He would then have transferred to a secondary school. However, depending on where he lived, he might have been involved in a first school, middle school, upper school organization. In addition he might have moved about from one authority area to another. Whichever system he had inflicted on him he would have been taught by many teachers. They would have discovered a great deal about his personality, background, abilities, handicaps and problems. Much of this important information would have been lost in transfer from one school to another. He would also have been subjected to sudden and confusing changes in teaching methods, particularly in mathematics.

All changes of school are significant for any pupil, though the change from primary to secondary must surely be the most important. There is no legal compulsion on schools to co-operate over such transfer apart from the obligation to forward names, dates of birth, addresses and test scores, if these have been set at the authority's instruction. If the authority issues a standard record card then the secondary school would be entitled to receive that but the information recorded on it might well be only superficial. Obviously, some of the information regarding pupils may be such that primary school staff would not be prepared to put it in writing. Since it is likely to be given in an informal manner it is important that contacts between the staffs of primary and secondary schools are based on frankness and professional trust. The schools together need to decide on the information needed by the secondary school and the kind of information the primary school feels it is prepared to give. If there is no suitable system to use then schools should devise their own.

If staff teaching first year pupils in the secondary schools were more aware of the material taught and the methods used in the primary schools they could do far more to ease the problems caused by transfer. Meetings of specialist secondary staff with the staff of primary schools, visits by specialist secondary staff to primary schools and exchange of staff on a short term basis are devices that can help. It is equally important for primary school staff to understand the workings of a large secondary school, the subjects taught and the methods used so that during the last year in primary schools pupils can be prepared for the change.

The following might serve as a basis for the kind of information that should be available on transfer:

Name.
Address.

Date of birth.
Family, including brothers and sisters at school.
Parental contact, copies of letters received from parents and sent to them.
Medical, references to illnesses, poor eyesight, hygiene, deafness, operations.
Educational assessment, including up-to-date test scores.
Learning problems, details of remedial work, contact with educational psychologist.
Social problems, e.g. a 'loner', needing help to adjust to new situations in a large school.
Teaching methods, ITA used or Fletcher maths perhaps.

This needs to be supported by face to face discussion between the primary school class teacher and someone at the secondary school who will have close contact with the pupil in the first year, by visits to the secondary school by primary school pupils and by efforts on the part of the secondary school to explain its organization to parents and make them feel welcome in the school.

British schools are famous for their autonomy. Each school may organize itself in almost any way that it wishes. It may teach the curriculum that it wishes with the exception of religious instruction. It may have close and informal parental contact or it may keep parents at arm's length. It may well be that this is about to change. There have been attempts recently to establish some notion of a common curriculum. The suggestions are not very positive and one would think that the majority of schools were well in advance of them anyway. The likelihood of a curriculum enforced from the centre, as happens in many countries, seems unlikely here. However, problems of falling rolls would seem to mean that in the future there will be an increasing number of sixth form or tertiary colleges set up and where this does not happen co-operation between schools on a consortium basis will be essential, certainly for sixth form provision and perhaps at a lower level still.

If a sixth form college takes pupils from a number of eleven to sixteen schools then it is suggested that, for the sake of the pupils, the curriculum of those schools cannot be left to the goodwill of their particular heads and that some kind of compulsory linking of the secondary school curriculum with that of the college will be necessary.

Where consortium arrangements take place and schools join 'A' level groups together, even if only in minority subjects, then decisions will have to be taken compulsorily over examining boards, syllabuses, staffing and transport. Again, the arrangements cannot just be left to the goodwill of those concerned – though that goodwill will also be a necessary ingredient.

10.13 Neighbours

One of our rugby pitches was, by force of circumstances, once situated on the side of a sports field next to a private housing estate. Wayward kicks from time to time caused the ball to land in gardens – usually it seemed to be in Mrs L's patch. Boys went to retrieve the ball and used Mrs L's front gate. She did not claim damage but wrote as follows:

> 'I am sick and tired of your boys coming into my garden to fetch rugby balls. One day something is going to be broken, probably my front window. While writing let me also complain about the crisp bags and drink cans your pupils throw over my hedge. Also there's smoking behind the sports hall, I can see it from my bedroom window. . . .'

I put Mrs L's garden out of bounds. We must have had a good rugby team that year as kicking from touch from then on always seemed to result in the ball landing in gardens other than Mrs L's. As soon as we could we moved the pitch.

In fact, Mrs L might have had a good case though nothing exactly like it has been tested in an English court, as far as I know. It has occurred in New Zealand.

In *Matheson* v. *Northcote College Board of Governors* (1975) it was alleged that pupils of a secondary school had stolen apples, hit golf balls into the garden, thrown fire crackers, deposited rubbish and trampled on flower beds belonging to the plaintiff. The action was brought under what is known as a *Rylands Fletcher* tort where the defendant has allowed something dangerous to 'escape' from his land – the pupils presumably! The court dismissed the action as it was not covered by that particular tort but went on to say that an action could have been brought on the grounds of the commission of a private nuisance.

Nuisance is an indirect interference with a person's enjoyment of his land, as against trespass which is a direct interference with a right to enjoy possession of land. The children who stole apples, deposited rubbish, and trampled on flower beds were trespassing – the court seemed to be saying that the school staff were committing a nuisance by allowing them to do so.

As far as neighbours are concerned a school is in the same position as a private householder. It owes a duty of care to neighbours. It may sue neighbours e.g. where a neighbour's tree overhangs a school fence and a branch breaks off and damages equipment (in this situation the school would be entitled to trim the tree at the boundary line). It may be sued by neighbours e.g. where it has a responsibility to fence and has not done so properly, or when its negligence has caused damage to the neighbour's property. In the case of county schools it would be the authority who would sue or be sued and in the case of a voluntary school it would be the governors.

When a school feels that a neighbour could be in the mood to take legal action the facts should be reported to the authority. A mention of possible legal action would be the best way to bring a swift response! Where a school feels that legal action might be taken against a neighbour then proceedings are likely to be very slow. The best approach is a formal one through the governing body. Where it can be shown that the action of a neighbour, or his lack of action, could lead to physical harm to pupils or staff this should be stressed as it would undoubtedly act as a spur to the authority.

10.14 Publishers, photographers and other sales promoters

In the days of expanding school rolls, the opening of new schools and reasonable capitation allowances schools were often besieged by representatives of commercial concerns. Some of their methods were doubtful. Although the present financial climate has altered this situation to some extent, education is still big business. It is the greatest charge upon a local authority. Children must be educated and books and equipment supplied. The financial plight of schools has led to increased trade for firms in the fund-raising business.

Reputable publishers do not present a problem for schools. They supply catalogues, leaflets and inspection copies on request. Most have a system where, by previous arrangement, a representative (often an ex-teacher) will visit the school and display samples of the books and equipment sold by his firm. He does not sell books direct but discusses his firm's products with interested staff and may take orders for inspection copies. Publishers often use teachers' centres for joint exhibitions of books and materials.

Publishers' representatives have their own association, the Association of Publishers' Representatives and this has its own code of conduct. This lays down that a school should not be visited more than once a year and then only by permission of the education authority or the head; that no direct sales should be made in school or orders taken; that no attempt should be made to sell to pupils; and that no teacher should be visited at his private address, unless he has specifically requested it. Complaints may be made to the association but, if there is any real difficulty, the simple solution is to ban a particular firm from visiting the school. Problems may arise with encyclopaedia salesmen and representatives of lesser-known companies. Some authorities do not allow representatives to visit schools unless they have written permission to do so. Where this is the case, the school's position is clear – it turns the representative away. When the authority leaves the decision to the head then he should at least insist on an appointment being made and require some proof of the salesman's authority. This will usually give the address of his head office and the head may then take up any complaint direct. If a salesman causes problems the head should declare him a trespasser, order him from the premises and inform the authority in writing of what has happened.

Most schools have visits from photographers and the work of many of these is of a good standard and excellent value for money, with a percentage allowed for school funds. Records of sports teams, classes etc. are of interest to both school and pupils. The individual photographs, usually taken well in time for Christmas, are valuable where a free small copy of each is given to the school for fixing on to record cards. In a large school such photographs attached to record cards are of great use for quick identification of pupils. Schools should insist that all pupils are photographed and that the school is only charged for those which are purchased by pupils.

Salesmen who approach the school with regard to other products should be treated with some caution. If they are selling some wonderful new duplicating machine or computer then the problem may not just be one of initial purchase but of safety and future maintenance. If a school is in a position to purchase equipment out of private school funds, or through a parents' association, that may not be the end of the matter. Most authorities insist that only equipment approved by themselves as being safe should be used in their schools. A school could find itself banned from using equipment it had purchased if it did not make the purchase through the authority or at least with its blessing. Also, even if the authority does approve the initial purchase of the equipment, it may not agree to pay for future maintenance and this aspect should be checked before purchase.

A school is not a 'person' in law and so it cannot make contracts. A head who signs a maintenance agreement without the express consent of the authority may find that he has made himself a party to the contract and may be sued personally if any breach occurs. A similar position may arise where the school installs a vending machine for drinks or confectionery. The safest method here (though the least profitable) is where the firm installs and services a machine, takes all risk over vandalism and gives the school a percentage of the profits. Where such machines are installed it is always best to obtain the authority's permission and to ensure that any electrical or plumbing work is carried out by qualified persons.

Schools often raise funds by selling pens, combs, sweat shirts, track suits and so on. They should be careful to obtain samples and keep them. If the goods eventually sold are defective then the parents may have an action against the school as the seller – possibly against the head or whoever has placed the order. Under the Sale of Goods Act goods supplied in bulk must be of the same quality as the sample so an action for breach of contract against the supplier would be possible where his bulk delivery was sub-standard.

10.15 Political groups

There is a good case for saying that all pupils in school should learn something of law, government and politics. How may they take a place in our society if they do not? The difficulty of bringing politics into the school curriculum is that of avoiding bias. Many of those prepared to talk about politics, or teach it in schools, are seriously committed to one party and, try as they will, cannot present a balanced view. Nevertheless, some effort needs to be made to explain the working of the system and the policies of the parties.

One method used in schools is to invite the local representative from each main party to talk to senior pupils for ten minutes, say, about their beliefs and then answer questions. The difficulty here will usually be that of preventing the politicians from getting at each other's throats in question time. Occasionally, at election time, a school may organize a mock election, obtaining literature from the parties and allowing volunteer pupils (not staff – that might be brainwashing) to stand as candidates with all the trappings of voting booths, poll clerks, ballot boxes and a returning officer. I remember one very quiet and insignificant boy who, in such circumstances, offered to stand as a communist candidate. When addressing the assembled school he began, in a quiet voice, 'First I will abolish the Queen and Parliament . . .'. This brought the house down, though he wasn't elected.

Teachers should be careful not to abuse their position by attempting to influence pupils over political matters. Even giving a child a 'Vote for X' badge or sticker can be seen in a bad light by parents, governors and the public. Neither should pupils be allowed to put up political posters on school notice-boards or distribute literature of a political nature.

Attempts have been made by organizations such as the National Union of School Students and the National Front to influence school pupils, either by attempting direct entry using members of the school, or distributing literature outside the gates. If pupils wish to belong to such groups then that is a matter for themselves and their parents but a school would certainly be within its rights to ban their activities inside the school boundaries and to discipline any pupil who disobeyed. Activities outside the school gates are a different matter. As we have seen, the school may use disciplinary measures against its own pupils for incidents outside school but it has no powers against other parties.

The police may be able to help. It is an offence against public order for a person in a public place to use threatening, abusive or insulting behaviour or to display or distribute literature or writing which is threatening, abusive or insulting with an intent to commit a breach of the peace or where a breach of the peace is likely to occur. If racial hatred is likely to be stirred up by such conduct then it is an offence. The publications of some groups could certainly be said to do so. School premises are not a 'public place' – a street is.

11 Defamation, records and references

11.1 A quartet of case studies

Consider the following incidents and write your comments in the boxes below. Each case will be assessed at the end of the chapter.

Maria Marten

The teacher, Mr Redbarn, wrote on Maria's report:

'This girl is thoroughly lazy and dishonest. She often fails to do her homework and tells lies to excuse herself. Her low standard in English may be due to the bad teaching in her previous school but she makes no effort to improve.'

The head received a long, rambling letter from Mrs Marten. Here is an extract to give the flavour of it:

'A lot of overpaid layabouts who don't try to help kids and only think of drinking in the staffroom, beer too I expect. They don't know the answers themselves. That's why they don't teach properly. . . . And another thing you tell that teacher to leave Maria alone. She says he keeps on touching her where it's not nice. . . .

The head showed the letter to the teacher but did not reply immediately. The teacher, somewhat tactlessly, said something to Maria about the rude letter received from her mother.

Mrs Marten came into school the next day with all guns firing. The head took her into his office. She demanded to see the teacher and the head refused so the broadside was turned on him. His competence, his parentage and his morals were all commented upon loudly and unfavourably and finally Mrs Marten departed, threatening to contact the police, the Chief Education Officer, her MP and 'Watchdog' on the television.

Norman Charles Mentis

Norman was creating severe behaviour problems in school. He was a very backward boy of ten who had a reading age of 6.5. He was absent from school frequently and when chided in any way by teachers he would burst into tears. On several occasions when other children teased him or he had been told off by a teacher he had run home.

He was referred to the educational psychologist and here is an extract from the school's report:

'Norman does not get on well with other children. He cries easily and is the subject of bullying. A number of small items, such as pencils and sweets, have gone missing from his class and he is suspected of petty thieving.

His mother is over-protective and supports his frequent absences with feeble excuses. There is no evidence of a father. Mrs Mentis says that he works away but local gossip has it that he is either "inside" or in a mental home. We suspect the latter. Norman himself behaves very erratically at times, claiming that "they" are going to get him. When asked who "they" are he becomes silent or gives a knowing look and says "Ah!". . . .'

Mr Irving

Mr Irving took up duties as a history master at a comprehensive school. It was his first post. He discovered that his predecessor had been a Mr Van Winkle who had left under a cloud having failed his probation. Mr Van Winkle had had disciplinary problems. He seemed to have been unable to prevent pupils from leaving his classroom by means of the windows and thus escaping over the roof-tops.

The head of the history department was a man who spoke his mind and when Mr Irving was teaching he entered the room and said in a loud voice that the work of the class was dreadful and this was largely due to the poor teaching received from Mr Van Winkle, who couldn't string two sentences together himself. If they worked hard, with Mr Irving's help all would be well.

Mr Irving was embarrassed but the comments reflected the feelings of both the pupils and their parents.

Mr Saggermaker

Mr Saggermaker, a pottery specialist in the school's art department, had applied for a post as second in the art department of another school. Here is an extract from the head's confidential report, written on request from the other school:

'Mr Saggermaker came to us three years ago as a potter of exceptional talent and a promising young teacher. His personal output of pottery is prodigiously high and his work features in national exhibitions. He is frequently absent from school for health reasons.

As a teacher, Mr Saggermaker promised much but has achieved little. With a few talented pupils he has produced excellent pieces of work but he is not successful with pupils of less ability. He tends to concentrate on the interested few and allows the others to amuse themselves by throwing clay at the walls of his room. As you will gather, discipline is poor and has improved little during his time here.

In school Mr Saggermaker is popular both with pupils and colleagues. He is a courteous and pleasant young man. Outside school he is, apparently, living with a married woman who has left her husband.'

11.2 Defamation

The writing of letters, reports and references relating to parents, pupils and colleagues are frequent occurrences in the busy life of any teacher. So are encounters of a verbal kind. The law as it relates to defamation may be significant in all such matters.

There is no such thing as a 'free' country, if by 'free' we indicate the right to do exactly as one pleases. The rights of individuals have to be balanced against the overall needs of the society they live in and being a member of any society necessarily involves restrictions of some sort on individuals. Ours is a 'free' country by comparison, say, with Russia but this does not mean that our vaunted right of free speech allows us to say anything we like, where we like or when we like. Our society believes that no man's reputation should be ruined by others making false statements about him. The law of defamation is his defence.

Winfield defines defamation as: 'The publication of a statement which tends to lower a person in the estimation of right thinking members of society generally, or which tends to make them shun or avoid that person.' This definition needs to be examined carefully.

Publication

This simply means that the defamatory statement must be communicated to a third party. If a teacher keeps a child behind in the classroom alone and makes defamatory statements about him, they have not been published. If a head calls a member of staff into his office and makes a defamatory statement about him to his face, it has not been published. If a parent writes a defamatory letter to a teacher it has not been published but, if the letter is addressed to the head and makes references to the teacher, then publication has taken place.

Publication does not take place in communications between husband and wife about a third party. Thus, if a head were interviewing a mother and father the parents could say anything they liked to each other about the head – such remarks would not be actionable. If the head passed a remark about the husband in the wife's presence that could be actionable, since publication would have taken place.

A post-card is always published since the postman, or others, could possibly have read what was on it. What about a letter, addressed to a head and opened and read by the school secretary, which contained a defamatory statement relating to the head? It seems reasonable for anyone to be aware that a secretary will open the mail and thus publication will have taken place. If, however, the letter was marked PRIVATE AND CONFIDENTIAL then the opening of the letter by the secretary would probably be an unauthorized act and thus publication would not have taken place.

Each separate publication gives rise to a new source of action so the repetition of a defamatory statement is always actionable.

Statement

The statement must be a false one. If the statement is true then that is a complete defence in normal circumstances. The statement may be in words, writing or gestures. It may also be by innuendo. Suppose a teacher discovered two boys who had stolen sweets from others and brought them to the front of the class and told everyone about the incident. If he then called on another boy to come and join the two culprits he would be implying that boy no. 3 was a thief, even if he did not say so in so many words.

Right thinking members of society

Who are these worthy folk? They are ordinary, decent, law-abiding citizens. In one famous case it was held that to criticize a man for giving information to the police regarding a breach of the law could not be defamatory. It is the citizen's moral duty to do so and right thinking members of society would applaud him.

11.3 Libel

There are two kinds of defamation – libel and slander. Libel is defamation in a permanent form; slander is defamation in a transitory form. The most obvious form of libel is in printing or writing. A child's report, a comment on a reference for a teacher, a remark in a letter from a parent to a teacher, or vice versa, will be libel. Words daubed on a wall with an aerosol will be libel. A famous test case in 1934 decided that a talking film was libel. The position over radio, television broadcasts and tape recordings is not so clear. The Defamation Act of 1952 makes it clear that programmes put out generally for all to hear on radio programmes or television broadcasts are to be considered as permanent in form – and therefore libel. The Act did not cover closed transmission as between radio 'hams' or police cars. It could not have foreseen closed circuit television, the use of video tape recorders and CB radio, so issues over these remain as yet undecided. Under the Theatres Act of 1968 the publication of statements in a theatrical performance is considered to be libel. So a school production lampooning local worthies would be in that category.

11.4 Slander

Slander is defamation in an impermanent form. Usually, this is by word of mouth but gestures may also constitute slander. A teacher who called a pupil 'an illiterate ignoramus' in front of his classmates would be liable in slander – though he might well have a good case for saying that the statement was true. A teacher who called a colleague 'an incompetent nincompoop' in front of colleagues or pupils would be in the same position.

11.5 Differences between libel and slander

The reader may well be wondering why all this fuss is made in establishing two categories of defamation. The differences between them are very important in law.

Libel is a tort that is actionable *per se*. This means that it is actionable in itself without any proof of damage. Thus, if one teacher writes a defamatory statement relating to another and publishes this then the other teacher may bring an action for damages whether the publication has caused him any real harm or not. Slander is only actionable, however, if the plaintiff can prove that he suffered some damage. There are exceptions to this, however, where slander is actionable *per se* and one in particular is of great importance to teachers:

1 A suggestion that the plaintiff has committed an offence for which the punishment is imprisonment. Since theft is such an offence, to call a pupil a thief is slander but is actionable without proof of damage. Teachers are particularly careless in the use of the word 'thief' when questioning pupils.
2 A suggestion that a woman is unchaste or has committed adultery (no such rule relating to men, you notice!). Again, staff questioning senior girl pupils need to be careful here.
3 A suggestion that the plaintiff has a disease of such a nature that others will avoid him. There appear to be no modern cases on this aspect but in the past venereal disease, plague and leprosy have all been held to be covered by this rule. Perhaps if a teacher told a class that one pupil had eczema and they should keep away from him this might be actionable.
4 A suggestion that the plaintiff is incompetent or unfit to carry on his trade, profession or calling. Before the Defamation Act of 1952 this rule was a very strict one and the statement had to refer clearly to the functions of the office itself. So, in a case in 1919, where a schoolmaster was alleged to have had an adulterous relationship with a school cleaner, it was held that

damage had to be proved. Today, however, any statement likely to injure a teacher's good name as a professional person would be actionable without proof of damage.

For teachers the rule is important since it means that parents who pass comments on a teacher's competence to third parties will be laying themselves open to an action for damages.

11.6 What has to be proved

The burden of proof is on the plaintiff. To bring an action in defamation he must show that the statement was untrue in fact and that it was defamatory in the sense of Winfield's definition above i.e. that it made decent people think badly of him. He must show that the statement referred to him and this may be by innuendo. He must show that it was the defendant who published the statement. Where necessary he must prove damage has resulted.

Can there be defamation of a group of persons? If a parent writes a letter to the education authority alleging that all the staff of a particular school are incompetent layabouts, or stands up at a parents' meeting and voices a similar opinion, can anything be done?

Statements about a class of persons cannot usually lead to an action in defamation. To publish a statement that all teachers are incompetent could not lead to actions by teachers. If, however, the group that was defamed was a small one so that particular individuals might be identified and have their reputations ruined, then each and every one might be able to bring a separate action against the defendant – there could not be a group action.

Actions for defamation are heard in a civil court, either the County Court or the Queen's Bench. Juries are rarely used in civil actions but they may be called to serve in actions for defamation. Where this happens, the judge will decide whether the statement at issue is capable of being defamatory. If he rules that it is, then the function of the jury is to take into account all the relevant facts and decide, in the light of reasonableness, whether the statement amounted to defamation in this particular case or not.

The common law remedy for a successful action is damages. At the court's discretion the equitable remedy of an injunction might be used to prevent a defendant from repeating a defamatory statement e.g. by reprinting an article or a book.

11.7 Defences

There are various defences that may be put up in answer to an action in defamation.

Justification

If the defendant can prove that the statement is true, then that is a complete defence. The defamatory statement does not have to be true in its entirety. If it is substantially true then that will be enough. If the defendant has made a number of statements and almost all of them are true then this will also amount to justification. A child's report containing a number of defamatory statements regarding his honesty or reliability would be justified, even though in one isolated case it could be shown that the statement was incorrect.

Consent

If the defendant has consented to the publication of the defamatory statement e.g. agreed to an article or a cartoon being published in a school magazine then he will not succeed in his action. The defence here is basically the same as in an action for negligence, discussed earlier.

Fair comment on a matter of public interest

In this country our freedom of speech allows us to be very critical of government, authority generally, politicians, celebrities in the world of sport and entertainment and so on. 'Public interest' is taken as a very broad term and means any activity in which the public has a right to be interested – not just those concerns in which it is actually involved. This defence would certainly be available to someone publishing defamatory statements about an education authority or one of its schools.

The comment, however, must be one of opinion and not of fact, though the difference is not always easy to define. 'The headmaster is a thief' is a statement of fact, since a thief is one who has been convicted of theft by a properly constituted court of law. 'I consider Miss A is a better teacher of English than Miss B' is a statement of opinion but into which category would we place 'the headmaster is inefficient'? A court hearing would be needed in order to decide.

The comment must be fair, that is it must be based on facts that are true, or which the defendant genuinely believes to be true, and the view, in the light of all the evidence, must be an honest expression of opinion. It is not for the court to agree or disagree with that opinion, only to decide whether the defendant made it in all honesty.

If there is evidence that the defendant has shown malice in making his comment then that will make negative the defence. A parent who asked for his child to be moved from Class B to Class A and was refused and who then bombarded the local press with defamatory statements about the general conduct of the school might be said to be acting from a malicious motive.

Parents who make statements about a school to an education authority, an MP, a local councillor or the media may well use this defence successfully.

Privilege

There are occasions when it is clear that people should be able to express opinions without the fear of legal consequences, where the value of a forthright expression of views should outweigh the protection of individual reputations. Such occasions may be protected by the defence of privilege – either absolute or qualified.

Absolute privilege

Here the person who makes the defamatory statement has complete immunity, even if he acts maliciously, even if the statement is untrue.

All statements made in Parliament are covered by this defence. Parliament may take its own disciplinary proceedings against its members who defame others but there can be no redress in the law courts. Recently an MP made allegations in the House regarding an employee of Rolls Royce. He would not repeat his remarks outside the House, though he later withdrew them. The Rolls Royce man could take no legal action.

Absolute privilege also covers all papers published by order of Parliament. It also applies to statements made in judicial proceedings by judge, jury, parties, lawyers and witnesses but the comments must be in relation to the case before the court. Thus, statements made on a report prepared by a school for a juvenile court hearing would be protected absolutely.

Fair and accurate reports of court proceedings in newspapers, on radio or television, are protected, if they are made near the time of the trial but not if made at some considerable time afterwards.

Qualified privilege

It seems right to restrict absolute privilege to very few instances but there are many other situations where it also seems fair for people who have a right or duty to make statements to have some measure of protection. These situations are covered by qualified privilege.

The difference between the two types of privilege is that if it can be shown that the defendant acted with malice or that the statement was published more widely than was necessary, then the defence of qualified privilege will not hold, whereas absolute privilege has no restrictions.

Accurate reports on parliamentary proceedings and extracts from parliamentary papers are covered. So are reports of public meetings and meetings of local authority committees, either in newspapers, on the radio or on television. So are any reports of judicial proceedings which are not covered by absolute privilege. So is the statement made to protect an interest, particularly a public interest. A complaint made to an education authority that a teacher was not obeying its instructions in some way would be an example. It was allowed in one case where a statement was made to a bishop alleging that one of his vicars had had a fight with a local schoolmaster.

Mostly, however, this defence is used by those who have a legal, social or moral duty to make comments to another party concerning the third party. It is this defence that would be available to teachers in several situations if they were sued for damages in defamation.

As with most torts, in defamation it is open for anyone to sue or be sued. Teachers regularly make reports on pupils. These will be published as soon as they are read by other teachers, parents, prospective employers or by colleges or universities to whom they are addressed. If the report would make normal sensible people think badly of the pupil (and many are bound to do so) then the statements may be defamatory and the pupil may have a cause of action.

Consider the following: 'John's behaviour in class is very bad. He is a liar and has been caught cheating in tests.'

Strong stuff, but the teacher does have a duty to be frank with parents. If he does go as far as this then, in all fairness, he should be sure of his facts. There should be clear evidence of John's lies and of his cheating in class. Nevertheless, if the teacher is mistaken, or cannot provide concrete evidence to back up his comments, it will still be incumbent on John, through his parent, to prove that the statement was made maliciously.

Or this:

'As regards John's application to you for the post of trainee railway porter, I have to say that it seems to me that he is quite unsuitable. In the first place, although I can produce no clear evidence of theft having been committed, he has certainly been suspected of it. I could not recommend him to be trusted with the handling of property. In the second place, he is a very insolent boy. He adopts this attitude towards most people and would be likely to do so towards members of the public. He has been extremely rude to me personally and, frankly, I hope he does not obtain employment as he does not deserve to.'

Again, the school has a duty to be frank with employers. An ill-mannered youth who cannot be trusted with property is clearly unsuitable to carry out the duties of railway porter. However, this report does seem to contain malice.

Malice may show itself in several ways. It may lie in spreading the statement further than is necessary – if the teacher had shown his comments to persons other than British Rail e.g. colleagues in the staffroom, or even other pupils, then that could be malicious. The most obvious sign of malice, though, is personal spite. Here there is possible evidence of malice in the statement that John is suspected of theft, though the writer does make it clear that he is giving an opinion and actual theft has not been proved. His final statement, however, is clearly spite – the hope that John fails to obtain any job at all because of the rudeness the teacher has suffered at John's hands. The teacher may think John will not find employment but to say so in this way is vindictive. The defence of qualified privilege would not be available in such a situation.

Senior staff, particularly heads, are often quoted as referees and asked to write reports on other teachers who apply for posts elsewhere. Usually, of course, the teacher does not see such reports since they are confidential. The open testimonial, once required for all teaching posts, has now almost disappeared. No one seemed to have a bad one!

Sometimes the teacher may discover that the contents of a confidential report are not favourable towards him. In one instance a clerk in an education office placed such a report in a wrong envelope and the teacher received a report on himself through the post. If this should happen, then the writer also has the defence of qualified privilege. If he wrote the report in good faith and without malice then he will not be liable, even if, in fact, he has made a false statement in error which is defamatory.

Who decides whether a defamatory statement contains malice and therefore the defence of qualified privilege may not be used? The answer, again, is the jury of ordinary men and women taking a common-sense approach and bearing in mind all the relevant details in the case.

Earlier, it was stated that a complaint by a parent to an education authority would be protected by qualified privilege. Could a parent use such a defence to an action in defamation for remarks made in a letter to a head concerning disquiet over the teaching of his child by a particular member of staff? I would think so, though the courts have never considered the matter. It is in the public interest for the school to be run efficiently and the parent and head have a common interest in arranging efficient education for the child.

Unintentional defamation

Under the Defamation Act of 1952, Section 4, where there has been an unintentional defamation then this may be put forward as a defence. This defence may be used where the defamation was made innocently and all reasonable care was taken to avoid its publication. It may not be used where a statement was made recklessly, without regard as to whether it was true or not.

It may be used when the publisher did not intend to publish the words relating to the plaintiff and did not know of the circumstances in which they might be taken as referring to him. It may also be used where the words themselves were not defamatory on the face of it but could become so because of circumstances of which a publisher was unaware. If the defence is put forward, the defendant must offer to make a correction and an apology – this is called an offer of amends. The offer must be accompanied by a sworn statement (an affidavit) of the facts on which he relies to show that the publication was innocent. An effort must be made to retrieve copies of the offending statement and inform those who have received them already that the statement is alleged to be defamatory.

If the offer of amends is accepted then that settles the case. If not, then the offer is put forward as a defence.

Abuse

In everyday encounters people use words, either in a jocular or angry fashion, which could be defamatory if their true meaning was intended by a speaker, or interpreted as such by the hearer. It is well accepted in law, however, that 'mere vulgar abuse' does not constitute defamation. Abuse of this kind occurs as a part of general statements made in haste or colloquial usage and understood as such by those who hear them.

Suppose a teacher was driven to desperation by a badly behaved class and one boy in particular was causing trouble. Suppose the teacher lost control, turned on the boy and shouted at him, 'Shut up, you horrible little bastard!'. Since a bastard is someone born out of wedlock and, even today, the term carries some stigma with it, is the teacher's statement slanderous?

Certainly, it could be. The judge would be bound to declare that 'bastard' is capable of being defamatory. It would then be up to the jury to decide if, in the light of common sense and all the circumstances, the teacher meant to convey that the boy was illegitimate and meant the rest of the class to understand this. The teacher would be most unlikely to lose.

Do not take this as a licence to say all those things to pupils that one would like to! The unpleasantness of the publicity surrounding a defamation case would be nerve-racking. Also, to swear at pupils would undoubtedly be unprofessional conduct and could lead to disciplinary proceedings by an education authority.

Libel, by the way, can never be mere vulgar abuse since it is presumed that the writer or publisher has had sufficient time in which to consider the words he is using.

11.8 Rehabilitation of Offenders Act 1974

Schools may have noticed that when asked for references over candidates for some posts a note is enclosed with the request giving a short extract from this Act.

The Act was passed in order to assist in the rehabilitation of offenders by banning references to convictions that are 'spent'. This means that where offenders have received sentences which do not exceed thirty months' imprisonment, and where a specified time has elapsed, they must be treated as if they had never been committed, charged, prosecuted, convicted or sentenced at all. The time runs from the conviction and varies from five to ten years according to the sentence. The rehabilitation periods are halved for persons under seventeen years.

The Act means that once the specified time has elapsed in general a convicted person need not disclose details of his conviction on applications for insurance, credit, employment, etc. He does not have to disclose such information in a civil court unless the judge decides it is necessary in order for justice to be done. There are other exceptions to his right not to disclose.

Many of these concern applications for posts involving contact with young or vulnerable people – teaching in schools or colleges of further education; serving as a nurse or in some other capacity which involves contact with patients; work in Social Services which involves contact with the handicapped or young persons; work in the Careers Service involving contact with persons under eighteen; working with youth organizations; and serving as a policeman or a probation officer. In all these cases, convictions must be disclosed when applying for appointment, if the applicant is told that he must do so.

As far as the writing of reports and references are concerned the writer does not have to disclose spent convictions and is under no liability to the addressee if he fails to do so. He may do so, however, if he believes it is his duty and may use the defence of qualified privilege if such publication leads to an action in defamation. This may, of course, be rebutted by evidence of malice, which will apply even if the statement were true.

11.9 Reports on pupils

The school will often have to write reports on pupils that will go outside the school and it will also need to keep its own internal reports.

External reports

Such reports will go to parents at least once a year. In the past the standard method was a single sheet or a number of separate sheets collected in the form of a book, often beautifully printed with the school's name and crest on the front. The report was completed by subject teachers and one narrow line was left for each one with room for a class position, mark, brief comment and signature. The comment was brief too – 'average', 'excellent', 'needs to try harder' – vague phrases that could hardly raise the faintest glimmer of a legal problem. There was often a small box at the foot for a brief summing up of work and behaviour by the form teacher plus a comment by the head. The report gave a general idea of the pupil's standard of work and progress, but little else.

Today, schools use a variety of systems but a greater effort is made to give parents a picture of the pupil's standard of work, amount of effort and performance in relation to others in his class. One method used in many secondary schools is to have a separate self-carbonized small slip for each subject with enough room for the teacher to discuss in some detail the problems a child is encountering in the subject, suggestions for improvement and an explanation of his attitude towards the work. A separate slip is included for comments by pastoral staff. The slips are collected and stapled into a small booklet after the copy slips have been collected together to form a school record. The advantages of the system are that each school has its own slips printed according to its own needs; each subject teacher has enough room for a full discussion of each pupil; there is no time-lag in waiting for other staff to complete reports; parents have a copy that may be kept; and the school has a record of each child's report.

Such a scheme may easily be adapted for primary school use. Some primary schools now give reports to parents in the form of an open letter discussing a pupil's work, effort, attitude and behaviour.

Reports of this kind are valuable for parents but impose greater burdens on teachers. Not only must they be careful over their own spelling, grammar and punctuation, but they must think carefully over the actual statements made and the implications that arise. If the report contains defamatory statements then the defence of qualified privilege may be used, of course, but this will not hold if the statement was made maliciously.

The best safeguard is to have senior members of staff who check all reports. Hopefully, they will pick up the errors of style and also any tactless and ill-considered statements. These reports could then be discussed with the teachers concerned and rectified. If a teacher felt that changes were not justified then the matter could go to the head as final arbitrator.

External reports may be required for court hearings (discussed earlier) and

PUPIL'S REPORT

The grades which appear in this report are briefly explained below:

Effort	Attainment
A - Excellent	A - Exceptionally high standard
B - Good	B - Good work
C - Satisfactory	C - A reasonable standard
D - Not working hard enough	D - A low standard
E - Very poor	E - Exceptionally low

Grades will indicate pupil's performance within the teaching group, and do not indicate performance compared to the whole year. They should not be used as a basis on which to predict external examination success.

Name JOHN SMITH Form 31C Set

Subject HISTORY

Effort A Attainment C

John has worked very hard indeed since entering the Third Year, but has found some of the historical information difficult to master. He successfully handles the factual content of the course, but tends to struggle when required to elicit general ideas from a mass of information. Frequently his selection of material in answering essays is poor and often irrelevant. This is the major aspect of his work which will need careful attention in the future.

Subject Teacher M.A. Cane

Form Teacher's Comments

Name John Smith Attendance 318/322

John is a conscientious pupil who has worked hard in all his subjects, but the reports also reveal some problems which will need careful attention if his hard work is to receive just reward. John has continued to play an active part in the general life of the school and has represented the school at rugby and basketball. He has also proved an efficient form representative on the Year Council.

Form Teacher B. W. Morgan

A pleasing report. Well done, John.

Year Teacher [illegible signature]

although these are covered by absolute privilege it needs to be remembered that parents have a right to know the contents and in some areas it is the practice to show them the actual wording.

Other reports will usually be of a confidential nature. Where a child is referred to an educational psychologist, to a child psychiatrist or even to a medical specialist, a report will be needed. The most common of these will be the one written as part of a referral to an educational psychologist. Here the school is attempting to give the psychologist a picture of the child, his relationships with his fellows and teachers, his home background and a description of his problems. The report will contain facts but it will undoubtedly also contain a certain amount of opinion and feeling which is essential if the psychologist is ever to get to the heart of the problem. Such reports will be covered by qualified privilege.

Here is a report on the imaginary Dennis Noone:

'Dennis Noone is now in the middle of his first year with us, having come from Little Downside Primary School. He came to us with an IQ score of 87, a maths quotient of 82 and an English quotient of 80. His reading age was 9.2. His primary school felt that he was underachieving because of absence. They had wished to refer him to the educational psychologist but as his mother was opposed to this they had not done so. Dennis reacted badly to his transfer to a large secondary school. He was placed in a small class of slow learners but his attendance began to deteriorate from the start. There have always been written excuses from Mrs Noone. Usually they have been trivial – a cold, or having missed the bus because of oversleeping. After a few weeks with us Dennis ran out of school, after he had been mildly rebuked by a teacher, and walked home (about three miles away). His mother rang to say that he had done so. There have been several similar episodes, always because of criticism from a teacher or taunts from other pupils in class and in the playground. There is no evidence of real physical bullying.

We have had contacts with Mrs Noone through the EWO. She has visited the school on several occasions and seems most anxious to co-operate. She has consented to this referral. There is a Mr Noone but he remains a shadowy figure. He has not been seen and, according to Mrs Noone, he works away from home a good deal. The grapevine suggests that there is no Mr Noone in any kind of residence at all.

Mrs Noone herself is a large and emotional lady who has, on each occasion, emphasized her affection for the boy, stressed his frail condition (his medical report does not support this) and frequent illnesses and finally burst into tears. On one occasion she let slip that Dennis still shares her bed. We feel that she is over-protective of Dennis and over-anxious and this may be communicating itself to the boy.

Miss Robinson, his form teacher, is a sympathetic person who has tried to establish a relationship with Dennis. While he is not rude, she feels that he resents her attempts to be friendly and prefers to remain alone. He has no friends and while the other children do not shun him he seems to resent any overtures so they leave him to his own devices. His work, when in school, is adequate but he makes no great effort, being content to stare out of the window if allowed to do so. Miss Robinson says that she perceives sparks of intelligence at times and feels that he is under-achieving.'

External reports will also be required for pupils when applying for jobs and for entry to further and higher education courses. Usually, such reports require answers to specific questions and these will vary according to the demands of particular institutions so that the format of the report is already dictated. Those for higher education courses will give the greatest scope for the school's initiative but in all there is a need to ensure that an attempt is made to give an objective assessment of a pupil's strengths, weaknesses, achievements in school and potential for the future, concentrating on performance during the last year at school. Again, all such reports will be protected by qualified privilege.

When older pupils or ex-pupils wish to open bank accounts they often name the school as a referee, certifying that the pupil is the sort of person to whom normal banking facilities may be allowed. It is perfectly in order for the head or any teacher to sign such a reference, providing that it is not known that the pupil has been involved in theft or some kind of fraudulent activity. In doubtful cases the answer is to refuse altogether or to include some phrase such as 'to the best of my knowledge . . .'. A person who certified the trustworthiness of another, knowing of criminal convictions, could be liable to the bank in negligence, if the bank suffered a financial loss.

Sometimes pupils still ask for open testimonials. There is no obligation on a school to provide such a document – the pupil can always be told to use his final report. An open testimonial is vague and of comparatively little value since it

Do not detach this page

Confidential statement by referee (first read page 6 overleaf)

Name A. E. WILLIAMSON

Post/~~occupation~~/~~relationship~~ HEAD OF SIXTH FORM

Address

Telephone (including STD code)

Type of school or college		COMPREHENSIVE
Number on roll	Full-time	1200
	Part-time	
Number in Sixth form (upper plus lower) or equivalent group		110
Number normally proceeding to university each year		18

This form will be photographed and smaller copies made: please type with a good black ribbon or write in black ink on this side of the form only, within the frame. Typing is very much preferred. No continuation sheets can be accepted.

Name of candidate (*block capitals or type*) JACK SMITH

Jack's excellent Ordinary Level results give a fair reflection of his ability and motivation and his Advanced level studies suggest he has a promising academic future. At present he has no clear idea of a future vocation but his choice of History as a first degree course is a very suitable one for a boy with an open, enquiring, disciplined mind. Below are some comments made by subject staff on the boy's work in the Lower Sixth.

History

Possesses a very fluent style and has an excellent memory and recall. Very good at producing synthesis of ideas and prepared to challenge accepted ideas. He is sound at evaluating evidence and in producing argumentative essays which call for the weighing up of divergent ideas. Expected grade: A.

English

Displays good understanding and clear, orderly essay expression and organisation. Work is always thorough and allusions testify to wide reading and the ability to apply it to deepen his understanding. At present he needs a little more maturity, and confidence in his critical ability when dealing with unseen passages. Expected grade: B.

Mathematics

He makes excellent use of previously learned methods and has the ability and imagination to devise original approaches and solutions to unfamiliar problems. Extremely quick to grasp new ideas and concepts and their implications. He has a wide, intelligent interest in the subject andhe discusses problems in a clear, fluent manner. Expected grade: A.

Jack has made an excellent contribution to General Studies lessons. He is positive in his attitude and his dry sense of humour has enlivened and stimulated many classes. Jack has a deep interest in classical music and he is an active member of the School orchestra and choir. He has a pleasant confident manner and he has been an effective Deputy Head Boy and Captain of the School Rugby team.

Jack is a mature, courteous boy and he will readily adjust to the demands and benefits of life and study at University.

Jack's health has always been good and he comes from an interested home background.

Sections 6 and 7 checked: Yes/~~No~~

Signed A. E. Williamson

Applicant's fee enclosed: Yes/~~No~~

Date

The referee is asked to return this completed form, with the applicant's fee attached, to UCCA without delay. See page 6 for closing dates.

Page 3

cannot be directed at a specific job. If a teacher gives such a document he should beware of using terms such as 'trustworthy' if he cannot in all sincerity do so. Liability can certainly arise from untrue or negligent misstatements.

11.10 Comments from parents

A parent certainly has a right to comment on the education his child is receiving. He may make such comment verbally or in writing to the teacher, to the head or to the education authority, to his MP and through him to the ombudsman. He may write to newspapers or comment on radio or television. All this is permissible providing his views are couched in moderate terms and can be construed as fair comment on a matter of public interest.

When a parent makes personal attacks on individual teachers, however, he is on dangerous ground. Slanging matches at parents' evenings are rare but unpleasant. They do, however, create the easiest situation in which an action for defamation may arise – others are certain to be within earshot and therefore the slanderous statements would certainly be published and, if they referred to a teacher's professional ability, no damage would have to be proved.

The most monstrous statement can be made to a teacher within the confines of a small office and the slander will not have been published. Neither will it be actionable if the defamatory statement is libel contained in a sealed letter addressed personally to the teacher.

If the statement is made to the head about a teacher then it will have been published, if it is made to the head about the head and no one else is present then it will not be actionable, neither will it be so if it refers to the head and is in writing and delivered to the head personally. It may be published if it is opened by a secretary.

A statement made to any person outside school or a letter written to anyone other than the teacher concerned will, of course, be published.

The best advice to teachers on the receiving end of defamatory statements is not to become involved in a legal action if that can be avoided. Most parents who say things in the heat of the moment, even in writing, are sorry for it afterwards. Where it is felt that some action must be taken then the best course is to consult a solicitor. Teacher associations will take up a case and the larger ones retain the services of local solicitors who will give advice at the association's expense and write a letter of warning to the parent.

11.11 Others with an interest

Since education is financed from public funds then presumably the public generally has a right to comment in a reasonable way on the service that is provided, but not to make personal attacks on individual teachers. School governors certainly have a right to make comments on schools and possibly on individual members of the teaching staff if they can show a close knowledge of the working of the school for which they are reponsible. In one case it was held that the secretary of an old boys' association (he was also a parent) had a right to criticize a teacher to pupils. The court held that he had done so for the good of the school and, as he had not acted maliciously, the defence of qualified privilege would be allowed.

The media always have an interest, particularly if something happens in a school which can make banner headlines and suggest torture, abuse of power, drugs or sex. I always feel that this may be a reflection on the kind of schooldays experienced by editors and reporters themselves – though no doubt it sells copy, particularly in the immediate locality of the school. This was brought home to me when, a short while ago, a girl who had just left my sixth form was murdered in a town a few miles away, after being sexually assaulted. For days we were besieged by callers from major national newspapers both in person and on the telephone hoping it seemed to find some suggestion that the poor girl had been promiscuous or at least had had an unusual number of boyfriends.

Newspaper reports which contain defamatory statements may put up the defences of qualified privilege or fair comment – the latter in articles about schools. Newspapers are usually well experienced in just how far to go to avoid legal action but there are examples of teachers succeeding in cases against them.

Mr Hardwick and the infant's trousers

Julie, aged six, came to a school infants' Christmas party dressed in a trouser suit. The head, Mr Hardwick, did not allow pupils to come to school dressed in this fashion (shades of *Spiers* v. *Warrington Corporation*!) and sent her home to change. The pupils had been told not to come dressed in such a fashion. She did not come back to school so the head said she could attend the juniors' party on the next day instead and she did so.

Julie's mother contacted the *Daily Express* which published an article under the heading 'NO TROUSERS – THE HEAD BANS JULIE, 6, FROM SCHOOL CHRISTMAS PARTY' and included posed photographs of Julie. A further article at a later date also discussed the affair and the paper refused to apologize to Mr Hardwick.

He considered that the articles made him out to be something of a martinet, to be narrow-minded and unreasonable and presented an unfair picture both of himself and the way he ran his school.

The court said that a trivial incident had been deliberately blown up into something of importance by the newspaper and awarded Mr Hardwick damages of £1000. *Hardwick* v. *Daily Express* (1972).

How should a school handle relations with the media? In moderation, publicity of a favourable kind is good for the school's image, interesting for parents and good for the morale of pupils since it fosters a pride in their own establishment. A willingness to give information relating to the work of the school and the successes of pupils is always appreciated by the local press, who are often short of material. A school which is ready to co-operate in this way will then usually receive sympathetic treatment when an ugly situation develops – a school which keeps the press at arm's length may not be so fortunate.

A suggested method is to have a member of staff designated as press officer – in a small school the head will probably act as such himself. Staff are then asked to submit items which they consider worthwhile to the press officer and he will keep an eye open for school events which would make good news stories. Sports results, individual successes, plays, concerts, charity work, community service, fund-raising efforts, new equipment and teaching methods and school visits are all items that deserve recognition and help parents to understand more of the life of the school. The press officer then collects such items together, say on a monthly basis, and sends a newssheet to the various local papers, allowing them to take up any further items that interest them.

When a crisis occurs and the national newspapers and TV cameramen move in then life becomes more difficult. If the school refuses to discuss the matter, bans reporters from the premises and hides behind a 'no comment' screen, then views will inevitably be sought from others – parents at home perhaps or pupils interviewed as they leave the school – and this may distort the picture even more. The refusal to comment may also suggest that there is something to hide. Silence may be the best course but the issue of a carefully worded statement giving the facts of the situation without the use of emotive language could be a big help in diffusing the situation. Talking to reporters over the phone should always be avoided, they will be rapidly making notes in shorthand and throwing out leading questions at the same time. Invite them into school, make a clear simple statement and then shut up.

Where the situation is likely to reflect on the staff or school or authority no admission should be made and individual teachers are advised to consult their professional association. The head should be in touch with his chairman of governors and the education authority.

11.12 Reports on staff

As with pupils, the reports may be internal or external.

Internal

Apart from one or two unusual establishments, pupils in schools do not write reports on their teachers though it might be a salutary experience for some staff if this happened. It is not often that the staff are asked to report on their colleagues but it may be necessary in some instances.

The head of department may be expected to write a report on the work of his department or may be asked to give a verbal report to his headteacher. This will often require a mention of staffing problems and may involve comments on individual colleagues. By communication to the head such comments are published and thus actionable, though certainly the defence of qualified privilege would be available. It was held to apply in a case where a senior member of staff in a boarding school reported to the headmaster on the drunken habits of a junior member of staff. The NUT, and perhaps other associations, consider it to be unprofessional for one teacher to make a report on another without acquainting him of the contents of it. Senior staff need to be careful and tactful in these situations. Staffing problems have to be discussed – perhaps they are best dealt with in an informal way unless the position is such that disciplinary procedures are being contemplated. If this is the case, then the adverse comments should be recorded officially and put clearly to the teacher. Where disciplinary procedures are undertaken then the head will, of course, need to make full reports to the governors and the education authority in accordance with the regulations described in an earlier chapter. Again, such reports have the protection of qualified privilege.

The position over teachers on probation is simple enough. The onus is on the teacher to prove himself capable. The school has a duty to assist as far as it can and it must prepare reports (usually three) on which a decision may be taken by the authority as to whether the teacher should pass probation or not. In a large school a senior member of staff should be designated as having responsibility for probationers and he should prepare the reports in consultation with heads of departments. The contents of the reports should be made known to the teacher and, if he is in danger of failing his probation, this should be made clear to him together with the reasons and suggestions as to how he may put matters right.

External

Apart from reports made to the authority as a part of disciplinary proceedings, mentioned above, external reports will be those on teachers who have applied for posts outside the school.

Open testimonials are now rarely used, though heads and senior staff may be asked occasionally to write one. The usual situation is for a teacher to ask the head or a senior member of staff to act as a referee. It is discourteous to name a person as a referee without asking permission, since he is always at liberty to refuse. When acting as a referee it is certainly not necessary to tell the teacher of the contents of the report, indeed to do so would often detract from the frankness and value of it. Obviously, every effort should be made for accuracy and objectivity but opinion is bound to colour the report to some degree. Even if errors occur or defamatory statements are made qualified privilege will be a defence.

Here is a typical report written about a young primary school teacher applying for a deputy headship:

MISS EYRE

Miss Jane Eyre joined the staff of this six teacher primary school just over three years ago. It was her second post. Previously, she had taught for several years in a primary school at Haworth in Yorkshire and came to us, she said, to broaden her experience and specialize in art and craftwork. She receives a scale 2 post for this.

During her time here Miss Eyre has been form mistress of a mixed group of eight to nine year olds and she has taken them for all general subjects. In addition she has taken all classes in the junior section of the school for craftwork – a double period with each class per week. Her work in general has shown a good grasp of educational principles and she has produced excellent results in most areas, her weakness, if any, being in the teaching of mathematics. I have been particularly impressed with her ability to improve the reading of slower children in her class and the quality of the craftwork (particularly needlecraft) produced by some pupils. Miss Eyre has also helped with our annual field studies week on the Yorkshire moors and the girls' netball team. She is also a member of the PTA committee.

She expects good standards of behaviour from her classes and usually obtains them without a great deal of fuss or shouting. Usually she is sympathetic and friendly but can be very firm if the occasion demands it. The children like and respect her. Her dealings with parents too have been cordial in most cases though there have been one or two occasions when Miss Eyre has had arguments because of her strongly held views over progressive teaching methods – she is particularly interested in free expression methods in English lessons.

Her relationships with colleagues have generally been excellent though her strongly held feminist views have not always gone down well with older members of staff. She puts forward these views forcibly but in a courteous and acceptable manner.

During her time here Miss Eyre has attended various courses on the teaching of reading, child psychology and craftwork in the primary school. At present she is attending an evening course which will eventually lead to a certificate in primary school management.

She is an ambitious young lady with a great deal about her. She has an attractive presence, good voice, pleasant personality and a welcome sense of purpose and order. She would certainly make a good deputy head eventually but perhaps needs a little more experience of handling staff before she is ready for such a move. Nevertheless, I would say she is a candidate well worth interviewing even at this stage.

Edward Rochester, Headmaster

You may like to ask yourself just what this tells us about Miss Eyre, both on the surface and at a deeper level, or perhaps what it tells us about the headmaster!

The reference makes clear Miss Eyre's present position and duties in the school. It comments on her work in the classroom and outside it. It deals with her relationships with pupils, parents, colleagues and the head himself. It indicates her efforts to improve herself as a teacher and assesses her readiness for promotion. There is an attempt to include both her strengths and weaknesses.

If a reference contained nothing but praise one would be suspicious. If it contained nothing but condemnation one would be equally wary. To promote by false praise and to retain by false criticism are both old tricks of the trade used by a few unscrupulous people. Most of us have good and bad points and a reference should be honest enough to show this. Pointers may sometimes be given, of course, by what is omitted rather than by what is said. A reference must mention discipline or class control in some way or the applicant is almost certainly damned.

11.13 Case studies – comments

Now for some comments on the case studies with which we began this chapter.

Maria Marten

Mrs Marten has undoubtedly uttered defamatory statements. She has defamed the teacher who wrote the report (by alleging some kind of sexual assault). She had defamed the entire staff (by suggesting their incompetence and unprofessional conduct). She has defamed the headmaster (by commenting on his professional competence and his parentage). However, the last seems to have been said in his office and unless some one else was in earshot it has not been published so that the head has no cause of action.

While individual members of a small group who are defamed may have a cause of action the statement here is so vague that they are unlikely to succeed unless it was a small school with only two or three staff concerned.

The teacher who wrote the report has a clear cause of action. There is an allegation of the commission of a criminal offence.

Does Maria have an action? The report is strongly worded but unless Maria can prove malice, the defence of qualified privilege will apply here.

Does anyone else have an action? The teacher has very foolishly uttered a defamatory statement regarding Maria's teachers in her previous school so someone there could sue, if he can show that the statement referred to him. It would, of course, be unprofessional to make such a comment.

A further point that arises from this incident is the allegation that Mr Redbarn may have committed a criminal offence. If Mrs Marten does go to the police then there will be a criminal investigation. The head will need to be alive to the possibility of there being some truth in her statement, even if Mrs Marten does not take things further.

Norman Mentis

A report to an educational psychologist that contained only proven facts would be unlikely to give him clues that might lead to a discovery of the nature of a child's problems and thus being able to offer help. The opinions and feelings of teachers regarding his behaviour, his home background, his work and his relationships with others are of considerable importance. Such remarks are clearly protected by qualified privilege. They may even be in the nature of guesses but if they are made honestly, without malice, then even if they are very wide of the mark no action for defamation is likely to succeed.

The comments here are defamatory of Norman (theft) and of Mr Mentis, if he exists, (conviction of a criminal offence or an implication of lunacy). Possibly there is also an innuendo in the last remark that Norman himself is also mentally unstable.

Mr Irving

Most teachers, and certainly all teacher associations, would consider it unprofessional for one teacher to criticize another in front of pupils, colleagues, parents or anyone else for that matter. To do so does not necessarily lead to a liability in defamation though. If the evidence of Mr Winkle's incompetence is as strong as it appears to be, including the failing of his probation, the head of department could plead justification, however tactless we might consider him to be.

The statement is slander, not libel, since it is spoken. It is, however, in one of the excepted categories mentioned earlier in the chapter and so damage would not have to be proved. If Mr Winkle did bring an action it would be sufficient for him to show that his professional ability as a teacher had been wrongly impugned.

Mr Saggermaker

One who is quoted as a referee and is then asked to write a confidential report is certainly entitled to give his opinions frankly and to put forward relevant facts as he understands them. If those facts are incorrect, and if his opinions are obviously wrong, he will still be protected by qualified privilege providing there is no malice – that is he made them honestly, believing them to be true.

The head seems to make at least three statements capable of being defamatory. He implies that Mr Saggermarker pretends to be ill in order to work privately on his own production of pottery. He states that his classroom discipline is bad. He also appears to condemn Mr Saggermaker for adultery with an unknown lady.

If the head honestly believes that the talented potter pretends to be ill in order to carry on with his own work his suggestion is not necessarily malicious. He is entitled, indeed expected, to comment on discipline but if the reference to lumps of clay being thrown at the walls is untrue then that would certainly indicate malice.

What of the potter taken in adultery? Fifty years ago such a comment might have been in order, indeed such facts reported to an authority might well have led to dismissal. Attitudes change. Today, if Mr Saggermaker keeps his sex life out of school then no authority would attempt to dismiss him, unless he was convicted of some kind of sexual assault which could possibly create a hazard in his relationships with pupils. Even if he sets up a ménage with another member of the same staff it is unlikely that any authority would take action. There is no suggestion in the reference that our potter's conduct in school is affected by his love life (though it might have been linked to his absence!) and the statement could well be held to be malicious.

12 Copyright, licensing and lotteries

12.1 Copyright

While most property that one can possess has a physical existence, this is not always so in law. A person can own a right to something or to control the use of something. A cheque is a good example. The paper itself is of no real value, the value lies in the right of the person named as payee to a stated amount of money which will then be debited to the account of the writer of the cheque. The right to the amount of money can even be assigned to another by the payee signing the back of the cheque and handing it to the other person. The cheque is a negotiable instrument and can be transferred from person to person before it is actually paid into a bank.

If I write a poem, paint a picture or compose a piece of music, then I have created something original (however poor it may be) and I then have a legal right to control its use. This is the law of copyright. Copyright does not protect ideas but the vehicle in which they are expressed and that expression is the property of the creator. Like other property copyright may be sold or left to others by will.

Owners of copyright may be authors, composers, artists, photographers, publishers, film makers, makers of tapes or gramophone records or makers of video cassettes.

Copyright today is one of the most confused and inappropriate areas of law. The rapid growth in technology over the last twenty years or so has not been dealt with by suitable changes in copyright law. Tape recording, video recording, photocopying and television broadcasting are all dealt with inadequately, if dealt with at all. The result is a misunderstanding of the law and breaches by all and sundry at frequent intervals.

The complexity of the problem can be illustrated by taking the case of a 'pop' song with music and lyrics written by different individuals and recorded by a group. The composer of the music has copyright, so does the writer of the lyric. The group who actually perform have a right under the Performers Protection Act and the company who made the recording have copyright in the recording.

12.2 Questions

In which of the following circumstances might a breach of copyright have taken place?

1. A teacher wishes to use a poem with a class. He has only one copy in an anthology so he has copies of the poem duplicated.
2. A short extract is taken from a modern novel and appears on a mock 'O' level English paper as a comprehension exercise.
3. Photocopies are made of a diagram from a geography book for use with a class.
4. A teacher writes a short poem on the blackboard and tells the class to copy it into their exercise books.
5. A pupil writes a story in class. This is so good that the teacher has it typed, duplicated and distributed to other classes as an example of good work.
6. *A Midsummer Night's Dream* is produced by a school for which tickets are sold to the public.
7. In the production recordings of Mendelssohn's Overture to 'A Midsummer Night's Dream' are played.
8. A fifth former photocopies a short extract from a book for his CSE project.
9. The school makes a video recording of a BBC schools' broadcast.
10. The school makes a video recording of an Independent Television programme on 'The Life of the Whale'.

12.3 The Copyright Act 1956

Virtually the whole law of copyright is to be found in this Act, though performers themselves have some rights under the Act mentioned in 12.1 above.

The 1956 Act gives the right of control to copyright holders. The holder may control the publishing of his material. He may decide whether or not a public performance of his work shall take place. He may decide whether it is to be reproduced in any way, including recording or filming. He may control the broadcasting of his work and whether it may be transmitted through a diffusion service. He may control the translation, adaptation or arranging of his work and the publishing, public performance, reproduction or broadcasting of such a translation, adaptation or arrangement.

When a tape, record or film is made then the maker may control its use in public performance, its use in broadcasting, its use in a diffusion service or the making of a subsequent tape, record or film of the original.

Naturally, any holder of copyright may agree to his material being used, with or without a charge and subject to any conditions he lays down.

The 1956 Act also set up a Performing Rights Tribunal. This body deals with disputes between groups such as the Performing Rights Society and its licensees.

12.4 Exceptions

The act allows a number of exceptions, the main ones which may affect schools being as follows:

Fair dealing

Section 6 (2) of the 1956 Act states:

> 'No fair dealing with a literary, dramatic or musical work shall constitute an infringement of the copyright in the work if it is for purposes of criticism or review, whether of that work or of another work and is accompanied by a sufficient acknowledgement.'

'Fair dealing' is a vague term and the amount of quotation that may be reasonable in a criticism or review varies from one situation to another. The Society of Authors and the Publishers' Association have stated that in their view an extract of up to 400 words, or a series of extracts with comments interposed totalling 800 words, where no one extract exceeds 300 words, is acceptable. An extract or extracts of up to 40 lines from a poem is reasonable, but this must not exceed one quarter of the whole poem. The acknowledgement must have a clear identification of the work and author.

Section 49 (1) of the Act makes it clear that there is no infringement of copyright unless there is copying of a substantial part of the work. What amounts to a substantial part is left to be decided by the courts in individual cases. The Society of Authors and the Publishers' Association when referring to the limitations of photocopying which may be allowed as fair dealing in the course of research and private study state that a single extract not exceeding 4000 words, or a series of extracts not exceeding a total of 8000 words (none of which exceeds 3000 words), is acceptable. No extract must amount to more than ten per cent of the entire work. In the case of an anthology of poems or essays, each poem or essay would amount to an entire work in itself.

Since copyright is intended to protect the interests of the owner, to reproduce a summary of a book or a graph or design that summed up a whole article would amount to copying a substantial part.

There can be little doubt, again, that copyright is being flouted in many cases by the use of substantial extracts from works and also by using material in such a way as to take a core from a work which will deter readers or students from going to the original itself. The most recent instance of this comes in the judgement over Coles notes. These are well known study notes produced in Canada and sold extensively in this country. Three authors were concerned in bringing the action – Alan Sillitoe, Laurie Lee and the representative of the estate of G. B. Shaw, the books referred to in particular being, *The Loneliness of the Long Distance Runner*, *Cider with Rosie* and *St Joan*. The court found that the substantial quotation from the texts, without acknowledgement or permission, was in breach of copyright – the implication being that students would 'swot' for examinations from the study notes rather than go to the original. Clearly, many study notes could not be objected to in this way but many others are likely to be affected by the judgement.

Research and private study

A pupil may make a copy of protected material as part of his school work but this exception would not allow him to make more than one copy and then give copies to his friends.

'Private study' is not the same as 'private use'. A teenager who tapes a record from the radio or makes a copy of an extract from a book or photocopies a photograph at home just for amusement is in breach of copyright. A teacher who tapes music at home and then uses it with a class is in breach. The widespread practice of home copying and the difficulty of taking any action illustrates the absurdity of modern copyright law.

In the course of instruction

The Copyright Act allows reproduction 'in the course of instruction' and for use in schools so that schools in fact may sometimes be in a stronger position than, say, a college of further education. Reproduction in the course of instruction must, when made by a pupil or teacher, be otherwise than by a duplicating process. A duplicating process is the production of multiple copies by mechanical means. Hand copying is permitted, therefore, and presumably dictation but photocopying and similar methods are not.

Libraries

Libraries have a limited right to photocopying under the Copyright Regulations 1957. Libraries of schools, colleges or universities may make single copies of individual articles from periodicals or single copies of a reasonable proportion from other works. When they are asked to do so the person who makes the request must certify that the extract is required for research or private study and if the library is aware of the identity of the owner of the copyright then permission must be obtained.

The Society of Authors and the Publishers' Association have indicated that all libraries, not just those mentioned above, need not observe the requirement of a statement from the researcher or an approach to the copyright holder if the extracts conform to the limits mentioned under 'fair dealing'.

Examinations

The use of extracts of copyright material is permitted, if they form part of examination questions set internally by a school, so comprehension and context questions in English literature examinations would not constitute a breach. Public examinations are not included.

School performances

Where a play, opera, musical concert or poetry reading is presented in school it may be exempt from obtaining permission from the copyright holder. It would certainly be so if the work were presented in a classroom situation. It will also be so if the work is presented by teachers and pupils to an audience consisting of teachers, pupils and others directly connected with the work of the school. Unfortunately, parents do not come into this category as far as the law of copyright is concerned.

A similar exemption extends to films, records and television broadcasts.

12.5 Music

The position with regard to music is somewhat different from that relating to other material. The position of music used in the classroom is the same as for literary material but there is a difference when performance is involved.

In 1980 the Wolverhampton authority was ordered to pay £1000 in damages to the Music Publishers' Association for allowing infringements of music copyright to take place within its schools.

In 1981 the Association brought an action against Oakham School, an independent school with a strong tradition of music which had several orchestras, a band, a choir and other musical groups. Such a school needs a lot of music and the court held that this had been illegally copied over a period of time and awarded damages of over £4000.

The position over music is complicated because there may be more than one copyright involved, that of the composer and the writer of the words.

On the other hand there have been more positive attempts to regularize the arrangements for the performance of music than for most other forms. This is largely due to the work of the Performing Rights Society. Where broadcasting authorities or any other organizations allow music to be performed then the payment of an annual fee to the Society will cover the use of material covered by the Society and that of affiliated societies from other countries. These arrangements include schools as well as such other places as clubs, restaurants and shops.

Where the authority pays the fee, which is a very reasonable one, schools may perform the music concerned in public. The authority must give the Society a list of premises on which performances may take place and a return of items used.

12.6 Records, tapes and video cassettes

The position becomes even more complicated. In a recording of a song the composer, the lyric writer, the performer and the record company will all have rights. Fortunately, a system of licensing has been introduced which helps to simplify the situation.

An education authority may now take out an annual licence from the Mechanical Copyright Protection Society, which acts on behalf of the British Phonographic Industries Copyright Association and the British Copyright Protection Association. This will enable schools to re-record records and tapes for the purposes of the curriculum and, say, for storing in a resources centre. The licence also covers the recording of live music covered by copyright, if the consent of the performers is obtained. The licence does not cover a teacher who wishes to re-record for his own private use at home. Independent schools may obtain their own licence.

A second type of licence is available from the same source whereby teachers' centres or resources centres may supply a number of schools with re-recorded material. This material may only be made or used on the licensee's premises in connection with the work of the curriculum. Private use is forbidden. There are a number of restrictions – for example only short extracts may be recorded, each extract not exceeding four minutes, and no recording may be made from a film track or video tape – though permission may be obtained from the owners of the copyright, of course.

These licences do not cover public performances. When it is proposed to use records or tapes in such performances then separate permission must be obtained. This may be from the owners of the copyright or from Phonographic Performance Ltd which represents most major record companies. An annual or occasional licence may be obtained to cover all use of such records and tapes for public performance. This only covers the right to use the mechanical recording itself. If there is copyright in the material used on the record then permission must be obtained from the owners or from the Performing Rights Society.

12.7 Radio and television

By special arrangements, both the BBC and the Independent Television companies allow their educational broadcasts to be copied for use in schools, colleges and universities. This applies only to those programmes clearly intended for such establishments and advertised as such. It does not include Open University programmes. The BBC does not require formalities for this but the ITA requires the bodies concerned to take out an annual licence for a small fee. Before taping Independent Television programmes schools should check that their particular education authority is a subscriber.

Teachers' centres may also copy radio and television programmes for use in a number of institutions but, if so, a licence must be obtained from the Mechanical Copyright Protection Society Ltd. Records must be kept of the material used and the institution involved. Recordings must be erased after three years.

12.8 Language laboratories

Here common sense seems to have prevailed. Since the master tapes must be copied if the system is to work at all the producers of the tapes make a higher charge for them on the understanding that such copying as is essential may take place.

12.9 Home produce

One does not have to be a well-known writer, artist or composer to own copyright. Anyone who creates an original work is entitled to control its use. An infants' teacher who writes a story at home to read to her class, an art teacher or pupil who designs the cover of a school magazine, or a pupil who contributes a poem to it, all have a right to say if and when it shall be used.

Where a form or school magazine is printed it is not usual to seek permission from pupils to use their work but, strictly speaking, this ought to be done.

A possible exception is where staff are seconded or perhaps specially appointed by an authority to prepare visual aid materials or computer programmes. If they are doing this as a term of their contracts then the employers may well have rights in relation to copyright.

Incidentally, the law does not seem as yet to have caught up with computers but there can be little doubt that the law of copyright does apply to programmes written for them.

12.10 Length of copyright

For published literary, dramatic, musical and artistic works, also unpublished artistic works (except photographs and engravings), copyright lasts for fifty years from the death of the author.

For published sound recordings, films, radio and TV broadcasts, photographs and government publications under Crown copyright, the limit is fifty years from publication.

Where literary, dramatic and musical works, photographs, films, engravings and sound recordings are unpublished they are protected indefinitely.

12.11 The Green Paper

The Whitford Committee was appointed in 1973 to examine the field of law relating to copyright. It reported in 1977. In 1981 the government issued a Green Paper but no new legislation has as yet been introduced. As far as schools are concerned, there are few changes of any significance suggested by the Green Paper except to tighten up on the existing law.

An effort is to be made to remove the present abuses over the freedom to copy for purposes of research and private study. Damages for flagrant infringements will be broadened. Computer programmes will be covered. The perpetual copyright on unpublished works will be replaced by a term of fifty years from the death of the author. The broadening of the functions of the Performing Rights Tribunal will be considered.

One important change, though it is unlikely to affect schools, is to create a new criminal offence of being in possession of an infringing copy in the course of trade.

12.12 Answers

By now you will probably have dealt with all the questions posed in 12.2 but, if not, here are the answers.

1 A clear breach of copyright, unless the poet has been dead for fifty years. Even then there would be a breach if the modern edition had been photocopied.

2 This is permitted.
3 One copy could be used in the course of instruction and even that could be a breach if the diagram constituted the core of the work. The production of a number of copies would be a breach.
4 This is permitted.
5 Technically, a breach of copyright. The child's permission is needed.
6 The production would not constitute a breach, since Shakespeare has been dead a long time, but if the modern edition used was reproduced on a photocopy for the cast then a breach would take place.
7 There is a breach unless the school is covered by a licence to use records in public performances. The breach would be to the orchestra and the recording company.
8 This is permitted for research and private study.
9 This is permitted.
10 Unless this is clearly advertised as an educational programme for schools and colleges then there is a breach of copyright.

12.13 Licensing – dramatic performances

Schools are used for a number of purposes which require the obtaining of a licence. It should be remembered that not only may the school be involved in such matters on its own account but, if it allows the premises to be used by outside organizations for stage plays or dances, then it may become involved where the law is broken by those outsiders.

Almost all secondary schools, as well as many primary schools, present dramatic performances from time to time. If these are internal and only watched by pupils and members of staff then the law has no interest in them. If they are 'public' performances then they are subject to the regulations set out in the Theatres Act 1968. A public performance is one where outsiders are admitted and parents are in that category. Whether a charge is made or not is immaterial.

The 1968 Act lays down that no premises are to be used for the public performance of a play except under licence and according to the terms of that licence. 'Premises' means any place. A play is any dramatic performance, the major part of which involves the playing of roles by an actor or actors, whether by speech, singing or action. It includes operas, mimes and ballet. Where the music used forms less than a quarter of the entire performance then no further licence for music is necessary.

In London licences are issued by the Greater London Council and elsewhere they are issued by District Councils. Each authority has powers to vary its rules to some extent. The licence may be an annual one or for shorter terms, and occasional licences may be obtained. When a licence is first taken out twenty-one days' notice must be given, both to the council and the police. Twenty-eight days' notice must be given to the council only, where renewal has to be applied for. For school plays it is not usual for a charge to be made.

A main purpose of the law on this subject is to ensure public safety. The Public Health Act of 1936 requires premises used for public performances to have suitable exits and gangways which are unobstructed. It is important to check local regulations but these will usually include a clear marking and illumination of exits with an alternate system of lighting (often battery operated); chairs to be fastened to the floor or battened together in units of not less than four; gangways, passageways and stairs to be unobstructed; gangways to be at least 42 inches wide, the space in front of the seating to be 28 inches wide, no seat to be more than 12 feet from a gangway and all gangways to lead directly to exits; adequate fire-fighting apparatus to be provided and access for fire-fighting services; fire-proofed curtains; and at least one attendant to each 150 persons present or one attendant to each 100 children present. The conditions may apply to the auditorium and back-stage. A further condition is usually that of the power of any police constable or fire officer on duty to enter at any time when the premises are open to the public to see that the conditions are being observed.

The censorship of dramatic performances is abolished but any public performance that is obscene, defamatory, offends against the race relations act or sets out to cause a breach of the peace may be subject to a criminal prosecution.

Schools should note that where a public performance takes place in unlicensed premises liability rests not only upon any person concerned in the organization and management of the performance but also on any other person who allowed the premises to be used, knowing that an offence would be committed.

Where a condition is broken the licence holder will be liable, unless he can show that the offence took place without his knowledge and that he had exercised reasonable care to see that the condition was observed.

Apart from licensing the premises, the school must obtain permission to perform from the owner of the copyright in the work if this exists. This is usually obtained from the publisher of the play but it may have to be sought from the playwright himself. Royalties may then be payable.

If the play is an original one written, say, by a member of staff, or even by a group of staff and pupils working together, then at least one month before the first public performance a copy of the script must be delivered free of charge to the British Museum. It is an offence not to do so.

12.14 Licensing – music and dancing

Again, many secondary schools are used for dances and similar social activities and so are some primary schools, particularly those that have a strong PTA. Such dances are pleasant social occasions, bring parents into school in an informal way and help to raise valuable funds.

The position regarding the licensing of schools for music and dancing is not always clear. In the first place, only those schools where music and dancing for the public takes place habitually need to be licensed. The court decides on the meaning of 'habitual' but it has been held that once a month on a regular basis qualifies. Parents are members of the public and payment is immaterial. In the second place, in some areas there is no requirement to license for music and dancing at all.

There is special legislation affecting London and the Home Counties. Some other authorities have special powers granted by local Acts of Parliament. In other areas the local authority has adopted provisions contained in the Local Government (Miscellaneous Provisions) Act of 1982 and decided that these shall apply to their area. If a school is in an area which does not fall into one of these categories then a licence is not needed. A check should be made with the local authority to discover just what the position is.

It is usual for the head to be the applicant and he must give twenty-eight days' notice to the local authority, the police and fire authority. The police will report to the authority on the applicant and the suitability of the premises and may object to the grant of a licence or its renewal. The Fire Service will also be asked to report on the premises from the points of view of fire risk and safety precautions.

Conditions may be attached to the granting of the licence. The most common ones are those relating to the latest hour at which events must cease; days on which there shall be no entertainment, usually Sundays; and regulations relating to the conduct of the premises. These regulations usually insist on lighting so that the whole area can be seen clearly at one time (discos today are often in breach of this); lighting in lavatories and cloakrooms; no admission or re-admission after a certain time; corridors not to be used as cloakrooms; no consumption of liquor allowed, unless there is a liquor licence; and the right of any constable on duty to enter the premises while the event is in progress.

Where a licence is granted then a permanent notice must be fixed on the door or near the entrance in a conspicuous position. It must read 'licensed in pursuance of Act of Parliament for . . .' and be completed with words indicating the scope of the licence.

Under the Hypnotism Act of 1952 a condition may be attached that no hypnotic performance may form part of the entertainment. It is, incidentally, an offence to hypnotize any young person under the age of eighteen years at a public performance.

For a breach of the law regarding licensing for music and dancing actions are brought by a local authority, not the police, so where the police discover that an offence has been committed they will make the report to the local authority.

12.15 Licensing – liquor in schools

Until fairly recently events where alcohol was consumed were not allowed on school premises in most areas. Times have changed and many authorities now allow the hiring of schools for dances and other activities where alcohol is not only consumed but is sold openly.

Intoxicating liquor may only be sold to the public by those who hold an on-licence (such as publicans) or an off-licence (such as certain shops). Intoxicating liquor includes spirits, wine, beer or cider. It also includes any fermented, distilled or spirituous liquor. Beer and lemonade shandy is also included. Liquors under 2 per cent proof are not.

Under the Licensing (Occasional Permissions) Act of 1983 it is now possible for an approved organization such as a PTA to take out an occasional licence on four occasions during the year. This enables them to sell alcohol at say a dance or a cheese and wine party.

An application for an occasional licence must be made by serving two copies of the application on the Clerk to the Licensing Justices not less than one month before the date of the function. One copy will be sent to the police and if they have objections the licensee will be required to appear before the magistrates.

The permitted hours for the licence will be stated. It is important to note that during those hours the premises, for all legal purposes, become licensed premises. This means that the rules relating to the entry of police, selling of liquor to minors and those who are drunk apply as if the building were part of a public house. Before and after the stated hours the premises are not licensed. It would, therefore, be an offence to sell liquor before or after the hours stated, but the law relating to 'drinking up' would not apply.

The licensee or his employee should be present and primarily he will be liable if a breach of the licence occurs. However, a head who knowingly allowed the law to be broken would also be risking prosecution himself.

12.16 Lotteries

Schools and PTAs frequently resort to raffles, draws and similar competitions in order to raise funds. When they do so their activities are subject to the Lotteries and Amusements Act 1976.

This Act declares all lotteries to be unlawful except those classified as art union lotteries, small lotteries incidental to other entertainments, private lotteries, society lotteries and local lotteries. The first and last of these will be of no concern to schools, but the others may well be.

Private lotteries

A private lottery, which does not have to be registered, is one promoted on behalf of members of the same club or organization (not specifically established for the purpose) and where the sale of tickets is restricted to members of that club or organization or to those who work or live on the same premises. The promoters must be persons to whom tickets could be sold and must be authorized in writing by the society. Clearly, members of a PTA could organize such a competition.

The conditions attached to a private lottery are that all proceeds (less printing expenses) must go either entirely to the society or to prizes and the residue to the society. The only advertisements allowed are on the tickets or in the premises of the organization. Tickets must only be sold at the one price and this must be displayed on the tickets. The tickets must also bear the names and addresses of the promoters, a statement of the persons to whom sale of the tickets is restricted and a statement to the effect that prizes will only be given to the actual purchasers of the winning tickets. No money may be returned and no tickets sent through the post.

Small lotteries

Fêtes, coffee mornings, jumble sales, dances and similar social and fund-raising occasions are known as 'exempt entertainments'. Small lotteries such as raffles may be held as part of the proceedings and registration is not required. There are conditions however.

After the deduction of prize money and expenses, all proceeds must go to purposes other than to private gain. There must be no money prizes and the value of the prizes must not exceed £50. The tickets must only be issued and sold on the premises while the entertainment is in progress. The result must also be declared during the proceedings. The lottery must not be the only inducement for persons to attend.

Society lotteries

These are lotteries where tickets are sold outside the organization and to members of the public.

The lottery must be promoted on behalf of a society established wholly or mainly for charitable purposes, support of sporting or cultural activities or some other similar purpose, which is not part of a commercial undertaking or for private gain. All proceeds, less prizes and expenses, must go to the society. There must be a scheme approved by the society and the society must be registered. If the tickets or chances to be sold are over £5000 the society must deposit details of its scheme with the registration authority, but this is not essential where amounts below £5000 are involved.

Where the amount is £5000 or less the registration authority is in the City of London, London Borough or District Council, as appropriate. For larger sums registration must be made with the Gaming Board for Great Britain.

Where a society, such as a PTA, wishes to run lotteries from time to time with tickets on sale to the public then it is convenient to take out an annual registration. The application must set out the purposes of the society clearly and enclose the appropriate fee, which is renewable on 1 January each year. The promoter must be a member of the society and authorized in writing by it. Tickets, notices and advertisements must specify the society, give the name and address of the promoter and the date when the lottery is to be drawn. Returns have to be submitted to the registration authority giving details of proceeds, expenses, prizes etc. and these are open to public inspection.

Other conditions are that no ticket must cost more than 25p; all tickets must be the same price and as stated on the tickets; and no ticket money may be returned. Not more than fifty-two lotteries may be held in any twelve months. Prizes must not amount to more than half the proceeds and expenses are limited to 25 per cent of the proceeds.

Schools should note that if it is proposed to organize lotteries involving prizes of more than £1000 there are special conditions and a check should be made.

A registration authority may refuse to grant registration and if a breach of the Act occurs then the promoter, or any person party to the breach, may be prosecuted.

Appendix 1

STAFFORDSHIRE COUNTY COUNCIL EDUCATION COMMITTEE

GRIEVANCE PROCEDURE FOR TEACHERS IN COUNTY, VOLUNTARY CONTROLLED AND SPECIAL AGREEMENT PRIMARY AND SECONDARY SCHOOLS

TO MEET THE REQUIREMENTS OF THE CONTRACTS OF EMPLOYMENT ACT, 1972

Teachers' grievances can arise from a variety of sources. They can arise among members of the teaching staff or with the head teacher. They can be of a relatively simple nature or of fundamental importance. They can involve the managers or governors of the school or the administration of the school and the local authority. To meet this situation it seems desirable to set out:

> first, a procedure which may enable a grievance to be resolved informally and without recourse to any subsequent stage; secondly, a completely formal procedure where the first kind of procedure is inappropriate or has failed.

Advice on a similar procedure for head teachers in their relations with their managers or governors or the local authority follows a section dealing with members of the teaching staff.

A. **Members of the Teaching Staff**

A.1 (i) Where a member of the teaching staff has a grievance with the local authority or with the managers or governors which does not involve any other member of the staff, a direct approach should be made to the chief education officer or the managers or governors, as may be appropriate.

A.1 (ii) Where a teacher has a grievance which involves other members of the staff he should first of all endeavour to resolve the matter by direct approach to the member of staff involved or in discussion with the head of department, or other appropriate senior member of staff or, if necessary, in discussion with the head teacher.

A.1(iii) Where a member of staff requests a personal interview with head of department or other appropriate senior member of staff or head teacher it should be granted within five working days of the request being made.

A.1(iv) The head of department or other appropriate senior member of staff or the head teacher (as in (iii) above) should seek to resolve the problem personally or, by mutual agreement, in consultation with other member(s) of the staff. The head teacher may also, by mutual agreement, seek consultation with the chairman of the managers or governors, officers of the LEA, or with representatives of the teachers' organisation(s) as may be thought appropriate.

A.2 (i) Where the matter has not been resolved under any of the procedures referred to above, the member of staff concerned should submit a formal written notice of the grievance to the head teacher, and to the person concerned, if other than the head teacher. The head teacher should then forthwith make a formal written report to the managers or governors and send a copy to the chief education officer.

A.2 (ii) The managers or governors, in consultation, where appropriate, with the chief education officer or his representative, should seek to settle the problem. All relevant documents should be submitted to them and they should allow the parties concerned, if they so wish, to make their submissions, each of them being accompanied, if they so wish, by a friend or an official representative of their union or association.

The meeting for this purpose should be arranged within ten days.

A.2(iii) There should be a right of appeal on the part of any person or body involved in the issue to such standing or ad hoc body as may be agreed locally in consultation between the authority and the organisations of teachers in the area.

A.2(iv) All relevant documents should be submitted to the body so constituted, which should meet within ten days or as soon as practicable thereafter and should allow the parties concerned, if they so wish, to make their submissions, each of them being accompanied by a friend or an official representative of their union or association.

B. **Head Teachers**

B.1 (i) Where a head teacher has a grievance he should first of all endeavour to resolve the matter by direct approach to the person concerned. If not resolved he should then discuss the matter personally with the appropriate officer of the local education authority, who may be a member of the advisory staff of the authority or a member of the administrative staff.

B.1 (ii) Where the matter remains unresolved the head teacher should discuss it with the chief education officer or his representative, who may, also by mutual agreement, seek consultation with the Chairman of the managers or governors or with representatives of the teachers' organisation(s) concerned, as may be thought appropriate.

B.2 (i) Where the matter is not resolved under B.1 above the head teacher should submit a formal written notice of the grievance to the chief education officer and/or to the managers or governors of the school, as the nature of the grievance makes appropriate.

B.2 (ii) Where the grievance lies with the managers or governors a meeting should be arranged by them within ten days, or as soon as is practicable thereafter. The head and any other teacher who may be involved should be entitled to be accompanied by a friend or by a representative of the teachers' organisation(s) concerned.

B.2 (iii) Where the grievance lies with the local education authority, whether or not the support of the managers or governors of the school has been sought by the head teacher, the chief education officer should refer the grievance to the appropriate committee or sub-committee of the local education authority with all the relevant documents and, where this is relevant, with the observations of the managers or governors of the school. Such a meeting should be arranged within ten days or as soon as is practicable thereafter. The parties should be entitled to be accompanied by a friend or an official representative of their union or association.

B.2 (iv) Where the grievance has been with the managers or governors and the appropriate procedure under B.2 (ii) above has been applied, reference will be to the appropriate committee or sub-committee of the local education authority. Again all relevant documents should be placed before the committee concerned and a meeting should be arranged within ten days or as soon as is practicable thereafter to resolve the issue. The parties should be entitled to be accompanied by a friend or an official representative of their union or association.

B.2 (v) Where the procedures outlined in B.2 (ii), (iii) and (iv) above have been followed, and the problem is still unresolved there shall remain a right of appeal as under A.2 (iii) and (iv) above.

The Education Committee and the Joint Advisory Committee (Primary and Secondary) have agreed that the constitution of the ad hoc Appeals Body referred to in Section A.2 (iii) shall consist of

Three members to be appointed by the Local Education Authority.

Three members to be appointed by the Teachers' Panel of the Joint Advisory Committee.

The Chairman shall be appointed from within the Appeals Body and he or she shall not have a casting vote. In the event of an equal division of opinion, the appeal will not be upheld. The Appeals Body will be ad hoc to deal with each appeal with teacher representatives appointed by the Panel according to the subject matter of the grievance and the teacher and the teachers' organisations involved.

Appendix 2

NATIONAL CONFEDERATION
OF
PARENT-TEACHER ASSOCIATIONS

A SUGGESTED P.T.A. CONSTITUTION

---

43 Stonebridge Road, Northfleet, Gravesend, Kent.
Telephone: Gravesend 60618.

This is a draft document and may be varied to suit the particular circumstances of each PTA. For your assistance, comments on various clauses have been added. WILL YOU PLEASE NOTE, HOWEVER, THE IMPORTANCE OF THE WORDING OF CLAUSES, 2, 18 and 21.

1. The NAME of the Association shall be ....

   ....

2. The OBJECTS of the Association are to advance the education of the pupils of the School by providing and assisting in the provision of facilities for education at the School (not normally provided by the Local Education Authority) and as an ancillary thereto and in furtherance of this object the Association may:

   (a) foster more extended relationships between the staff, parents and others associated with the school; and

   (b) engage in activities which support the School and advance the education of the pupils attending it.

   (IT IS ESSENTIAL THAT THIS CLAUSE BE ADOPTED WITHOUT ALTERATION. This wording has been agreed between the Chief Inspector of Taxes, the Charity Commissioners and the Department of Education and Science as being acceptable for use by Parent Teacher Associations. Any variation could render an Association liable to income tax on their investment income).

3. The Association shall be Non-Political.

4. The President of the Association shall be the Head Teacher. (This clause is not essential. For example, some Head Teachers are Chairman of their Associations.)

5. The names of Vice-Presidents shall be submitted at the Annual General Meeting. (These are usually people the Association wishes to honour.)

6. The Annual Subscription shall be (..................) per household, becoming due at the Annual General Meeting. (A growing number of PTAs no longer have subscriptions, thinking they are restrictive and difficult to collect and administer. Where subscriptions are levied, the amount is usually 25p per family.)

7. The Management and control of the Association shall be vested in a Committee which shall consist of the following:–

   The Head of the School and the following officers, who shall be elected annually at the AGM:

   1. Chairman
   2. Treasurer (Parent)
   3. Secretary

Other members from the following sources – Parents representing the First and subsequent years. – Members of the Staff of the School. – Members from friends of the School. (This is a possible arrangement, and can be varied in many ways. For example, in some schools the Secretary is a member of the Staff appointed and paid for that duty. Again, while some schools have committee members representing year groups, others have class representation, or, more usually, election of those parents generally considered suitable.)

8. (..................) members of the said committee shall constitute a quorum for the Committee.

9. Committee meetings shall be held at least once each term at such times and places as the Committee shall direct. (It may also be thought desirable to specify the frequency of ordinary meetings.)

10. The Annual General Meeting of the Association shall be held on (..................) of each year. At the Annual General Meeting the Chair shall be taken by the Chairman, or in his/her absence by the Vice-Chairman of the Committee. Additional meetings shall be held of the sub-sections of the Association, and these may be in addition to those called by the convenor from time to time.

11. (..................) members shall constitute a quorum at the Annual General Meeting.

12. The Committee shall have the power to co-opt up to (..................) members, and to appoint any sub-committee, and shall prescribe the function of any such sub-committee.

13. A special General Meeting shall be convened at the request in writing, to the Secretary, of TEN members of the Association. Such a meeting shall be held within THIRTY days of the request. Agenda and motions submitted shall be circulated to all members.

14. Casual vacancies on the Committee may be filled by the Committee by co-option. Any person so co-opted shall serve only while the person in whose place he/she is co-opted would have served.

15. At the first Committee meeting after the Annual General Meeting the Committee shall elect a Vice-Chairman from among its members.

16. Where a child leaves school during the year then the parent, being a fully paid member of the Association, shall be deemed to continue as such until the next AGM.

17. Where parents no longer have children at the School, but wish to continue their interest in the School through the Association, such parents may be accepted as Friends of the School, on payment of the

Annual subscription, and shall be entitled to full membership with the exception that they may not hold office as Chairman, Secretary or Treasurer, or serve on the Committee.

18. No alteration of the rules may be made except at the Annual General Meeting or at a Special Meeting called for this purpose. No alteration or amendment shall be made to the objects clause or dissolution clause which would cause the Association to cease to be a charity at law. (This is another ESSENTIAL CLAUSE that must not be varied.)

19. The Honorary Treasurer shall keep an account of all income and expenditure and shall submit accounts, duly audited, at the AGM. The Banking Account shall be in the name of the Association and withdrawals shall be made in the name of the Association on the signature of any two of the following:
    a. Chairman
    b. Treasurer
    c. Secretary

20. Two auditors, not being members of the Committee shall be appointed annually at the Annual General Meeting to Audit the accounts and books of the Association.

21. Any assets remaining on dissolution of the Association after satisfying any outstanding debts and liabilities shall not be distributed amongst the members of the Association but will be given to the School for the benefit of the children of the School in any manner which is exclusively charitable at law. (This is another ESSENTIAL CLAUSE that must not be varied.)

22. The Association shall take out Public Liability Insurance to cover all its meetings and activities. (Membership of the National Confederation of PTAs automatically provides this.)

23. That any matter not provided for in the Constitution shall be dealt with by the Committee, whose decision shall be deemed final.

(It must be realised that on all educational matters the Head Teacher has the ultimate responsibility. Should your Association wish to mention this in its constitution, an additional clause could be inserted, e.g., "The Head Teacher shall have the ultimate decision on all educational matters.")

10/73

Appendix 3

Check list for a school prospectus

Admission
Attendance
Buses
Camps
Careers
Class organization
Clubs and societies
Curriculum
Departments
Discipline
Examinations
Field trips
Games
Governors
Head's letters
Homework
Library
Lost property
Lunches
Medical
Minibuses
Overseas travel
Parental contact (letters home/evenings)
Pastoral system
PE kit
Prefects
PTA
Religious education and worship
Remedial help
Rules
School day (times)
School fund
Staff contacts for parents
Staff list
Uniform

Appendix 4

Check list for staff handbook

Absence (staff and pupils)
Addresses
Aims of the school
Assemblies
Ancillary staff
Car parking
Clerical assistance
Cloakrooms
Clubs and societies
Courses
Damage to premises and property
Discipline
Duties
Fire drill
Governors
Homework
Litter
Lockers
Lost property
Lunches
Management structure
Mail
Medical
Minibuses
Money
Notice boards
Parental contact
Pastoral system
PTA
Publicity
Pupil records
School day
School fund
Staff meetings
Staff records
Student teachers
Supervision
Telephones
Travelling expenses
Visits

Bibliography

General

James, P. S. (1976), *An Introduction to English Law*, Butterworth

Walker, M. G. and Walker, R. J. (1976), *The English Legal System*, Butterworth

Education

Advisory Centre for Education, *The School in its Setting*

Barrell, G. R. (1978), *Teachers and the Law*, Methuen

Harrison, G. H. and Bloy, D. (1980), *Essential Law for Teachers*, Oyez

Taylor, G. T. and Sanders, J. B. (1976), *The Law of Education*, Butterworth

Wilby, P. (1980), *Parents' Rights*, Franklin Watts

Employment

Curson, C. (1977), *'Education' Guide to Industrial Relations*, Swift Publications

Selwyn, N. M. (1981), *Law of Health and Safety at Work*, Butterworth

Selwyn, N. M. (1982), *Law of Employment*, Butterworth

Tort

Williams, G. L. and Hepple, B. A. (1976), *Foundations of the Law of Tort*, Butterworth

Winfield and Jolowicz (1979), *Tort*, Sweet and Maxwell

Family Law

Bevan, H. K. (1973), *The Law Relating to Children*, Butterworth

Bromley (1976), *Family Law*, Butterworth

Hoggett (1977), *Parents and Children*, Sweet and Maxwell

The Courts

Smith, R. (1979), *Children and the Courts*, Sweet and Maxwell

Criminal Law

Cross and Jones (1980), *An Introduction to Criminal Law*, Butterworth

Case Law

Barrell, G. R. (1970), *Legal Cases for Teachers*, Methuen

Safety

DES Safety booklets, HMSO:

No. 1 Safety in Outdoor Pursuits (1972)

No. 2 Safety in Science Laboratories (1973)

No. 3 Safety in Practical Departments (1973)

No. 4 Safety in Physical Education (1974)

No. 5 Safety in Further Education (1976)

No. 6 Safety at School – General Advice (1979)

Useful addresses

Advisory Centre for Education, 18 Victoria Park Square, London, E2 9PB

Assessment of Performance Unit, Elizabeth House, York Road, London, SE1 7PH

Assistant Masters and Mistresses Association, 29 Gordon Square, London, WC1 0PX

Association of Careers Teachers, Hillsboro, Castledine Street, Loughborough, Leics.

Association of County Councils, Eaton House, 66a Eaton Square, London, SW1W 9BH

Association of Metropolitan Authorities, 36 Old Queen Street, London, SW1H 9JE

Association of Principals in Sixth Form Colleges, Brockenhurst College, Brockenhurst, Hants.

Association of Principals of Colleges, East Herts. College, Turnford, Broxbourne, Herts.

Association of Voluntary Aided Secondary Schools, 10e Reddons Road, Beckenham, Kent

Careers Research and Advisory Centre, Bateman Street, Cambridge, CB2 1LZ

Catholic Education Council, 41 Cromwell Road, London, SW7 2DJ

Central Register & Clearing House, 3 Crawford Place, London, W1H 2BN

College of Preceptors, Coppice Row, Theydon Bois, Epping, Essex, CM16 7DN

Council for Educational Technology, 3 Devonshire Street, London, W1N 2BA

Council for National Academic Awards, 344–354 Grays Inn Road, London, WC1X 8BP

Council of Local Education Authorities, 66a Eaton Square, London, SW1W 9BH

Department of Education & Science, Elizabeth House, York Road, London, SE1 7PH

Equal Opportunities Commission, Overseas House, Quay Street, Manchester M33 HN

Health Education Council, 78 New Oxford Street, London, WC1A 1AH

Health & Safety Executive, Regina House, 259–269 Old Marylebone Road, London, NW1 5RR

National Association of Governors & Managers, 81 Rustlings Road, Sheffield, S11 7AB

National Association of Head Teachers, Holly House, 6 Paddockhall Road, Haywards Heath, West Sussex, PH16 1RG
National Association of Schoolmasters and Union of Women Teachers, Hillscourt Education Centre, Rose Hill, Rednal, Birmingham, B45 8RS
National Confederation of Parent Teacher Associations, 43 Stonebridge Road, Northfleet, Gravesend, Kent, DA11 9DS
National Foundation for Educational Research, The Mere, Upton Park, Slough, SL1 2DQ
National Society for the Prevention of Cruelty to Children, 1–3 Riding House Street, London, W1P 8AA
Open University, Walton Hall, Milton Keynes, MK7 6AA
Professional Association of Teachers, 99 Friar Gate, Derby, DE1 1EZ
Secondary Heads Association, 29 Gordon Square, London, WC1H 0PS
Universities Central Council on Admissions, PO Box 28, Cheltenham, Gloucestershire, GL50 1HY
National Union of Teachers, Hamilton House, Mabledon Place, London, WC1H 9BD

Index